CARE OF THE PATIENT IN
DIAGNOSTIC RADIOGRAPHY

CARE OF THE PATIENT
IN DIAGNOSTIC
RADIOGRAPHY

D. NOREEN CHESNEY
F.S.R. T.E.

Group Superintendent Radiographer
Coventry and Warwickshire Hospital

and

MURIEL O. CHESNEY
F.S.R. T.E.

Teacher-Principal, School of Radiography
The United Birmingham Hospitals

FOURTH EDITION

BLACKWELL SCIENTIFIC PUBLICATIONS

OXFORD LONDON EDINBURGH MELBOURNE

ISBN 0 632 09210 6

FIRST PUBLISHED 1962
SECOND EDITION 1966
THIRD EDITION 1970
FOURTH EDITION 1973

Printed in Great Britain by
WESTERN PRINTING SERVICES LTD, BRISTOL
and bound by
THE KEMP HALL BINDERY, OXFORD

The authors of this book dedicate it to each other for doing the difficult bits, and to their students, but for whom there would have been no necessity to do any of it

CONTENTS

LIST OF ILLUSTRATIONS

PLATES

FIGURES

PREFACE TO FOURTH EDITION

The worst of writing a book is that we are expected to know what is in it. A decade has elapsed since the first publication of this book. Such a period of time was long enough to convince us, when we came to plan a fourth edition, that—whatever else we might do— we should begin by totally re-reading the first, in order to discover what we thought and said ten years ago about the care of patients in diagnostic X-ray departments.

Fortunately for ourselves certain principles of patient-care do not change and we have not found it necessary to re-write the book. However, some of the original material is now 'old-fashioned' without a doubt. Awareness of this has led us to alter much of Chapter III (Drugs in the X-ray Department); to extend earlier emphasis on the use of pre-sterilized and disposable equipment and to omit entirely the last section of Chapter IV which offered notes on the cleansing and sterilizing of specific articles (this instruction we consider now to be generally irrelevant to departmental practice).

Besides our concern with modernizing it, we wish to keep the book aligned with such changes as may occur in the syllabus of training for the Diploma of the Society of Radiographers. This has resulted in the inclusion in this fourth edition of sections on the care required of the radiographer for the patient who has a colostomy or has a tracheostomy and on the use of suction apparatus.

Other alterations—whether additional or subtractive—are minor in character but have been made with the same intention of tuning the book to current clinical procedure. We could not have realized this aim without help from the practical experts and we are pleased to acknowledge our debt in this connection to the library of the School of Nursing at the Queen Elizabeth Medical Centre, Birmingham; to senior pharmacists and nursing staff at the Coventry and Warwickshire and Walsgrave Hospitals, Coventry; and to the pharmaceutical manufacturing companies whose pamphlets contain

much advanced technical and clinical information. We are grateful
for their effectual aid.

D.N.C.
M.O.C.

1972

PREFACE TO FIRST EDITION

This book has been written because there seemed to be a need for it. Care of patients in the X-ray department has long been a responsibility accepted by radiographers, and it is possible that a textbook on the subject is overdue. Now recent changes in the syllabus of training and the examinations for the Diploma of Membership of the Society of Radiographers have made it necessary for students to receive formal instruction in this aspect of their work. We hope that this book will be of some help to them, and perhaps also to their teachers.

At the same time we have not felt that this section of the syllabus of training should rigidly define the boundaries of the book, and we know that we have included more detail than is likely to be required by the student preparing for Part I of the M.S.R. examination. We hope that senior students and perhaps also some radiographers may find it of value.

For the sake of clarity it has been necessary to attribute a specified sex to the patient, and it will be seen that we have described a male patient except when it was obviously unsuitable to do so. It must be understood that in this book as in others man embraces woman.

However, we have not ventured to predict the sex of the radiographer. Assiduous readers will notice that a certain section of Chapter II is the only part of the book in which a female radiographer makes determined appearance. This has been done because the opposition of the female attendant to the male patient adds clarity to explanation. We challenge anyone to write this particular section without the use of personal pronouns which must ascribe a sex to the radiographer while at the same time maintaining at least the semblance of lucidity.

We are pleased to find opportunity here to express thanks to those who have given us assistance. In particular we are grateful to our always helpful consultant radiologists at the General Hospital, Birmingham, and at the Coventry and Warwickshire Hospital, Coventry. Dr J.C. Bishop, Dr J.E. Glasgow, Dr J.B. Hearn, Dr J.F. K. Hutton, Dr P. Jacobs and Dr G.A. Macdonald were good enough to read various parts of the manuscript, and between them covered Chapters i to xi and Chapters xiii to xvii. We are indebted to them for the gift of their time and interest, for their helpful and detailed comments, and for the encouragement with which they sustained us. Mr R.F. Farr, Chief Physicist at the Department of Physics of the United Birmingham Hospitals, was kind enough to read Chapter xix and a section of Chapter xvii, and gave us the help of his comments. We are grateful to Dr F.G.M. Ross of the United Bristol Hospitals for a personal communication in connection with spleno-portal venography. Photography was undertaken by Mr T.F. Dee of the Department of Medical Photography at the Queen Elizabeth Hospital, Birmingham. We are glad to express our thanks to him, and to Miss W.L. Brookman, Superintendent Radiographer of the Radiodiagnostic Department, to members of her staff, to student radiographers, and to a patient for co-operation and help willingly given for these photographic illustrations. For the bulk of the remaining illustrations we are grateful to the following for the loan of blocks and art material and permission to reproduce in publication: Baillière, Tindall, & Cox Ltd; Bowater-Scott Corporation Ltd; Messrs A.C. Cossor & Son (Surgical) Ltd; Down Bros. and Mayer & Phelps Ltd; J.G. Franklin & Sons Ltd; The Genito-Urinary Manufacturing Co. Ltd; Macarthy's (Wholesale Chemists) Ltd; Her Majesty's Stationery Office; Charles F. Thackray Ltd; and Watson & Sons (Electro-Medical) Ltd.

Lastly, or perhaps firstly, we wish to thank Mr Per Saugman of Blackwell Scientific Publications for being always so helpful and for beginning it all.

D.N.C.
M.O.C.

CHAPTER I

THE HOSPITAL, THE PATIENT AND THE RADIOGRAPHER

Care of the patient in radiography is not a static subject. Radiographic techniques extend in their complexity and produce ramifications in patient-care with which radiographers must become familiar. The apparatus used may grow in the scope of its automation, but care of patients can never be placed within the function of any mechanical or electrical progression and must remain in the human hands of the radiographer. This is something which radiographers have long recognized as their responsibility. Whatever additions may be built on to it, there is a certain basic structure always unchanged.

The patient and the radiographer must first of all be seen in relation to the hospital as a whole. All hospitals, even small ones, are complex organizations in which are employed many different skills. Some of these skills may seem to be more easily replaced than others. It is, for example, easier to train a new lift operator than a new heart surgeon. Yet no one of them is entirely independent of the others, and whatsoever their variety they all have one feature in common. They all serve the patient.

Even when they are not seen to serve the patient directly they still do so. The surgeon may be able to mend a man's heart, but the patient would not do very well if there were no electrician to keep the theatre lights in order during the operation, and no laundry assistant to provide clean linen.

The patient therefore is the *reason* for the existence of the whole organization, which has no life, no purpose, and no value without him. This makes the patient the most important person in the hospital, although he will seldom look and unfortunately will rarely feel as if he were.

As the hospital personnel share the common purpose of being there to serve the patient, so the patients have in common the feature of being in need of help. The help they need may be small or great in degree, it may be possible to cure them, it may be possible only to alleviate their ills; their preceding history of pain, worry and dysfunction may be long and severe, or it may be trifling. None of these variations is relevant to alter the important and simple fact that the patient is in need of help and we as hospital personnel are there to give it. This is the basis of our responsibility towards him. Recognition of the fact that we are dealing with a fellow human being adds breadth to the base.

The responsibility which radiographers carry for patients in their departments may be considered as having three branches. These are:

    (i) clinical responsibility;
    (ii) ethical responsibility;
    (iii) legal responsibility.

CLINICAL RESPONSIBILITY

To meet their clinical responsibility radiographers need some knowledge of many practical procedures in the care of patients; some knowledge of pathology and disease processes so that they do not inadvertently worsen a diseased condition by uninformed handling of the patient; some knowledge of first aid and what to do in an emergency so that they will be able to help the patient until medical assistance arrives. These are practical matters; but it is also necessary for the radiographer to have as part of the required clinical expertise an understanding of the patient's psychological state.

To the patient the many individuals with whom he comes in contact represent the hospital, even the most junior encountered for the briefest time. Whether he regards the hospital as a 'good' hospital to which he willingly and confidently entrusts himself, or as a 'bad' hospital which he regards with apprehension and uncertainty, depends not only on what is actually done for him but also upon the *way* in which it is done. In many cases in the patient's judgment the latter is the more significant feature.

It is recognized that a patient's response to treatment may be influenced by his response to his environment. His general impression of his environment must be significantly (though not entirely) formed by the sum of individual encounters with those who serve him while he is in hospital. Any one of us who leaves him with an unfavourable or depressing influence—and it takes not deliberate cruelty but only a few moments' lack of thought to do this—may thus inflict more damage than can be calculated. All of us should recognize our potential in this, and should appreciate that if we can surround the patient with the right atmosphere we provide not merely the negative benefit of absence of injury, but a positive contribution to the patient's treatment.

To say that it is necessary to surround the patient with the right atmosphere is to make a very generalized statement which perhaps leaves the new student in the X-ray department wondering how this can be done. However, a little thought shows how it can be done, for we have our own humanity in common with this patient and we have only to put ourselves in his place to see how we must behave towards him.

It must be remembered that the patient is often in a hypersensitive state emotionally, and can be hurt and upset by occurrences that may seem to us trivial. We often find a patient extremely (and to us disproportionately) grateful for a service that is small. This indicates that some lack of consideration towards him may be far more distressing than we realize. He will usually be readier to give expression to his gratitude than to find words for his unease, but this does not alter the fact that distress may be there. In our dealings with him we must bear in mind this susceptibility.

There are two separate aspects of the radiographer with which the patient will be concerned, and on which he will feel the need of reassurance when he is first sent to the X-ray department. To him it is a very strange department that he must view at best with uncertainty in the first instance, if not with alarm. He will want to be reassured first of all as to certain personal qualities in the radiographer; he will want also to be assured of professional capability.

The personal qualities required are that the radiographer should seem sympathetic, understanding, cheerful, and interested in the patient. It is appreciated that these features are not always readily displayed and often a conscious effort may have to be made to maintain them. This effort must be made, however, and as responsible and trained professional people we should find enough self-control to make it even when it is not easy to do so. Small details combine to form the total effect made upon the patient.

A smile from the radiographer can go a very long way towards establishing an easy relationship and reducing tension in the patient. Oddly enough it also reduces tension in the radiographer even when an effort has had to be made to start the smile. Many radiographers do not smile at their patients enough, and they fail to realize as they

B

give instructions to them and bid them come hither and thither that a manner that is meant to seem efficient too often seems forbidding. A smile removes the impression of sternness.

It is also encouraging to the patients to find themselves addressed by name, correctly prefixed by Mr, Mrs, or Miss. The distinction between Mrs and Miss can be troublesome but it is important, for either group seem to feel equally indignant when misplaced in the other, and although the patient may forgive a radiographer for making a mistake about it once, she will be hurt if the radiographer is so thoughtless as to continue in failure to find the proper form.

The use of the name is reassuring because one of the feelings which trouble a patient when he comes to hospital is a sense of loss of identity and of loss of control in the direction of his affairs. He feels that he is no longer the master of himself but has been placed in the charge of other people. When he hears his name being used he feels re-established as a significant entity.

The indiscriminate use by radiographers of such forms of address as 'Dad' or 'Dear' may be well intentioned, but it seems to imply a certain condescension as if the radiographer were on a higher plane and descending to a casual familiarity. It conveys also a suggestion of indifference as if the radiographer could not be troubled to remember the patient's name. The use of the surname only is inexcusably impolite.

It would be foolish of any radiographer not to realize that the work involves encounter with aspects of patients that are displeasing or actively distressing, and we must all of us be prepared for this. Our distaste may be a physical reaction to a physical stimulus. For example, disease processes may give rise to disturbing sights and unpleasant smells which the unfortunate patients must carry with them when they come to our departments. We have frequently to concern ourselves with functions of the body that do not seem particularly attractive. We shall often meet patients who seem to us to have arrived in their several situations through failure to live knowledgeably according to the best principles; our X-ray films will show such sorry results as broken jaws after tavern brawls and pregnancy in the unmarried.

Recognizing that we shall encounter this aspect of our work, we must recognize also the necessity that we shall control our reaction towards it. No radiographer should reveal to the patient any sign of distaste or dismay whatever may occur, nor the least suggestion of moral censure for what may already have occurred. We must always present to our patients a manner that is friendly yet impersonal, and convey to them a confidence in our ability to take control of the situation and care for them while they are with us.

To a newcomer to the department this may sound an exacting thing to do, especially when there are features of the patient which the average person will find disturbing. Of course work with sick people *is* exacting, but it is by no means as difficult as might be thought to present to the patient a manner unchanged by accompanying circumstances. To help us we have the uses of training and custom. We have a job to do for this patient, and while we are thinking of this job and concentrating upon it and the patient, there seems no opportunity to let range our personal reactions.

It is, of course, true that patients in many different ways can test the self-control of a radiographer. We have all of us met the patient, often not very ill, who is difficult to please and impatient of delay and almost seems to imply that he is doing us a favour by letting us X-ray him. The radiographer who can see such a one as a challenge to professional ability to handle people is in no danger of loss of forbearance, and can indeed find a satisfying sense of success in leaving this patient smoother than he was before.

In any circumstances there must be no loss of temper by the radiographer, however severe the provocation. Once we have lost our tempers we have lost any control of the situation and allowed the patient to determine our behaviour. Clearly this should not be so, since it destroys altogether the correct professional relationship.

It was said a little earlier that the patient wants to find a cheerful radiographer, and in general this is true. Certainly he never wants his visit to the X-ray department to be marked by an atmosphere of unrelenting gloom. However, there is scope for different interpretations of the word 'cheerful'.

Obviously it must always stop short of the hilarious and when the patient is very ill, and knows it, he will find something heartless in a radiographer whose exuberant demeanour has a quality that seems to ignore the graver aspects of the situation and his own physical difficulties. At its ridiculous extreme this gives us a caricature of a radiographer saying 'Just jump up on the X-ray table' in a bright and encouraging tone to a patient disabled with arthritis, but it is possible to seem callously animated in many lesser degrees than this. The best interpretation of the word 'cheerful' is perhaps the shade of meaning conveyed by the phrase 'of good cheer' so that the ill patient feels an atmosphere of confidence and hope.

As well as persuading the patient of a sympathetic response towards him, the radiographer has to convince him of professional capability. To the radiographer the X-ray examination is doubtless one of many to be undertaken in a day's work, either more or less difficult according to its nature, the condition of the patient, and the experience of the radiographer. To the patient the X-ray examination is important and unique because it is his own. Upon the results will depend the determination of his ailment, its treatment, and thus features of his immediate and indeed even far distant future. Obviously he wishes to be assured that this examination will be carried out at the highest level of efficiency and that no mistake will be made.

The first thing then is for the radiographer to *look* efficient. This is one of the reasons why it is important to pay attention to the details of appearance when on duty. It is not simply a meaningless necessity to comply with what may seem tiresome hospital requirements in the matter of uniform.

No patient can feel any confidence at all in a radiographer whose white coat is dirty, whose hair is untidy, whose hands and nails look in need of soap and water, whose shoes look in need of both cleaning and repair. This radiographer may be highly qualified and knowledgeable in the technicalities of the job, but these things do not appear to the patient. Confronted by such radiographers, all the patient can see is a group of people who do not look well able to take care of themselves. How can he rely on their ability to take care of him?

The question of appearance on duty has perhaps more pitfalls for the female than for the male radiographer, since feminine dress and adornment have the greater range. So long as he looks clean and neat, does not appear to be in need of a deodorant, and avoids such informalities as open-necked shirts, sweaters, sandals and jeans, the male radiographer is not likely to be unsuitable in his person.

His female colleague has more to consider. Long nails and coloured varnish do not fit well to the handling of patients. Length may cause nails to scratch the patient, and is in any case difficult to maintain unbroken on hands constantly used to manipulate equipment; brightly coloured nails in a hospital setting may offend the sensitized patient because he thinks they look either inappropriately gay or unfortunately too like blood. Jewellery also presents a hazard to the patient who may be scratched by the setting of a ring or the fastening of a brooch, and as a result may develop a bedsore which will cause neither the victim nor the nursing staff on the ward to feel appreciative of the X-ray department.

The radiographer's hair should be neat and cosmetics should be used with discretion; what is agreeable at a ball looks unacceptably gaudy against a clinical background, and as we should never think of wearing a ball dress in the X-ray department so we should have the sense also to discard the facial accessories we may choose to go with it. In fact, of course, the secret of looking well dressed on duty is to look suitably dressed (as indeed it always is whatever the occasion). Let us not lightly dismiss the therapeutic effect upon the patient when his eye beholds a radiographer who looks both efficient and attractive. So we have every reason to make the best we can of ourselves, guided by the principle that the total effect must seem suitable to our work and its nature.

After looking efficient, the radiographer next has to be concerned with *sounding* efficient. One feature of this is that we must speak as if we had our minds on the job immediately before us—the X-ray examination which can be to us so familiar a routine and to the patient so unique. This means that radiographers working together in an X-ray room should restrict spoken exchanges between each other to technicalities relating to the examination.

From these there must be elimination of anything not reassuring. Remarks such as 'You can't use the Bucky at less than 0.5. It's a terrible old thing', or 'The mA's all over the place. I wonder if the tube's going?' speak to the uncomprehending patient of major risks which imperil the soundness of the examination and even his own personal safety among this peculiar equipment.

Radiographers should never begin a general conversation of their own on irrelevant themes such as football matches, hair styles, or what the radiologist said about yesterday's films. They may (and indeed should) have with the patient such general conversation as may ease his mind and create an agreeable atmosphere. Even this requires to be nicely graded so that the patient does not wish that the radiographer would stop talking and get on with the job, and the radiographer does not wish that the patient would stop talking, let the job be done, and free the X-ray room for Mrs Smith who is waiting outside. The talkative patient needs tact, as in the interests of others we clearly cannot allow him to monopolize our time, yet we must not send him away with his feelings hurt.

Care must be used with *any* words spoken in the patient's hearing. Comments such as 'That chest's too thin' may be taken by Mrs Jones as a wounding description of her physical characteristics. 'I can't see anything on the lumbar spine' may describe a radiological appearance that is normal, but can leave the patient thinking that the film is useless. A radiographer describing fracture displacements to a student discovered with surprise that a patient was concluding that her broken wrist would be deformed for the rest of her life. It is only too easy for the patient to form such erroneous impressions when he cannot fully understand what he hears. More often he will carry such anxieties away to worry over them unspoken than acquaint us with his concern.

The Child Patient

Radiographers in diagnostic X-ray departments deal with patients of all ages and children very often come their way. The management of the child patient can seem difficult in busy general X-ray departments where there is pressure on each radiographer to carry out the examinations as quickly as is consistent with efficiency. There is no simple answer to the problem—each child needs individual treatment—but it may be of help in guiding the radiographer's approach to the child if we state here some reminders on the child's psychological state. To go further than that is somewhat beyond the scope of this book.

Firstly let it be said that all children are fearful of many things, the causes of fear varying at different stages in the child's development. The young baby, for example, is frightened by sudden loud noises and rough movements; the toddler is frightened when left alone (after all, he hardly ever is left alone in his daily life). Knowing these facts, the radiographer can take care that the infant or child is not placed in situations which elicit fear from these causes. This means, do not handle him roughly, expose him to sudden loud noises or leave him alone with only himself and his fears for companionship.

Young children are fearful when they find themselves in a novel situation so anything that can be done to make the X-ray room and its procedures seem less strange is of help—for example the presence of a favourite toy, or nursery-rhyme characters among the wall decorations, or an explanation that seeks to relate the examination to something that the child has done before (such as having his picture taken or looking at television).

It is important that all radiographers dealing with children should realize that the experiences of a child coming to hospital, perhaps being separated from parents on admission, certainly encountering unfamiliar faces and novel situations, can be emotionally devastating to the child. The child may be precipitated into acute panic states, extremes of distress and fear the full extent of which our dulled adult perceptions may not be able to appreciate.

A child in such a state is intractable and unmanageable—a very difficult subject for radiography. But there are much worse effects than simply the making of a radiographer's task difficult or impossible. It is thought that experiencing these states of mind affects the child for a very long time after the precipitating causes have ceased to be effective. Long after he has left the hospital he may carry the marks that the experience has scored upon him psychologically. An infant may be changed from a happy, chattering little person to one who is silent and withdrawn, less ready to explore life; an older child may have persistent enuresis. Such are the effects which have been attributed to the damage of experiences in hospital.

ETHICAL RESPONSIBILITY

Ethics may be defined as the science of human duty in its widest extent, and although the ethical side of patient-care is intangible it is a most important factor in the radiographer-patient relationship. True understanding of it marks the radiographer as a professional person, as distinct from someone whose training is wholly technical.

We must recognize that we have both a human need and a professional obligation to believe in certain assumptions: that human life is worth saving, that the conditions of our fellows are worth alleviating, that certain human rights exist. Most of us have little difficulty in seeing the importance of these assumptions as they apply to *ourselves*. When we work in hospital dealing with our fellows as patients, we make decisions about them and undertake upon them procedures which potentially can have far-reaching effects on their lives and well-being, and indeed on the lives and well-being of their kin. We must remember that these humanitarian assumptions must be applied to every human creature. We must follow the old but still valid injunction to do as we would be done by.

In the United Kingdom one of the functions of the Radiographers' Board of the Council for Professions Supplementary to Medicine is to promote high standards of professional conduct. The Board has said in a statement (July 1965) that 'These standards are required not solely or even principally for the benefit of the profession but for the safeguarding of treatment which can be given to a patient and for the patient's protection.' So this is a clear reminder that we carry an ethical responsibility in respect of our patients.

There are two special elements in this responsibility to which the reader's attention is here drawn. The first is discretion in speech and the absolute necessity not to reveal information about patients which is confidential. This is discussed more fully in Chapter XVIII, with further reference to the rulings of the Radiographers' Board of the Council for the Professions Supplementary to Medicine.

The second matter concerns radiation hazard and the radiographer's inescapable duty to use radiation so that all patients receive the smallest dose which is necessary. This is explained and discussed in Chapter XIX.

LEGAL RESPONSIBILITY

The medico-legal responsibility of radiographers is most likely to be brought into question when something has gone wrong. We have given these matters a chapter to themselves and the reader is referred to Chapter XVIII.

THE RADIOGRAPHER AND THE HOSPITAL

In the present chapter the radiographer has been defined in relation to the patient. Now something more should be said in regard to the student radiographer and the X-ray department, and the X-ray department and the rest of the hospital.

The X-ray department must be seen by the rest of the hospital as an important one since it is one with which they will nearly all of them have business. With very few exceptions, all the wards and out-patient clinics, theatres, and special departments will need to use the diagnostic X-ray service for their patients, and of course we frequently make X-ray examinations on the staff themselves.

There is thus sound basis for our professional self-respect in seeing ourselves as people with a significant contribution to make in the work of the hospital by reason of our specialized knowledge. We should not, however, think that this removes us from any need to consider the work of others. Because we work in a prominent position, serving many outside the X-ray department and having many points of contact with the rest of the hospital, it is the more important that we should work well with them.

This is done by recognizing that they also have a job to do that is worthy and important to the patient, and that they also have certain problems even as we do. We hope that those outside the X-ray department will try to understand *our* difficulties so that the work will be easier. Human nature being what it is, one way to make it certain that they will not try to understand is ourselves to make no effort at consideration towards them. Consideration of other departments usually carries a bonus of consideration towards ours. The lack of it certainly results in a reciprocal lack towards us.

In practice this appreciation of the problems of others will prevent the X-ray department, for example, from sending for ward patients a long while before it is ready to carry out the examination, or fetching down the very ill patient at a time when there are many others in the department. It will keep us from insistence that we do the non-urgent case with the mobile set at a period when the ward sister is trying to see that the patients are served with lunch. It will cause us to organize our work in the department and arrange the different examinations so far as is possible in order to make the best use of staff and X-ray rooms, and thus reduce waiting time both for patients and for medical staff who may be requiring the films.

Student radiographers newly arrived to work in the hospital generally bring with them some knowledge of the hierarchy of authority within it, gathered from accounts in novels and other books and depictions in cinema and television programmes. It will be understood that the matron or principal nursing officer is in overall charge of the nursing staff, and that each ward and some of the special departments such as the accident department are in the charge of a sister or other nursing officer. In administration the matron or principal nursing officer has the help of a deputy and assistants while the ward sisters will have the help of their senior staff nurses. Less well-known perhaps will be the function of the secretary of the hospital, but it will soon be appreciated that he is in charge of hospital staff other than the nursing group.

On the medical side the highest authority is invested in consultant physicians and consultant surgeons. These are all experienced and highly qualified specialist doctors, each of whom is aided by a registrar (who might be described as occupying the next lower rungs in the ladder), and under the registrar a house physician or house surgeon, who is a young doctor gaining experience in medicine or surgery.

The X-ray department has its own gradations of authority as the student very quickly discovers. The medical man in charge of the department is the consultant radiologist, whose specialist training qualifies him to interpret X-ray films and conduct diagnostic X-ray examinations. In a large department the radiologist who acts as the director will have the assistance of other consultant radiologists and also a radiological registrar, or perhaps several registrars. The radiographers, who are the technical assistants of the radiologists, are in the charge of the superintendent radiographer. The superintendent will be aided by a deputy superintendent and senior radiographers varying in number according to the size and scope of the department. In the X-ray room the student will be working as assistant to and under the supervision of a qualified radiographer.

The work of those in authority first presents itself to the new student in an aspect of control, perhaps even primarily in an aspect of veto. The superintendent radiographer may be seen mainly as someone who says what must or may not be done, and the radiologist may be seen as someone who gives instructions for repeat examinations and additional films without regard to the fact that you have enough work to do already.

It will be of help in understanding the reason for various restrictions and rules of procedure in the department if some effort is made to appreciate that these people who wield authority and direction, and to whom we may be responsible, themselves carry responsibility and are responsible to others. The superintendent radiographer is responsible to the chief radiologist for the smooth and efficient running of the department, the maintenance of a good standard of radiographic technique, and the care of patients in the department. The radiologist is responsible for the provision of an

X-ray service giving diagnostic facilities to his medical colleagues in the hospital, and he carries the weight of decision on the practice of various X-ray examinations, the welfare of the patient, and the interpretation of X-ray appearances which are shown.

To look beyond the X-ray department from this point of view is to see the ward sister responsible for the treatment and care of patients in her ward, and to see the matron or principal nursing officer responsible to the governing body of the hospital for the provision of an efficient nursing service.

Consideration of this aspect of authority, which is now seen to have a face of duty, helps us to appreciate the integration of the hospital as a single unit, working (as has been said) for the patient, and to see our own place as members of the team.

CHAPTER II

FEATURES OF GENERAL PATIENT CARE

Something of the required approach to the patient has been indicated in the previous chapter, and it will now be considered in further and more practical detail.

It is certain that in discussing work in the department radiographers will express themselves in terms of the type of examination to be done rather than of the individual on whom the examination is to be made. Thus the radiographer on duty in the X-ray room may be told to expect 'a bronchogram' at ten o'clock. The radiologist as he begins his screening session by asking about the cases may learn that he has 'two follow throughs, three meals, and a barium swallow'. Coming into the viewing room to look at films a radiographer will say 'Is that skull through yet?'

This is a necessary method of communication for it is explicit and time-saving, and it would be impractical to undertake technical discussion in any other way. At the same time we realize, if we pause to think, that when we wish to assess any examination in terms of the degree of departmental effort and time which it will consume, there are really three factors in the equation; (i) the actual nature of the examination, (ii) the skill and experience of the staff, (iii) the condition of the patient.

The condition of the patient is just as important as the others. This can be seen in many instances that are known even to those who have worked only a short time in X-ray departments. It is, for example, easier and quicker to produce films of the wrist of a young man who walks into the accident department saying that he came off his motor cycle last Saturday than it is to undertake the same examination on an old woman who has fallen down a flight of stairs and comes to the X-ray department as a stretcher patient in a state of shock.

Merely as a technical factor influencing others the patient is an important variable, and we must assess him as carefully as the rest. No other factor is more variable or more difficult fully to assess.

Leaving aside humanitarian aspects, merely to make the required examination easier for ourselves we have to secure the co-operation of the patient. We shall do this more certainly if we can understand him, and we shall understand him only if, having appreciated him as a technical factor, we then consider him as an individual.

Thus we may leave the X-ray room and go to the waiting-room to fetch the 'next lumbar spine', but by the time we get there we must have stopped thinking about the examination of a body region or a clinical condition; we must have read the name on the request form and we must be ready to greet Mr Smith *as a person.*

We must now see him as an individual and we must not let him hear us refer to him in the terms previously described. It has been known for patients to be amused to realize that they were being described as a 'row of barium meals waiting to be screened', but many will be hurt. In any case, whatever the patient's reaction may be, it must lower the professional status of the radiographer in the patient's estimation when he realizes that he is so regarded.

GENERAL PRELIMINARIES TO THE EXAMINATION

In the moment of contact when the first impression is to be made upon the patient, he must be greeted by name with a smile as if the radiographer were pleased to see him. When he is taken to the X-ray room all must be ready to receive him, and the room must have been tidied after the previous examination. To enter the X-ray room and find it muddled and untidy leaves the patient with an impression of inefficiency in both the radiographer and the department which it will be difficult to change. He may well ask himself 'Do these people really know what they are doing?'

An explanation should be given to the patient of the procedure in which he is to play so important a part. This explanation will reassure him and make his co-operation easier and more certain. Radiographers often feel that patients strain their forbearance by seeming stupid and unco-operative, and in some cases this is true. At the same time we should ask ourselves whether our explanations are as lucid and adequate as they should be; when they are, they certainly help both the patient and ourselves.

It must be ascertained that the right patient has been found, and his full name and the examination to be undertaken should be checked carefully with the patient and the request form. If he has had to undergo special preparation he should be asked whether this has been done, before he is told to get undressed ready for the X-ray examination.

MOVING CHAIR AND STRETCHER PATIENTS

If the patient is fully mobile getting him on to the X-ray table will present little difficulty, once an explanation has been given of what is required. It will be necessary to give him only such assistance as makes certain that he is in fact able to get on the X-ray table, that he does not fall off the step or the table while he is doing it, and that he does not knock himself on any overhanging parts of the apparatus. It must be remembered that the X-ray room and its equipment are strange to him, and in his concentration on trying to do what he is told and lie down on the X-ray table, the patient can completely fail to notice the presence of the X-ray tube just above him, though to us this is very obvious. It is wise therefore to draw his attention to any hazards of this nature which exist. A patient who is not ambulant requires special study. He will reach the X-ray department in any of three forms of transport:

   (i) a wheel-chair;
   (ii) a stretcher;
   (iii) the bed which he occupies on the ward.

The Patient in a Wheel-chair

The patient in a wheel-chair will require assistance, in relation to the degree of co-operation he can give. The chair should be brought close to the X-ray table and parallel to it, the patient facing towards the end of the X-ray table at which it is designed to put his feet when he lies down.

In controlling the wheel-chair itself there are two points to watch; (i) that it does not slide away from the patient as he rises, and (ii) that he does not tip the whole thing forwards by standing on the foot-rest. In some chairs the foot-rest can be slid underneath so that it is impossible for the patient to stand on it and he puts his feet on the floor on rising; in such a chair the foot-rest must be put away before the patient begins to get up. Others are designed to have stability so that even with someone standing on the foot-rest the chair does not tip.

Probably the patient will be able to rise with help and transfer himself to the X-ray table. If the wheels of the chair can be locked or an assistant is available to act as a brake, the radiographer may face the patient, ask him to put both hands on her shoulders, and with both her own hands under his armpits assist him to rise.

If alone and required to act as a brake on the chair, the radiographer must stand to one side of the chair (the side furthest from the X-ray table) and place a foot behind one wheel. The patient is then best helped by the radiographer putting one arm along the back of the chair, and the other hand and arm under the patient's armpit. Once the patient is on his feet he should be turned so that his back is towards the X-ray table; he should be close up against it at this stage if the chair has been properly placed initially. He can then mount backwards on to the step, assisted by the radiographer's hand under his arm, and sit on the X-ray table. From this position he can be helped to lie down.

It sometimes happens that a patient coming to the X-ray department in a wheel-chair is unable to give this degree of co-operation, and it may be necessary to lift such a patient from the chair and transfer him to the X-ray table without the intermediate stage of his standing on the floor. Two people are required for this, and a third to act as the brake on the chair if that is necessary.

The chair should again be placed parallel to the X-ray table and close to it, the patient at this stage facing towards the end of the X-ray table which will be occupied subsequently by his feet. The two radiographers who are to lift him stand on each side of the chair facing the patient and towards the head of the X-ray table. The one on his *left* puts her *left* shoulder under his *left* axilla, and her *left* arm under his thighs in the hollow at juction of thigh and buttock. The radiographer on the patient's *right* side puts her *right* shoulder under his *right* axilla, and her *right* arm under his thighs, grasping the left wrist of the radiographer on the opposite side.

Both radiographers should make certain that their arms are well under the *upper* part of the patient's thighs in the gluteal fold. The tempting and accessible hollow under the knees is not in fact useful and may make successful lifting nearly impossible, as the patient can fold up like a jack-knife at the hips and slide backwards out of the seat which the radiographers are trying to provide. The radiographers should join their free arms, the hand of one grasping the wrist of the other, as supports across the patient's back.

He can now be lifted bodily out of the chair on the word of command from the leader of the proceedings, and transferred to the

X-ray table by the radiographers' stepping backwards and turning sideways. He is then assisted to lie down.

If the patient is unable to take any weight upon his shoulders an alternative method must be used. The patient's arms are best folded across his chest, and the radiographers stand as before on each side of him. The one on his *left* puts her *left* arm under the gluteal fold as before, and her *right* arm across the small of the patient's back. The radiographer on his *right* puts her *right* arm similarly under his upper thighs, and her *left* arm across his back. Both radiographers as before join hands, each gripping with one hand and having the wrist of the other gripped by her partner.

If it is necessary to bend to lift the patient (and the height of the chair will probably necessitate some stooping by the lifters), the radiographers should not bend from the waist, but should keep their backs as straight as possible and stoop by bending at the knees. In this way, as they straighten up in lifting the patient the strain will be taken by the muscles of thigh and hip, and the stress upon their backs and shoulders will be reduced.

The Patient on a Stretcher

The *stretcher* patient can be moved on to the X-ray table from the stretcher in a variety of ways, choice depending on the condition of the patient and the general circumstances. If he can co-operate well he may be able to move himself over when the stretcher is brought parallel to the X-ray table, and firmly held close against it. If the stretcher and the X-ray table are the same height, there will be no great difficulty for the patient who can help himself in sliding across on to the X-ray table; he should be instructed to move his hips first, his shoulders next, and his legs last of all. If he is able to sit up on the stretcher and move himself in that position, the business is easier still.

If the stretcher is not the same height as the X-ray table a difficulty is introduced, for the patient will have to face both a climb and a drop on his double journey to and fro. Pillows laid over the junction between stretcher and table may be of help to him in making the passage smoother, but it may well be wiser to abandon this method of transfer.

It must always be ascertained that a stretcher patient is able for the task before he is allowed to undertake the business of moving

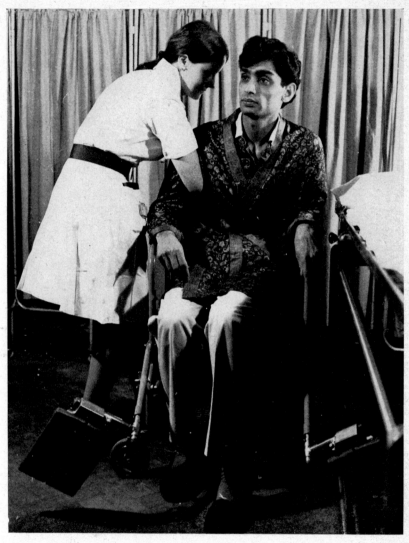

Plate I   Radiographer assisting from a wheel chair a patient who can help himself. The radiographer's left foot and left arm prevent the chair from moving back.

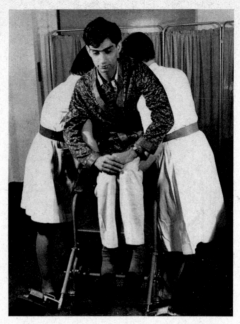

Plate II   Lifting from a wheel chair a patient unable to help himself. Note how each radiographer's shoulder is placed in the patient's axilla.

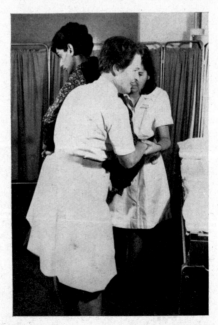

Plate III   The radiographers have stepped back and turned towards the X-ray table.

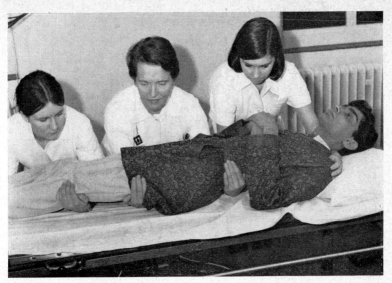

Plate IV   Getting ready to lift a stretcher patient.

Plate V   Lifting a stretcher patient. Note that the patient's weight
is taken by the upper arms of the lifters.

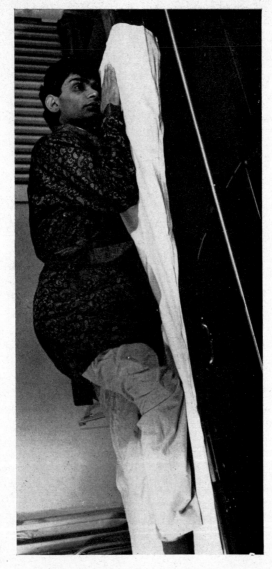

Plate VI   The semi-prone position.

himself. He must not be allowed to begin it under the impression that it is expected of him because it is less trouble to the staff than lifting, and he must not be called upon to make more effort than he is fit to exert.

When he is asked if he can move himself and it is explained to him how he will get from the stretcher to the X-ray table, it must at the same time be made clear that he can be lifted very easily and that the radiographers are used to lifting patients, so that even for big patients it is a practised and everyday procedure. If there is any doubt at all of the patient's ability to move himself, he should be lifted as if he were unable to help.

The patient who cannot help must be moved on to the X-ray table by others. This task must not be attempted by a radiographer unaided, and it is very important for both the staff and the patient that there should be sufficient assistance.

If the stretcher and the X-ray table are the same height and the stretcher is brought alongside the X-ray table, the patient (if he is not too heavy) may be drawn over on the sheet or blanket on which he lies. This can be done by two people standing on the far side of the X-ray table, and if there are three to do the job it will be easier still. This method must not be attempted at all if there is *any* disparity in height between the X-ray table and the stretcher, if the table and the stretcher cannot be made flush with each other, and if any metal fittings on the side of the table or stretcher are likely to give the patient a bumpy passage from one to the other.

The alternative is for three people to lift the patient, and this is not difficult if it is properly done. The three lifters stand on the same side of the patient and put their arms underneath him; one pair of arms is under his shoulders and mid-trunk, the second pair is under his pelvis and mid-thighs, and the third pair supports his legs. If he is not conscious, the radiographer supporting his shoulders must also support his head. The radiographers must put their arms well under the patient so that their hands emerge on the other side.

On the command of the leader of the team the radiographers lift the patient, rolling him towards themselves so that his weight is being borne by their upper arms and chests, and not by the weaker forearms. In this way a heavy patient can be lifted quite easily; he could even be lifted if necessary from the floor without undue difficulty by three practised lifters kneeling beside him on one knee, with the other leg bent and the foot firmly on the ground.

C

In moving him from stretcher to X-ray table, the amount of carrying to be done is reduced to a minimum if the stretcher is first placed at right angles to the X-ray table, the head of the stretcher at the foot of the table. If the radiographers then place themselves in the right angle between the X-ray table and the stretcher, they will find that all they have to do when they have lifted the patient is to turn through ninety degrees, and he can be placed quite conveniently on the X-ray table (Fig. 1).

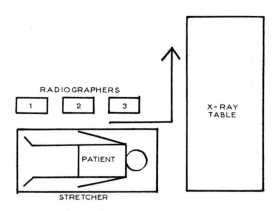

Fig. 1. First arrangement of stretcher relative to the X-ray table.

This manœuvre demands a certain amount of room. If space is not available to put the stretcher at right angles to the table, it may be possible to put the stretcher in tandem with the table, its head at the table's foot. The radiographers have then to take a few steps sideways with the patient in their arms and place him on the X-ray table (Fig. 2).

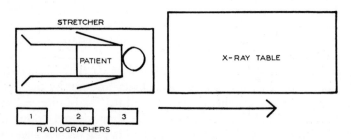

Fig. 2. Second arrangement of stretcher relative to the X-ray table.

If this is not possible, the stretcher may be set parallel to and at a little distance from the X-ray table, its head to the table's foot. The radiographers will then place the patient on the X-ray table by turning 'in formation' through one hundred and eighty degrees (Fig. 3).

A method of lifting which has been seen in use when space is very tight consists of placing the stretcher parallel to the X-ray table and making use of six lifters. They stand thus: three on the far side of the X-ray table, spread to take the patient's shoulders, pelvis and lower limbs, and the other three opposite to them on the far side of the stretcher. The patient is then lifted by the team of six grasping the edges of the sheet or blanket on which he lies. It can be done, but it is an uneconomic application of effort, for the three on the far side of the X-ray table have to stretch across it to reach the patient, and they are very poorly placed to exert their most force without strain to themselves. It takes six people acting with partial efficiency, instead of three acting with their forces properly applied.

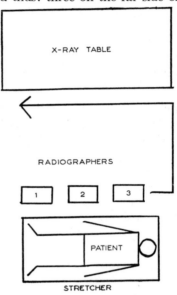

FIG. 3. Third arrangement of stretcher relative to the X-ray table.

It is frequently necessary to turn patients on the X-ray table on to one side for a lateral projection. If the patient is unable to help, it is again important to see that this is done in the proper way, so that both staff and patient are involved in the least expenditure of effort.

Since the X-ray table is not very wide it is wise to begin by pulling the patient from the centre of the table nearer to the edge towards which he is *not* going to turn. He is less likely then to find that as he turns he rolls perilously close to the table edge on the side towards which he is turning.

The turning procedure is begun by alteration in the position of the patient's limbs. If he is to be turned on to his *left* side, his left arm is brought away from his body, abducted at the shoulder. The right leg is brought across the trunk, flexed at hip and knee, and the right arm brought forward across the chest. This positioning of the limbs tilts the trunk in the direction of the patient's turn.

The radiographer who will do most of the work of turning the patient (and can in fact act unaided) then goes round the X-ray table to the patient's left side and puts both hands well under the patient, one under the shoulders and one under the pelvis. This is easy to do as the patient's body is already tilted by the weight of the limbs.

It is now possible smoothly and gently to roll the patient on to his left side by the radiographer leaning backwards and pressing with thighs and knees against the X-ray table. Some assistance can be given by another radiographer standing on the other side of the X-ray table, but it will probably not be necessary unless the patient is entirely a dead weight. A patient can be turned from the supine position on to his *right* side in a similar manner with the above procedure reversed as to side.

In moving and turning patients, in picking them up and in putting them down, and in assisting them to move themselves, it is important always to be as smooth and as gentle in action as possible. It is, for instance, very unpleasant for a patient who is being lifted on to the X-ray table to be put down upon it too quickly. There is no 'give' in an uncovered X-ray table that the patient can appreciate, and he is going to think it hard enough without making his first encounter with the surface a sudden one. Whenever the X-ray examination is likely to be prolonged in time, it is a kindness to the patient to make the table a softer bed by the use of the thin radiolucent mattresses which are available.

Before beginning any turning movements it is wise to find out if there is any particular part of the patient which is painful or tender. He will wish to guard it from sudden contacts, and it may be necessary to arrange special support for an injured limb, someone being detailed to care for this while the movements are undertaken.

It is also wise to think that the patient may know the best way in which he can be assisted. If a patient has been ill a long time and has lived with a particular pain or disability for some while, he will have learned how best to manage certain manœuvres with the least distress to himself. If he seems to know and wants to do it his way, he should not be disregarded.

In accident and emergency X-ray departments special casualty trolleys or transport tables are sometimes used. A patient occupying such equipment is seriously injured and should not be moved from it. The design of each system—there are several available—is intended to facilitate radiological investigation with minimum disturbance of the subject.

The Patient in Bed

In some hospitals the working method is to move a patient from the ward to other departments in his bed, unless he is fully ambulant. The patient is often well enough to transfer himself from bed to X-ray table with a small measure of supervision and assistance. If he is not fit for this he should be lifted. Several of the methods described for a stretcher patient are clearly applicable but it is not practical to use any in which radiographers have to stretch across the bed in moving the patient. Even hospital beds are much wider than a stretcher: the extension of the arms will totally prevent the proper application of forces and put the operator's back in considerable jeopardy.

THE ANAESTHETIZED PATIENT

With the increasing use in X-ray departments of procedures which involve the use of a general anaesthetic, care of the unconscious patient is becoming more frequently part of a radiographer's responsibility. Even though this care is of a temporary character and short duration for any particular patient, lack of knowledge can result in disasters which may occur very quickly. The radiographer must understand the mishaps which are liable to occur, and must know the simple yet important principles of care of such a patient, not only during the period of recovery from anaesthesia but also prior to and in the course of its induction.

Before Anaesthesia

A patient who comes to the X-ray department for any radiological procedure which requires the administration of an anaesthetic, either local or general, will be already under sedation by the time the radiographer receives him. This does not mean either that he will be unconscious or even that his aspect necessarily appears abnormal to a cursory observation. For these reasons it is particularly important to remember that this patient *is* in a drugged condition and affected by influences which may cause him to behave abnormally. He may become disorientated and restless and in his confusion attempt to leave the X-ray table or trolley on which he is lying; loss of muscular co-ordination, as a result of the administration of drugs, can then easily lead to a fall.

No sedated patient should be left alone at any time in the X-ray department unless he is in a bed with cot sides. He will arrive in the X-ray room in the company of a nurse but it is quite probable that the latter must then leave to return to her duties on the ward. The radiographer who receives the patient should observe the following procedure.

(1) Greet the patient by name, giving him also some words of comfort and confidence. Your purpose should be to make the patient feel important; to show him that he has your full attention and that you know what you are doing.

(2) Check carefully the patient's identity, referring to the case notes, the patient's hospital number, the X-ray requisition form and any previous radiographs.

(3) Check with the nurse, the case notes and personal observation that the patient has been prepared for the procedure, particularly that any denture normally worn has been removed.

(4) If the patient has to wait on the X-ray table make him as comfortable as possible.

(5) Be quiet. If others are in the room, unnecessary noise and conversation should be avoided, as such stimuli may excite or confuse the patient.

(6) If the patient wishes to talk, reply gently, briefly and reassuringly.

(7) Remain with the patient. If the patient becomes restless, either at this time or during induction of general anaesthesia, the radiographer should not struggle with him. As a rule he can be effectively restrained if the radiographer places one arm across his legs just above the knees and uses the other to hold down the patient's arms. Assistance should be obtained when necessary.

During induction of general anaesthesia, the anaesthetist is likely to require help from a member of the radiographic staff if a nurse is not available for this purpose. At this time conversation should be avoided as far as possible. If words are necessary they must be carefully chosen: as consciousness fades so hearing becomes more acute and a patient can be easily alarmed and upset by comments which he may not understand.

A number of ways of producing anaesthesia are available but their discussion is irrelevant to the purpose of this book. In the X-ray department the probable method will be by inhalation of gases, preceded by the intravenous injection of a rapidly acting agent such as Sodium Pentothal. Several stages of anaesthesia have been described.

(1) Analgesia. The nervous system remains under control but the patient loses peripheral sensation. During this stage he may make swallowing movements.

(2) Excitement, which may be observed in movements of the limbs and eyeballs, dilatation of the pupils and muscle spasm. The purpose of administering the short-acting anaesthetic is to avoid this stage. The patient usually falls rapidly and easily asleep.

(3) Surgical anaesthesia which will be moderate or deep depending upon the requirements of the operation or procedure; in the X-ray department only light or moderate anaesthesia should be required.

In attending the anaesthetist the radiographer's function may include the following:

(i) assisting with any intravenous injection (see Chapter XVI);

(ii) handing to the anaesthetist any instruments, drugs or apparatus he may need;

(iii) under his direction, adjusting the flow of a transfusion or checking the pulse or blood pressure of the patient (see Chapter XVI). At no stage of the procedure should the anaesthetist be left wholly alone with the patient, particularly during either induction or termination of the anaesthetic. Emergencies may occur which are difficult for him to handle without assistance of some kind. From another point of view, if the patient is a woman a male anaesthetist should have a chaperone present as a safeguard against hallucinatory allegations of unprofessional conduct towards her.

Following General Anaesthesia

Care of the unconscious patient should follow the same rules, whether his condition has resulted from anaesthesia or another cause. He must never be left alone while he is in the X-ray department but must be kept under observation. In the case of the anaesthetized patient the anaesthetist will terminate anaesthesia gradually and will indicate when the patient is fit to be moved from the table and to return to the ward.

In placing an unconscious patient either on the X-ray table or on a trolley it is important to see that his arms are not in such a position that he will be lying on them when he is laid down. Nor should they be allowed to dangle over the edges of the trolley or table and hang down towards the floor.

The commonest cause of death in the anaesthetized patient has been said to be obstruction of his airway produced by his relaxed tongue falling against the posterior wall of his pharynx; the patient is unable to breathe by reason of this obstruction. It is important, therefore, to see that a clear airway is maintained, and this is the first essential in looking after such a patient. In some cases a rubber airway may have been inserted, and there is then less likelihood of obstruction occurring. However if the patient is restless and tries to eject the airway, it is better removed.

If the patient has to lie supine, his lower jaw should be held forward. This is done by pulling the jaw forward so that the lower teeth are beyond the upper ones. (See description on p. 256 and illustrations on p. 255.) This keeps the tongue forward and the airway clear. If there is risk of the patient vomiting, his head should be turned to one side.

The vomiting patient is in danger of inhaling his own vomit. In the X-ray department this risk can be removed if the patient is put on a tilting table and tipped a few degrees head downwards. A tilting table is the best one for an unconscious patient. If he is not on a tilting table and he starts to vomit, his head should be turned to one side and the shoulders tilted sideways so that the head is really well turned. It should be ascertained that the airway is clear.

An advantageous position for the patient is one giving postural drainage. That is a semi-prone position, half-way between lying on his side and lying face downwards. (See Plate VI, facing page 19.) The arm of the side on which he is lying should be placed behind him (*not* underneath him). His head is turned on one side with the face rotated slightly downwards.

The patient's colour should be observed for cyanosis. The term cyanosis means that the patient is beginning to turn blue, and this will be observed in the face. It is a sign that the blood is lacking in oxygen. The blueness will show first in the tips of the ears and the nose, and immediate action should be taken. It should be made certain that the airway is clear, oxygen should be given by mask (see Chapter xvi) and medical advice sought.

If the patient stops breathing a method of artificial respiration which can be instantly and easily applied is one which is called expired air resuscitation (see Chapter xvii).

It is to be emphasized that these considerations in the care of the unconscious patient—the importance of seeing that a clear airway is maintained and that the patient can vomit in safety—apply whatever may be the reason for the patient's unconsciousness, whether it is due to anaesthesia or other causes. If the student radiographer is left alone with an unconscious patient and a change in the patient's condition is detected (for example he becomes cyanosed or stops breathing), the student should *not* run out of the room to fetch the assistance of seniors, leaving the patient alone. Instead the attention of others should be attracted by calling, and such procedures as seem immediately helpful should be initiated without delay.

If the patient is not completely unconscious but is semi-conscious, nothing should be given to him by mouth.

HYGIENE IN THE X-RAY DEPARTMENT

Although considerations of hygiene may be rated as secondary in a state of emergency, nevertheless the general practice of hygiene in the X-ray department is an important factor in patient-safety.

In this case the risk against which the patient is to be protected is cross infection—that is the acquiring of an infection which he did not have when he came to the hospital. It is important to protect from infection not only the patient but also the staff, and conditions of hygiene directed for the patient's benefit will assist also the staff. However, the staff have on their side the advantage of a tendency to acquire immunity, whereas the tendency of the patient is to acquire infection. He is already in a state of lowered resistance and is susceptible to invasion by bacteria.

The successful prevention of cross infection in hospitals depends upon every single member of its staff, not only those who handle patients but those who handle materials which will be in contact with patients and ward and departmental clinical staff. Much attention to detail is required from all concerned. For example, a laundry-bag can bring infection to the ward because at some stage in its transport it has been allowed to rest on the ground in the hospital yard.

As a contribution to general departmental hygiene, radiographers should pay attention to personal hygiene. In the previous chapter it was explained that a radiographer who looks clean and fresh makes a better impression on the patient, but the practical value of personal fastidiousness goes much further than external appearance.

Short clean nails, clean and tidy hair, clean shoes, and a fresh white coat are less likely to carry and transmit disease than are the same personal features in the opposite condition. Hands washed between the handling of patients, and after contact with such articles as bedpans, urinals, used instruments, dressings, etc., should be a practised routine so customary that it does not need to be remembered.

Hygiene for the patient must be maintained by ensuring that he has a clean gown to wear and a clean cubicle in which to undress. In the X-ray room clean linen and blankets should be provided for the X-ray table. Disposable paper sheets of various sizes are useful here, since they can be laid over the pillow case and over a linen sheet where the patient lies and fresh ones supplied for each patient.

Any utensils given to the patient for his use—for example bedpans, urinals, receivers, drinking mugs, containers for dentures, etc.—must be clean. In modern practice many of these items are disposable. These are a great aid to hygiene as they are used only once. Later chapters deal with the question of sterilization and the special case of the patient with a communicable disease (see Chapters IV and XV).

The radiolucent plastic foam pads which are accessories frequently found in X-ray departments should be washed often, and may conveniently be enclosed in polythene sheeting to save them from contamination by blood and other discharges. For drying the hands, ordinary roller towels should not be used as they provide a medium favourable to bacterial growth, and they should be replaced by disposable paper towels, or the type of towel dispenser which continuously provides a fresh area of towel for each user.

The darkroom also may be a good ground for the growth of bacteria. Tanks and water-jacket in a processing unit should be regularly cleaned out, not only because cleanliness is a necessary feature in photographic processing, but because the moisture, lack of sunlight, and even temperature of the surroundings are so favourable to the growth of bacterial organisms.

The X-ray rooms and changing rooms should be well ventilated and must be kept clean and tidy. Accessories such as the pads previously mentioned, head clamps, angle boards, and protractors should be kept in closed cupboards where they are more likely to escape dust. The top of the X-ray table and the front surface of the erect Potter-Bucky stand should be cleaned down with a suitable antiseptic solution (for example 70 per cent methylated spirit in an aerosol) and particular attention should be paid to this if the patient has been in direct contact with it as may occur in radiography of the skull and sinuses.

Aerosol sprays are very useful here as they allow quick, easy and hygienic application of the cleansing agent. It is good practice to keep an aerosol container of antiseptic in the X-ray room where skull and sinus examinations are carried out, together with a supply of disposable tissues for wiping dry the sprayed area.

It is part of the radiographer's responsibility to see that the department is clean, even if it is not necessary for the radiographer actually to undertake much cleaning. In most cases general cleaning will be done by the hospital cleaners, but the work of cleaning equipment and various accessories will be taken by the radiographer. No one should find the task beneath professional dignity, for the maintenance of clean conditions is an important part of departmental care, and is related to our responsibility towards the patient.

GENERAL COMFORT AND REASSURANCE FOR THE PATIENT

Patients of course spend periods of time in the X-ray department which vary according to the nature of the examination and the departmental conditions. The interval can vary from 20 minutes to a period of several hours. We must make the patient's stay, however brief, as pleasant as possible. This demands both attention to general conditions regarding adequate ventilation and provision of shelter from draughts, and time taken to see that the patient is comfortable. Often, for example, when a patient has to wait lying upon a stretcher, it needs but a slight rearrangement of the pillows and his position to make a great difference to his comfort. Even the busiest of us can spare the few seconds to do this.

If he has to wait a long while, the patient will do so with an easier mind if from time to time some explanation is given to him as to how matters are progressing. Even just a smile and a brief encouraging remark can make a difference, reassuring the patient that the radiographer remembers his existence and that his X-ray examination has not been forgotten. A patient who is alone in a waiting-room for some time has been known to convince himself that he was entirely alone in the department, everyone else having gone home. Ward patients worry sometimes over how they are going to get back to the ward.

The patient must always be fully instructed as to what he must do about food and drink during the waiting period.

There are many small general details of this nature which to the patient can be of very great importance, far more than we realize. They can add up to a large sum in the balance of his estimation, and can make a big difference to his ease while he is with us. Many of them are within the scope of the least experienced member of the department once sufficient insight and observation—valuable qualities in those who care for patients—have shown the need.

While there are many things which the student radiographer can undertake for the patient's well-being, anything untoward that happens to the patient while he is in the department should be reported to seniors in charge. The procedures required in the event of an accident are discussed in Chapter xviii.

CHAPTER III

DRUGS IN THE X-RAY DEPARTMENT

A drug is defined as 'an original simple medicinal substance'. Modern medical practice employs such a full range of materials administered to the patient that this dictionary definition may seem inadequate in its scope. In the X-ray department few substances given to the patient and introduced into his various anatomical and physiological systems are medicinal in the sense that they have healing properties, though they do have attributes adapted to medical use. The range of such substances is limited relative to the wide variety used throughout the hospital, and in this respect student radiographers may find themselves more fortunate than their medical and nursing colleagues. They have a shorter list to remember.

Defined for the purposes of consideration here as substances administered to the patient, drugs in the X-ray department will be seen to fall into three main groups.

(i) Drugs to be used in preparation of the patient.

(ii) Contrast agents for use in X-ray examination of the patient.

(iii) Drugs to be used in resuscitation.

The contrast agents form the largest and most extensively used group. An important feature of the other two groups is that they may include drugs which are classed as poisons and dangerous drugs, and certain regulations must be followed in keeping these drugs in the department. These regulations will be considered now.

POISONS AND DANGEROUS DRUGS

The term 'dangerous drugs' is used to mean here drugs controlled by the Dangerous Drugs Act, and they may be seen described as D.D.A. drugs. The drugs which come under this Act are those which are likely to cause drug addiction, and it is for this reason that the rules with regard to keeping and issuing them are so strict. Cocaine, heroin, morphine, opium, and pethidine are some examples of habit-forming drugs controlled by the Dangerous Drugs Act.

31

These drugs are issued to 'the man in the street' only on the written prescription of a medical practitioner, but hospital wards and special departments may keep a stock of some of the preparations. These must be requisitioned by an order in duplicate in a special book signed by an authorized responsible person in charge of the ward or department. The drugs must be in containers marked D.D.A., and they should be stored in a special locked cupboard of which the key is kept by the person in charge in the department responsible for the drugs.

Poisons and the regulations for their use are under the control of the Poisons and Pharmacy Act. This embraces a very wide range of substances capable of being toxic and dangerous, and it is divided into several separate schedules. In hospital the significant Schedules are Schedule I and Schedule IV, which can be grouped together. Drugs so scheduled can be obtained for the ward or department only on the written order of a medical officer or the responsible person in charge.

Scheduled Poisons must be clearly labelled and kept in a locked cupboard, the key being held by the person in charge. In practice on the wards it will be found usual to have a locked drug cupboard for the Schedule I and Schedule IV Poisons, with a small inside cupboard with separate lock and key for the D.D.A. drugs. Some of these cupboards have a red warning light which shows whenever the cupboard is unlocked and serves as a reminder that it must be locked again after use. Examples of drugs controlled by the Poisons and Pharmacy Act are atropine, hyoscine, adrenaline, digitalis, and others.

If the X-ray department has a D.D.A. Drugs and Poisons cupboard (as it must have if it keeps in stock any of the substances controlled by these Acts), then this cupboard is in the custody of the radiographer in charge of the department. The drugs concerned will be delivered to the department by being handed by an authorized person to the radiographer in charge (or deputy) in exchange for a signed order requesting them. The cupboard and its contents should be checked at regular intervals by the hospital pharmacist.

As a general rule poisons are issued from the hospital pharmacy in distinctive bottles. These may be in different coloured glass and are sometimes a special shape, often hexagonal and vertically ridged. Many drugs are prepared by the manufacturers in vacuum-sealed glass ampoules containing a standard amount, usually in individual dose for injection. In use these glass containers are broken open with the aid of a metal file and are then discarded after the drug has been used. The drug is drawn from the ampoule by means of a needle and syringe so that sterile technique may be maintained.

Another type of container is a glass bottle which holds more than one dose, the end being closed by a rubber diaphragm which is usually covered with a screw top. Such a bottle should be held by its sides so that the hands do not contaminate the rubber top. The contents are withdrawn by piercing the rubber diaphragm with a needle through which the drug is drawn into a syringe.

UNITS OF MEASUREMENT

In hospitals in the United Kingdom the metric system has by now replaced earlier systems of measurement which were often confusing, and thus were liable to be a source of error.

In the metric system weight is measured in kilograms, grammes, and milligrams. In writing, g is the symbol for a gramme, with kg, and mg for the multiple or fraction of it. Volume is measured in terms of the litre (l.), which is the volume of one kilogram of water at 4° C. A fraction of the litre is the millilitre (ml) which is the volume of one gramme of water at the same temperature. The cubic centimetre as an expression of volume is being discarded in favour of the millilitre, to which it is approximately equivalent.

Percentage Solutions

The term 'per cent' denotes the strength of a solution. If the solute is a solid it will be measured by weight, the liquid solvent being measured by volume. The strength of the solution will then be given by the expression 'Per cent W/V', meaning weight in volume. If the solute and the solvent are both liquids they are measured by volume, and the strength is then given by the expression 'Per cent V/V', meaning volume in volume.

DRUGS USED IN PREPARATION OF THE PATIENT

In the X-ray department drugs may be kept to be used in preparing the patient for X-ray examinations. The stock of these is not likely to be large nor will the range be wide. Certain X-ray examinations (for example angiography and encephalography) are very unlikely to be undertaken on out-patients, and if the patient is in hospital the responsibility for preparing him will rest with the ward. Drugs from the ward stock will be used in accordance with the recommendations of the X-ray department. However, there are some examinations for which some premedication is required which may well be done on out-patients (e.g., hysterosalpingography), and it may be useful to keep in the X-ray department a small stock of the necessary drugs. Certain X-ray examinations require the use of a local anaesthetic (for example bronchography) and this also is something that might be kept in the department.

It can be said that drugs used in preparation are likely to fall within the following general groupings.

(i) Aperients and suppositories.

(ii) Sedative drugs such as pethidine and luminal.

(iii) Preparations for local anaesthesia such as lignocaine.

(iv) Analgesics such as codeine and aspirin.

The important point in keeping these drugs is their correct segregation. Those which are Scheduled Poisons, such as codeine preparations over a certain strength and barbiturates, must be kept in a separate locked cupboard. Those, such as pethidine and preparations of cocaine over a certain strength, which are D.D.A. drugs must be kept in a separate locked cupboard; this is often, as has been said, a small inner cupboard within the poisons cupboard.

Aperients and suppositories should be kept separately in what is termed a medicine cupboard containing preparations for internal use; its contents can also include contrast agents for use in X-ray examinations. It is preferable that this cupboard should be capable of being locked, the key being kept in any convenient place.

This medicine cupboard should *not* be used also for the storing of preparations which are solely for external use (for example, antiseptic and disinfectant solutions). These should be kept in a separate lotions cupboard. Any system which puts into the same cupboard preparations which are for external application only and those materials which will be given internally (even though they be on separate shelves) is inadvisable, hazardous, and an invitation to error.

Regulations for the safe keeping of drugs are desirable and necessary but may have to be relaxed in particular circumstances.

These circumstances arise in the X-ray department in providing drugs which may be used in the resuscitation of a patient, suffering an adverse reaction to the administration of a radiological contrast agent. In this situation a needed drug which is under lock and key in a cupboard may not come to hand sufficiently quickly to help the patient.

The dilemma to be resolved—jointly by the consultant radiologist, the superintendent radiographer and the chief pharmacist—is to decide where the greater risk lies: in the open availability of small quantities of certain drugs; or in the occasional, but real danger to human life of them *not* being readily accessible? Some degree of compromise is possible and to this end the following points should be considered in equipping a resuscitation trolley.

(i) The trolley should not be kept in any place where many people—especially members of the public—would normally pass, for example in a corridor. It should stand, if possible, in an X-ray room where it is likely to be used.

(ii) The provision of a loose cover (of linen or plastic material) over the trolley serves the double purpose of protecting the equipment from dust and preventing its contents from being directly visible. Such a cover can be made to drape over the whole trolley like a cosy over a tea-pot and to be readily lifted by means of looped handles on the top.

CONTRAST AGENTS USED IN X-RAY EXAMINATIONS

The term *contrast agents* denotes substances which can be used to show organs or parts of the body in radiographic contrast to their surrounding tissues. The contrast material achieves this result in one of two ways. Either it is of low atomic number and causes the part in which it is placed to be *more* readily penetrated by X rays than is the surrounding tissue; this is called a negative contrast agent. Or it is of high atomic number and causes the part in which it is placed to be *less* readily penetrated by X rays than is the surrounding tissue; this is called a positive contrast agent and it may also be described as an opaque medium.

It should be noted that the expression *an opaque medium* is a correct singular form. The plural is *some opaque media*. The words

D

contrast medium and *contrast media* are often encountered in place of *contrast agent* and *contrast agents* and this is correct usage. Unfortunately the tiresome error of *contrast media* used as a *singular* is extremely widespread even among writers who should know better.

Negative Contrast Materials

The only negative contrast materials are gases such as air or oxygen or carbon dioxide. Air-filled parts are shown in the radiographic image of an ordinary X-ray film as black areas because the gas is letting through more X radiation to blacken the film, and on the fluorescent screen as light areas because more X radiation is being transmitted through the gas to make the screen fluoresce.

For diagnostic purposes air or oxygen or carbon dioxide may be put into tracts and cavities in various systems of the body. Some examples of organs suitable for the injection of a gas are the ventricles of the brain, the spinal canal, the colon, the peritoneal cavity of the abdomen, the joint spaces of the knee.

A natural demonstration of the effectiveness of gas as a negative contrast agent can be found in films of the abdomen taken with the patient erect. The normal 'gas bubble' present in the stomach is then seen readily, and it can be noted that part of the left side of the diaphragm is delineated by reason of its situation between the air-filled lungs above and the gas contained in the stomach immediately below.

Positive Contrast Materials

Positive contrast agents are all substances of high atomic number which absorb X radiation. Therefore in the radiographic image of the X-ray film they make structures in which they are present appear light in contrast to the surrounding tissue because less radiation is reaching the film to blacken it. Correspondingly they appear dark on the fluorescent screen because less X-radiation is reaching the screen to make it fluoresce.

These contrast materials are used in a variety of ways depending on the material and the part of the body which it is desired to examine. They can be introduced into tracts and cavities, and some of them can be allowed to pass into certain physiological systems so that the function of the organs concerned (for example the kidneys and gall bladder) can be examined radiographically.

Elements of high atomic number which are used to make these preparations are (i) barium and (ii) iodine.

BARIUM PREPARATIONS

Barium is employed as a radiographic contrast agent in the form of one of its salts—barium sulphate. It is used almost solely for examination of all parts of the alimentary tract (the pharynx and oesophagus, the stomach, the small bowel, the colon) though a special sterile preparation is sometimes introduced into the urinary bladder and the biliary ducts.

Barium sulphate is chosen for the following reasons.

(i) It has high atomic number.

(ii) It is insoluble and stable, and will pass through the intestinal tract without dissolving or changing to form substances poisonous to the patient. Salts of barium other than the sulphate are highly poisonous.

(iii) It causes little upset to the intestinal tract even in large doses, although it may aggravate a constipated condition.

(iv) It has the virtue of being cheap.

Barium sulphate is supplied commercially as a white powder, and may be prepared for use in the X-ray department by being mixed with water until the desired consistency is reached. It is probably a more common practice now to use the special preparations which are available under several proprietary names. These are suspensions of either 100 per cent W/V or 50 per cent W/V. If it is 100 per cent suspension each 100 ml contains 1 g in weight of barium sulphate, while the 50 per cent suspension contains, in each 100 ml, 0.5 g in weight of barium sulphate.

In some of these preparations the barium sulphate is kept in suspension by means of suspending agents such as water-soluble gums, and some of them are prepared with the barium sulphate in colloidal form (that is in very fine particles), so that suspending agents are not necessary.

These suspensions may be further diluted with water to obtain a concentration suitable to the wishes of the radiologist and the examination for which the contrast agent is being prepared. For examination of the oesophagus, a paste-like viscosity will often be needed, and special proprietary preparations with this characteristic are available; or barium sulphate powder may be mixed with water to obtain the desired consistency.

Fig. 4. Contrast agents used in X-ray examinations

AGENTS			USES	EXAMPLES OF PROPRIETARY NAMES
Negative agents	Gases		For filling certain tracts and cavities (1) Air (2) Oxygen (3) Carbon dioxide	
Positive agents	Barium preparations		For gastro-intestinal tract (1) Barium sulphate	Micropaque Baritop
	Iodine compounds	Organic iodine compounds	For urography and angiography (1) Sodium and meglumine diatrizoates (2) Sodium and meglumine iothalamates	Hypaque Urovison Conray
			For cholecystography intravenous (1) Iodipamide methylglucamine	(1) Biligrafin
			For cholecystography oral (1) Iopanoic acid (2) Calcium iopodate (3) Iobenzamic acid	(1) Telepaque (2) Biloptin (3) Osbil
			Other compounds for filling tracts and cavities (1) Propyliodone (2) Viscous sodium acetrizoate (3) Ethyl iodophenyl-undecylates	(1) Dionosil (2) Salpix (3) Myodil
			For gastro-intestinal tract (1) Sodium and methylglucamine salts of diatrizoate with flavouring and wetting agent	(1) Gastrografin
		Iodized oils	For filling tracts and cavities (1) Iodized fatty acids of poppyseed oil	(1) Lipiodol

One proprietary brand of barium sulphate at present on the market is a 100 per cent W/V suspension in which a quantity of carbon dioxide has been dissolved. The function of the gas is to increase adherence of barium particles to the mucous membranes of stomach and upper alimentary tract and thus to provide the double contrast of radio-opaque outlines to radio-parent organs. This preparation is available in an air-tight can which contains 300 ml and should be opened about 10 minutes before use, having been thoroughly shaken; for a barium meal the contents are given undiluted.

With regard to keeping and using barium sulphate preparations in the department, there are some points which should be borne in mind. These may seem so obvious that they take on the appearance of being insignificant, but errors arising from lack of attention to them are potentially disastrous in result. There are on record cases of barium examinations which have been lethal to the patient because of a 'simple' mistake.

The preparations used must be kept in clearly labelled containers, and the radiographer must check the container to make sure that the right preparation is being used. There is not likely to be any difficulty here in the case of the proprietary preparations, for these are of course supplied in containers clearly and durably labelled. If barium sulphate powder is used not as a proprietary preparation but supplied by the hospital pharmacy, it has been known for it to be kept in the X-ray department in a container which is unlabelled, or has entirely irrelevant indications of content on the outside (for example, it is a biscuit tin). This is a hazardous practice that should never be undertaken.

It is also a little unwise to prepare any of these contrast agents in a poorly-lit room. It may seem tiresomely punctilious to find risk from inadequate lighting when custom makes a procedure so familiar, and practice persuades us that nothing can go wrong. Yet some people have learned from irrevocable experience that had they been able to *see* fully the materials they were using, disaster would not have occurred.

Dry barium sulphate powder may be said to keep indefinitely in a well closed container, but the suspensions may be liable to contamination, and it should be ascertained by smell and by looking that this has not taken place. Dilutions from the suspensions should be prepared just before use.

Lastly, the simple rules of hygiene should not be overlooked. Vessels used in preparing the contrast medium and giving it to the patient should be clean, items such as glasses and spoons should not be interchanged between patients without being properly washed, and enema tubes inserted in the rectum must be washed after use unless they are disposable.

IODINE PREPARATIONS

Preparations in which molecules of iodine are the opaque agent form a very large group of contrast materials used in many different X-ray examinations. Some of them are of complex chemical composition, but they can be classified under two general headings.

(*a*) The organic iodine compounds.

(*b*) The iodized oils.

A feature which distinguishes the first and larger group is that many of the organic iodine compounds can be injected intravenously, and may take part in physiological processes in the body. The iodized oils are suitable only for filling tracts within the body by mechanical methods, and they are *not* suitable for injection into the blood stream.

An important requirement of all these preparations is that they must be stable compounds which do not break down after they have been given to the patient, with effects possibly dangerous to him.

(*a*) ORGANIC IODINE COMPOUNDS

These have a complex molecular structure, and as a result they tend to have full names which are lengthy and meaningless to those not learned in organic chemistry. In most cases they are called by a shortened name or by trade names under which these various preparations are sold.

Despite their complexity, the molecules of these compounds may be simply considered as having two constituent features; (i) the iodine which provides the radio-opaque element and makes the substance a contrast agent for radiography, and (ii) the chemical remainder which holds the iodine in stable combination and determines the chemical, physical, and physiological properties of the compound. In absorption of these agents iodine is excreted by the kidneys, but the carrier factor may remain and form a granulomatous residue which is potentially harmful. This eventuality is one of many which require consideration in the manufacture of new contrast agents.

Increase in the iodine content of each molecule increases the efficacy of the compound in providing contrast. Products which are now available have 3 atoms of iodine per molecule and are described as triiodinated compounds.

The organic iodine compounds can be considered from the point of view of the X-ray examinations for which they are used. These fall into three main groups. These groups are:

(i) organic iodine compounds for urography and angiography;

(ii) organic iodine compounds for cholecystography;

(iii) other organic iodine compounds which are *not* for intravenous injection, and are used for contrast examinations which are not included in the previous two groups.

(i) Organic Iodine Compounds for Urography and Angiography

There are several triiodinated organic iodine compounds which are suitable for injection intravenously or intra-arterially during urography or angiography. Examples are the sodium and meglumine salts of iothalamic acid and the corresponding salts of diatrizoic acid and acetrizoic acid; sometimes a product combines sodium and meglumine salts.

In the X-ray department these compounds are much more familiar to radiographers under their trade names. For instance 'Conray 280' is a meglumine iothalamate injection and 'Conray 420' a sodium iothalamate injection; 'Cardio-Conray' contains a combination of meglumine iothalamate and sodium iothalamate; 'Urovison' and 'Hypaque 85' are each a combination of sodium diatrizoate and meglumine diatrizoate.

The iodine content of these compounds varies considerably and influences the suitability of each for a particular kind of examination. Since many of the trade names include numerals it is easy for student radiographers—and indeed others who are supposedly older and wiser—to become confused about the possible meanings of these figures. Some of them refer to the W/V percentage of the solution: for example 'Hypaque 45' is a 45 per cent W/V aqueous solution of sodium diatrizoate. On the other hand, 'Conray 325' is a 54 per cent W/V aqueous solution of sodium iothalamate.

A more significant and memorable quantity for radiographers—

since it is a statement about the radio-opacity of the substance concerned—is the amount of iodine in one millilitre of the solution. In the 'Hypaque' preparation mentioned above this quantity is 270 mg of iodine and in the 'Conray' preparation it is 325 mg of iodine. Students should study manufacturers' leaflets and notice the amounts of iodine (mg/ml) contained in the contrast agents in use in their departments. It will be seen that, in general, organic iodine compounds employed for urography and cerebral angiography contain less iodine than those applicable to abdominal arteriography and angiocardiography.

(ii) Organic Iodine Compounds for Cholecystography

Organic iodine compounds appropriate for cholecystography can be administered in two different ways. There are at present (i) a single contrast agent suitable for intravenous injection, and (ii) a group of contrast agents suitable for oral administration.

The intravenous contrast agent for cholecystography is known as 'Biligrafin', which is a proprietary name: its approved chemical name is iodipamide. It is an iodine compound with 3 atoms of iodine per molecule, and it is available as a 30 per cent solution ('Biligrafin'), and a 50 per cent solution ('Biligrafin Forte').

This contrast medium is used particularly to show the ducts of the biliary tract as well as the gall bladder, and since its use depends on the excretory function of the *liver*, it will show the bile ducts even when the gall bladder has been surgically removed. It is also used as a means of examining the gall bladder when the oral method has failed to show any filling.

The oral contrast agents for cholecystography which are given to the patient by mouth usually depend upon the *functioning gall bladder* to become filled with the medium. The opaque material reaches the liver via the portal circulation, and is eventually concentrated by the gall bladder. The depth of contrast obtained, that is the degree of opacity of the organ as it appears on the radiograph, depends on the function of the gall bladder mucosa.

Many orally administered contrast agents for cholecystography are available and it is proposed to mention here only a few as examples.

'Osbil' (iobenzamic acid) is presented in tablet form, each tablet containing 0.5 g of iobenzamic acid; it is a triiodinated formula, the iodine content being 57.5 per cent. The usual dose is 3 g (six tablets) but in the case of an obese patient this may be increased to 4.5 g (nine tablets).

'Biloptin' and 'Solu-Biloptin' are a compound called calcium iopodate. 'Biloptin' is offered in capsule form, the normal dose being 6 capsules, comparable to the tablet preparations. 'Solu-Biloptin' appears as a powder, which is presented in packets containing a prepared dose of 3 g. The patient is instructed to put the contents of the sachet in an empty tumbler and stir in a small amount of water or diluted fruit squash before taking.

'Telepaque' is iopanoic acid and contains 66.68 per cent of organically bound iodine. The presentation is in tablet form, the normal adult dose being 3 g (six tablets); this may safely be doubled if necessary.

(iii) Other Organic Iodine Compounds

There is a group of organic iodine compounds which cannot be injected intravenously. They are used for examinations in which the method of application is the direct filling of a space or potential space, introduction of the material being made either through a natural body orifice or by means of a hollow needle or tube put into the space concerned. The regions for which these organic iodine compounds and these methods are used include principally the following: the spinal canal, the fourth ventricle of the brain, the bronchial tree, the urethra, the uterus, the nasal sinuses, the bile ducts post-operatively through a tube which has been left *in situ*, the pleural cavity, the ducts of the salivary glands, and the tracts of abnormal sinuses and fistulae.

Students will encounter in clinical use in their X-ray departments a number of these preparations which have an intra-cavitary application. A study of the manufacturer's information sheet which usually accompanies the packages is well worth while: it provides facts about the nature of the drug, indications, contra-indications and normal dosage. Here we can refer to only a few examples.

One of these compounds is 'Myodil' which is employed extensively for introduction into the spinal canal and has limited applications to ventriculography. 'Myodil' contains 30 per cent of iodine organically combined in a mixture of ethyl iodophenylundecylates; it is hardly necessary to observe that in the X-ray department everyone—from high to low—generally calls it 'Myodil'. 'Myodil' is not water soluble and absorbs only very slowly at a rate estimated to be 1 ml per year. This means that it will be visible on radiographs taken a long time after the first injection of the contrast agent. The dose for myelography is up to 6 ml and for ventriculography 0.5–2 ml. Preparations offered under the trade names of 'Ethiodan' and 'Pantopaque' are similar to 'Myodil'.

'Salpix' is the trade name of a contrast agent which is prepared for hysterosalpingography. The opacity to X rays is provided by sodium acetrizoate; this is combined with a carrier medium which is known for short as P.V.P. and is commonplace in many households—though no doubt unrecognized—as it is a binding agent used for aspirin and other tablets. 'Salpix' is water soluble and is excreted rapidly by the kidneys. A typical injection would consist of 10 ml.

'Dionosil' is an organic iodine compound employed for bronchography. Its shortened chemical name is propyliodone and it is di-iodinated (has 2 atoms of iodine per molecule). It is rapidly absorbed and is excreted by the kidneys. 'Dionosil' is offered in a 50 per cent aqueous solution ('Dionosil Aqueous'); as a 60 per cent suspension in arachis oil ('Dionosil Oily'); and in powder form. The dose for adults is between 12 and 18 ml of the fluids.

One further organic iodine compound should be mentioned. It is known by the proprietary name 'Gastrografin', and the contrast substance is the same as that in the medium for urography and angiography known as 'Urografin' (sodium-methylglucamine diatrizoate), but it has added to it some flavourings and a wetting agent. These additions mean that it is suitable only for examination of the alimentary tract. For this purpose it can be used in place of barium sulphate or in combination with it for special examinations. Unlike the barium sulphate, 'Gastrografin' is absorbable and is excreted by the kidneys.

Student radiographers are not expected to possess any detailed chemical knowledge of the many organic iodine compounds used in radiology. In this section we have mentioned a number which are appropriate only to mechanical introduction into a body cavity. It is this characteristic which is of serious significance to the radiographer, who—although not directly their user—is often the person preparing the instruments and materials for a particular procedure. The responsibility for administering a contrast agent to a patient is a medical one but this does not alter the desirability of radiographers' understanding the nature of these drugs and the dangers of any indiscriminate application.

At the beginning of this section we listed a number of bodily regions, for the examination of which this group of organic iodine compounds is suitable. It is possible to employ for certain of these procedures (for example, hysterosalpingography) some of the compounds designated for urography and angiography in a previous section of this chapter (see p. 41). However, the traffic is one way only: it is *not* possible to employ for intravenous or intra-arterial injection any of the compounds described here for intra-cavitary introduction.

(*b*) THE IODIZED OILS

In use the iodized oils may be linked with those organic compounds which cannot be injected intravenously or intra-arterially. The iodized oils can be neither injected into the blood stream nor passed into the body by a physiological process, and they must therefore be used only for direct introduction into spaces and tracts. They are thus used for a similar range of examinations. The regions examined include the bronchi, the pleural cavity, the nasal sinuses, the ducts of the salivary glands, the bladder and urethra, the biliary ducts where a tube has been left *in situ* at operation, the uterus, and abnormal sinus tracts.

The iodized oils are supplied in viscous form in different strengths and in fluid form. They are basically a combination of iodine and poppy seed oil. They are unabsorbable and a feature of their use in bronchography is that unless they are coughed up they will be retained in the bronchi for a period of time that may be months, whereas 'Dionosil' disappears in a few days. This may be significant if it is desired to repeat the bronchogram or perhaps to fill the other side shortly after the first examination.

The Use of Contrast Agents

When contrast agents are used in the X-ray department, there are certain points which have to be considered. First of all, the chance of reactions occurring as a result of their being given to the patient. This is particularly important in regard to the iodine compounds intravenously injected. Sensitivity to iodine is not uncommon, and the intravenous injection gives a rapid and systemic dispersal through the blood stream.

The reactions which occur may be mild, such as sensations of warmth, nausea, and faintness, but they can be severe resulting in a shock-like state, and they can be lethal. Methods of dealing with these reactions are discussed in another part of this book (Chapters VII and XVII).

In preparing to give *any* contrast medium to the patient the radiographer must first make sure that it is the right patient, checking the patient's name against the request form and the examination required. In certain cases the opaque medium will in fact be given to the patient by a doctor (for example, as an intravenous injection), but this does not absolve the radiographer from responsibility. The patient's name must be checked, the opaque agent must be checked when it is selected, when it is given to the patient, and again when the container is returned to wherever it is kept or the empty ampoule discarded. In the case of an intravenous injection the radiographer must see that the doctor also checks the substance before it is given.

Anything given to the patient should never be kept in or issued from an unlabelled container.

DRUGS USED IN RESUSCITATION

It has been indicated that reactions to contrast agents are possible, particularly when they are injected into the blood stream. Examinations of this type are being carried out by X-ray departments upon increasing numbers of patients. This must raise the risk of 'reaction incidents', and the X-ray department must prepare itself to meet these emergencies.

The time factor is important since for a severe reaction treatment must be instituted *at once*. It is therefore sound practice, indeed essential practice, to have in the X-ray room an emergency supply of various drugs and instruments. These may be in a box but better still are laid on a trolley where they are readily and instantly available. Chapters VII and XVII in this book deal with the treatment of reactions in more detail, but it can be said here that the probable drug contents of the emergency box or trolley are likely to include the following.

(i) Adrenaline (1 in 1000) plus adrenaline (1 in 10,000) to raise the blood pressure and increase cardiac output.

(ii) Analeptic drugs for injection. These are drugs which stimulate and restore. Examples are nikethamide which is a respiratory stimulant, aminophylline which stimulates the muscular tissue of the heart, Methedrine which stimulates the central nervous system.

(iii) Drugs which decrease cardiac excitability, such as Inderal and lignocaine (2 per cent).

(iv) Drugs which reduce allergic reactions in the body. Examples are the corticosteroids (for instance Hydrocortisone 100 mg) and the antihistamines (for instance Phenergan, Sparine).

(v) An intravenous anaesthetic, Pentothal.

(vi) Sterile distilled water.

If a patient collapses to the extent that his heart stops beating (cardiac arrest) and he stops breathing (respiratory arrest), clearly the first things that must be done for him are to restore the pumping action of the heart and to put air into his lungs by mechanical means (see Chapter XVII, page 250). Once the actions have been established, the medical team will proceed with a therapeutic plan and are likely to give the patient four substances. These are used (a) because the chemistry of the body has been disturbed by what is happening to the patient—his blood, for example, will be somewhat acid instead of being very slightly alkaline as it normally is; (b) because the heart muscle has lost its normal degree of tension and vigour (tone); (c) because the heart may not resume its normal rhythmic contractions but be in a state of abnormal twitching (fibrillation).

These conditions must be corrected and the substances used are:

(i) sodium bicarbonate to correct the metabolic acidosis;

(ii) adrenaline to restore the heart tone;

(iii) a calcium salt such as calcium chloride which also restores the heart tone and has an enhanced effect when used in conjunction with adrenaline;

(iv) Lignocaine, which is a local anaesthetic but in this instance is used for its specific properties affecting the heart muscle. It damps down the irritability of the heart muscle and assists in combating fibrillation.

The above observations are intended only for the general guidance of the student reader. Radiographers do not carry medical responsibility and do not make decisions involving the supply and use of drugs to be employed in a clinical emergency; nor can any particular selection of drugs be regarded as the only correct one in such a situation. Students who enquire about the provisions in their own hospital may find a much lengthier list of substances than the one given here, or may find confusingly different names and presentations. The choice will be influenced by the consultant cardiologist's own opinion of what is appropriate and perhaps also by the geographical situation of the X-ray department: whether it is very distant from effective clinical support or is close to a ward unit. Students who do not understand the contents of the box or trolley kept in the department where they work are well advised to make their own enquiry about it.

LABELLING AND ISSUING

It may be emphasized in conclusion that the labelling of all containers is most important. Labels must be placed on the body of the container and not upon the lid. They must be clear, they must not be altered, and if damaged they must be renewed. They should be renewed by returning the container to the hospital pharmacy where the labels will be properly replaced. It must be recognized that once any agents have been separated from their labelled containers opportunity has been made for an element of doubt as to their nature, and contents therefore must not be removed from their containers except for immediate use.

Many of the substances which we use in the X-ray department become very familiar to us, and we issue them to patients many times a week, never expecting that anything will go wrong. Yet we should always approach such procedures, even the simplest of them, with seriousness and attention to detail. It is when these features are absent that error enters easily through the door which we have left open by our lack of care.

CHAPTER IV

STERILIZATION AND STERILE TECHNIQUES

To sterilize anything for surgical purposes is to make it free from all living organisms. Among these living organisms will be included disease-producing bacteria. Surgical procedures in hospital carry risk of infection and sepsis for the patient, and even when the surgery seems of very minor character (for example, puncturing a vein with a needle to give an intravenous injection) the risk of infection, of bacteria entering the body and growing and multiplying in the tissues, is none the less there.

Patients are susceptible to infection. They are not in a state of full health, and are thus in a weakened condition and less able to combat bacterial invasion. In earlier days a patient who had to go into hospital saw his chances of emerging alive as not very great. If he did not die of whatever condition took him into the hospital, he had good opportunity of dying of infections acquired while he was there. The principle of asepsis in surgery—that is, of applying to surgery techniques which totally exclude the presence of disease-producing organisms—was introduced by Lister, and this gloomy picture of low survival rate was made to change a great deal.

Methods of preventing infection are based upon the fact that bacteria cannot effectively travel by themselves. The ways in which infection can be spread are therefore ways by which bacteria are carried. Bacteria can be conveyed from one person to another and from one place to another in the following ways.

(a) By direct contact. For example, a surgeon who operates with bacteria present on his clothes or hands may transfer these organisms directly to his instruments, and thus to the patient via the operation wound. It is to prevent this type of transfer of bacteria that surgeons not only use instruments and dressings which have been made free from living organisms by sterilization, but also wear sterile gowns over their theatre clothes and sterile gloves on their hands. Anyone assisting a surgeon and handling instruments he will use must take the same precautions.

(b) By aerial carriage. Dust or fluff from blankets may carry bacteria through the air. A less obvious but perhaps the most important way in which bacteria can be aerially conveyed is by droplet infection. This term refers to direct infection by droplet from the nose and mouth. Thus a surgeon, although he may have sought to sterilize his clothing, hands and instruments, could still convey bacteria into an operation wound by fine particles of moisture carried by his breath from his nose and mouth. Some of these bacteria might be innocuous to himself, so that he did not feel himself to be an infected person, but could be harmful to others. Certain diseases can be conveyed by those who give no evidence of having the disease and yet have the organisms present in their bodies; these people are called *carriers*. Diphtheria is an example of a disease which can be spread by droplet infection from carriers. In order to prevent spread of bacteria by droplet infection, hospital staff working with sterile equipment in conditions of surgical asepsis wear a mask which covers both mouth and nose and is designed to act as a barrier.

(*c*) *Food and water carriage.* Food and water are often vehicles for the transport of bacteria. Typhoid fever may be considered as a typical example of the way in which infection may be so conveyed from one place to another. Typhoid fever is a disease of the intestine, and the organisms are present in the faeces and sometimes the urine of infected persons; these people may have definite symptoms of the disease, or may be carriers as previously mentioned. Bad drainage systems and inefficient purification of drinking water can result in this being contaminated by excreta, and the infection is thus conveyed to others. In the U.K. the purification of most water supplies is so efficient as to make them safe for drinking purposes. *Food*, however, carries bacteria very readily, and certain foods (for example, re-heated meat dishes and carelessly made ice-cream) provide a good medium in which bacteria may multiply. The typhoid organisms, and of course many others, may be conveyed to food by the hands of people who are either actively infected with disease or are carriers. This is a particularly insidious form of spread, as it may be difficult to find the source. For this reason it is important that those who handle food should make sure that after using a lavatory they wash their hands to exclude contamination by excreta. The wrapping of bread and other foodstuffs at the source of production in order to reduce direct handling is another obvious safety measure.

(*d*) *Insect carriage*. We are most of us familiar with the fact that certain flying insects such as house-flies and blue-bottles spread disease by conveying organisms, for example, from infected faeces to food. Parasites and vermin (for example body lice and fleas) may also carry disease between people, and between animals and man. Malaria is conveyed to man by the bite of a particular mosquito which harbours the organisms.

Infection can be established in the body when bacteria have gained entry to it. For preventing the spread of infection, knowledge of how bacteria gain entry is as important as knowledge of how they are conveyed. They gain entry through a broken skin surface, and through natural orifices in the body such as the nose and mouth. Regions lined with mucous membrane give a warm moist environment which is favourable to bacterial growth.

Precautions are taken in hospital to prevent the spread of infection in any of the ways listed. During surgery direct contact and aerial spread by droplet infection are the most likely ways for bacteria to be carried to the patient, and sterile techniques and sterilization of instruments and materials are methods of prevention unfailingly applied. It is important for us to recognize how much the safety of the patient depends on the correct practice of these techniques in *every* detail of their application. We should realize too how much this correct practice depends upon *us*. By an instant's lack of attention any one of us can invalidate the whole careful technique, and thus endanger the patient's safety as surely as if we had pushed him off the X-ray table. We should aim at not allowing any slip to occur. If it does occur it should not be ignored or passed over, whether the fault be ours or another's. If just one link in the chain is faulty, the strength of the remainder is immaterial, and we must strictly supervise ourselves in this as keepers of the patient's safety.

Bacteria are microscopic single-cell organisms, and they live, reproduce, and die. In order to live they require the following.

(i) Food—protein, carbohydrate, and mineral salts taken from tissue cells.

(ii) Moisture.

(iii) Oxygen. Some bacteria require air for their oxygen, but others do not take it from the air, and in fact cannot live in air.

(iv) An even temperature—$37°$–$38°$ C ($98°$–$100°$ F).

(v) Generally an environment which is neither acid nor more than slightly alkaline and is unchanging.

E

The procedures used to achieve asepsis are directed to kill bacteria or prevent their growth by disturbance, in one way or another, of these conditions which they find favourable. Some bacteria when they discover themselves in unfavourable conditions are able to achieve a phase of resistance, and such bacteria are called spore-forming. In this state they can resist some degree of heat, lack of moisture, cold, and the action of disinfectants.

In procedures for which aseptic precautions are required all the utensils, instruments, and materials for dressings will be sterilized. It must be remembered that such articles are not to be allowed to come in contact with others which have not been sterilized, and they must be handled with sterile forceps or by hands covered with sterile rubber gloves. The lightest touch of any non-sterile surface against one which *is* sterile contaminates the latter and invalidates its sterility. To ensure that this technique is correctly performed requires an undeviating attention to detail.

METHODS OF STERILIZATION

Heat

Since heat kills all forms of bacteria it is the method of choice, unless it cannot be used because it will prove damaging to the article or material which is to be sterilized. In order to kill spore-forming bacteria it is necessary to achieve higher temperatures and longer periods of exposure than are lethal to the non-sporing type. Heat can be applied to sterilization in the following ways.

(i) By boiling.
(ii) By steam under pressure.
(iii) As dry heat in an oven.

STERILIZATION BY BOILING

Boiling in plain water has traditionally been used as a means of sterilization. The efficacy of the method is increased by raising the boiling temperature if sodium carbonate is added to the water to make a 2 per cent solution, and this also prevents the formation of rust on metal articles. However, for syringes only plain water must be used, as the addition of sodium carbonate will make the syringe alkaline, and this may affect any substance with which the syringe is

to be filled for the treatment of a patient. Nor should sodium carbonate be added to water in which rubber articles are to be boiled.

Boiling for 2 minutes destroys organisms which are not spore-
forming, but the usual practice is to extend the boiling time to 5
minutes to give added safety, provided that the article will stand 5
minutes' immersion in boiling water. Before use the boiled articles
must be allowed to cool.

Sterilization by boiling can of course be done in any container
which will hold the article and the boiling water and stand the
heat. A traditional piece of equipment is an electric sterilizer in
which several articles can be boiled together.

Fig. 5. Cheatle forceps. *By courtesy of Down Bros. and Mayer & Phelps Ltd.*

In using this sterilizer certain points must be noted if the method is
to be efficient.

First of all the articles must not be packed tightly, or stacked
closely one inside the other. Close packing prevents the full penetration of the moist heat. The water level in the sterilizer must be
high enough to cover all the articles which are in it, and the lid of
the sterilizer must be kept properly closed while the boiling is in
progress. The period of 5 minutes should be timed only after the
water has come to a 'full rolling boil' following the immersion of the
last unsterile article. Opening the lid of the sterilizer and putting in
more cold articles lowers the temperature, and if this is done the
water must be brought back to the boil, and the timing of the 5
minute period must be started again.

Modern hospital practice looks closely at techniques of sterilization for wards and departments, and whenever possible systems of
central sterile supplies (see page 59) are used. Some departments
may need such a number of sterilized instruments that they cannot

use the central sterile supplies and they do their own sterilizing. In some cases they have discarded the traditional sterilizer and use small autoclaves. These sterilize, not by means of boiling water but by means of steam under pressure (see page 55).

It must be remembered that once they have been sterilized, articles must be handled with sterile forceps and must not be allowed to make contact with unsterile surfaces. Sterile forceps for use in removing articles from a sterilizer or small autoclave are long handled and are known as Cheatle forceps. When not in use they are kept in a jar containing disinfectant solution, the jar being tall enough to keep immersed almost the whole length of the forceps, except the upper part of the handles. It must be recognized that unless they are kept and used with the utmost care, Cheatle forceps are a dangerous source of contamination.

This jar and the Cheatle forceps must be sterilized at least once a day, preferably just before use; too often the forceps sit in their container, with re-sterilization and renewal of the disinfectant fluid neglected even until there is a film of dust on the surface of the solution. This is very bad practice indeed.

It is better to have at least two pairs of Cheatle forceps. In a sterilizer, one pair and the jar are sterilized completely immersed; the other pair is placed with its handles resting on the edge of the sterilizer, the points and as much of the handles as possible being submerged in the boiling water. This pair is then used to remove the jar and the other forceps, the jar being raised from the sterilizer with some of the water in it. This reduces to a minimum contamination of the inside of the jar by air. The water can be 'topped up' with antiseptic solution and the jar used to receive the completely sterilized forceps. These will be employed to remove from the sterilizer other sterile equipment, and to undertake the tray or trolley setting for which sterilization is being done.

In using these forceps, it is necessary to take them straight from the jar without touching them to or tapping them against the unsterile edge and sides. The forceps must not be held vertically upwards or waved about, for the disinfectant solution can then run down them to the unsterile handles and then contaminate the points of the forceps by running in that direction again when the forceps are restored to the points-downward position.

Articles put into a sterilizer must be clean before they are put into it, and warm water and soap must be used to remove any barium, mucus, pus, blood, etc., with which they may be stained. The sterilizer itself requires regular cleaning with warm water and scouring powder.

STERILIZATION BY STEAM UNDER PRESSURE

Sterilization by steam under pressure is an efficient procedure. It is carried out in a piece of equipment called an autoclave. Articles put in an autoclave are subjected to the action of steam at pressures above atmospheric pressure and temperatures above the boiling point of water.

In hospital, large autoclaves are found in sterilizing departments. In order to make use of such autoclaves, the articles which are to be sterilized must be packed into a suitable container. This is traditionally a metal drum lined with lint, and having perforations at the sides and top which can be opened and closed. Before the drum is sent into the autoclave, the perforations are opened so that the steam can fully penetrate the interior, and they are then closed as soon as the drum comes out of the autoclave.

The container will return to the X-ray department with the perforations closed, and they must be left like that to preserve the sterility of the contents and not opened until the drum is being autoclaved again. The lining of the drum must provide for a covering over the contents, and when sterile articles are being removed care must be taken to see that no part of the lining becomes contaminated by touching the outside of the drum; the drum should be left open no longer than is necessary for removal of what is immediately needed. The drum must be packed loosely so that the steam may easily reach all the articles contained in it, and in a methodical manner so that specific articles may be readily recognized and removed without creating disorder among the contents which it is desired to leave for later use.

A modern development is the use of various materials to make a wrapping for articles to be autoclaved, an example being nylon film. Steam penetrates the nylon, which yet provides (so long as it is intact and sealed) a covering through which the contents cannot be contaminated from the outside. In opening such a pack, care must be taken to see that only the outside edges and corners are handled, and that these are not subsequently allowed to fall against the inner parts of the wrapping to contaminate the contents.

Another wrapping material in use is a special glycerin-impregnated paper. It has the virtue that it is very cheap, and the characteristic that when the pack is opened the paper falls away and lies flat very readily. Before autoclaving the articles are wrapped in this paper, and the pack is then enclosed in an outer wrapping or a paper bag thermally sealed or folded over and fastened. The paper wrappings are, of course, used once only and then discarded. Paper is a satisfactory bacterial barrier when kept dry. It would not be suitable as the only enclosure for the heavier surgical instruments.

The paper must be of a weight appropriate to what must be enclosed, and the packs must be stored in suitable conditions. These conditions must be dry and clean. Sterile packs in paper should be handled as little as possible. All separate packs must each bear outward evidence of sterilization, and this often takes the form of a special tape fastening the pack. The tape becomes striped after sterilization; this feature can be seen in Fig. 30 on page 223.

The hospital will use its autoclaving equipment as fully as possible, for it is not an economic procedure to bring it up to the required temperature and pressure, and hold it there for the necessary time unless the autoclave has a full load. In departmental practice it is therefore necessary to make a certain allowance of time for autoclaving to be done.

Drums and other containers of articles for sterilization are usually sent for autoclaving at certain times in the day, and are received back in the X-ray department either later the same day or on the following morning. The autoclaving process actually involves the loading of the autoclave, bringing it up to the correct temperature and pressure, and holding these for the required period. The time that this whole process needs depends upon several factors, the most important being the type of equipment in use. Modern high-pressure high vacuum equipment reaches higher temperatures more quickly, and sterilization is achieved in very much shorter times than would be possible with older apparatus. However, the time factor can be a problem when a busy clinic is sterilizing its own instruments in an autoclave installed in the clinic.

To check the efficacy of an autoclaving process, bacteriological tests can be carried out from time to time. It may be the practice to include among the contents of the packs to be put in for sterilization small glass tubes which contain a chemical that changes colour when the required temperature is reached.

STERILIZATION BY DRY HEAT

Moist heat is more penetrating and effective than dry heat, but hot dry air (or alternatively infra-red rays) can be used for efficient sterilization in an oven. In modern practice in sterilization departments, articles move slowly on a conveyor belt through an infrared oven at a rate which brings them to the other end of their travel in a condition of sterility. The method is suitable for fragile glass ware such as test-tubes and syringes.

Gamma Radiation

Gamma radiation, like heat, is a physical method of sterilization. Exposure to these electromagnetic radiations of very short wavelength is lethal to disease-producing organisms. It has the advantage that the penetrating character of the radiation enables it to be used to sterilize articles after they have been packaged; this makes it a valuable and commonly used method for manufacturers issuing pre-sterilized equipment. It may be used to sterilize articles which cannot be exposed to heat.

Chemical Disinfection

Chemical disinfectants and antiseptics (which may be called weak disinfectants) have certain limitations in use. The only way of achieving *complete* sterility is to expose the organisms to a great enough heat for a long enough time, but obviously this is not possible with all materials and all equipment at all times. Chemical methods will then have to be used, although they are regarded as the least efficient choice.

It is important to recognize two separate actions which these chemicals may have. They may (i) kill bacteria, or (ii) inhibit the growth of bacteria; the first of these effects is implied in the term *bactericidal* to describe any agent used, and the second is contained in the term *bacteriostatic*.

If it is desired to use a chemical agent to *kill* bacteria, it must be applied in greater strength and for a longer period of time than if the object is merely inhibition of growth. For example, tincture of chlorhexidine gluconate ('Hibitane') 0.5 per cent in 70 per cent industrial methylated spirit would be a suitable solution in which to store instruments which had been previously sterilized by heat, since the effect required from the solution is simply bacteriostatic. It would require a stronger solution of 'Hibitane' to be bactericidal. Twenty minutes' immersion in 2 per cent 'Hibitane' might be used as a chemical method of sterilization if heat could not be employed, although there is no method of chemical sterilization which is completely effective in the sense that it will kill *all* organisms. Spore-forming bacteria, for example, withstand the action of chemical disinfectants more easily than that of heat. However, a reliable preparation used in sufficient strength for a long enough time can be expected to kill *most* organisms.

Articles put into disinfectant must be cleaned with soap and water before they go in, as the solution will be unable to act efficiently upon parts covered with organic matter such as mucus, pus, blood, etc. The container holding the disinfectant solution must itself be sterilized before the solution is put in, and there must be enough solution in it entirely to cover the articles which are to be disinfected. These must be totally immersed in it for the length of time required for the solution to act.

The particular agent used for any given purpose will depend upon various factors—whether the required effect is bacteriostatic or bactericidal, the nature of what is to be disinfected (for example surgical instruments, skin surfaces, linen, sluice room floors), and the practice of those who are using the agent.

Many of the agents are long tried and accepted and there is a very wide range of them. They may be divided into certain general groups according to their basic nature and action. Some of them—such as hydrogen peroxide and formalin—have an oxidizing or reducing action. Some of them are heavy metallic salts—for example oxycyanide of mercury—which act by penetrating and killing bacteria. Chlorine, iodine, and bromine are non-metallic elements which kill bacteria by combining with protein in their cells. Cresol and phenol are two substances caustic in action which form the basis of many disinfectants and antiseptics. Carbolic acid is liquefied phenol, and Lysol is a solution of cresol in soap. Jeyes Fluid and Izal are disinfectant fluids which are preparations of phenol. Detergent solutions such as cetrimide are used for cleaning the skin and sterilizing plastic instruments, which cannot be autoclaved, and there is a detergent emulsion known as 'Phisohex' which can be used in place of soap to wash the hands. This has a bacterio-static action if used repeatedly, but there are certain organisms

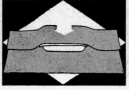
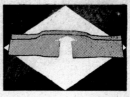

The contents of the pack —gauze, cotton wool, cellulose wadding etc.—are placed in a receiver in the centre of the INNER WRAPPER which acts as the sterile area when the pack is opened for use. Underneath is the OUTER PROTECTIVE wrapper.

The INNER WRAPPER is folded over in the manner shown so as to cover the contents.

The paper is again folded over so as to enclose the contents.

Both ends are neatly folded over the contents so that the wrapper can easily be opened when required.

The forceps in a paper bag or wrapper which will be used for opening the inner wrapper are then put on top.

A paper towel is put on top. This is for use as a sterile towel by the doctor or nurse who will be using the pack.

One corner of the OUTER WRAPPER is now folded over so as to cover the top of the contents and the corner folded back on top.

In a similar manner the paper is folded over to the centre of the pack and the corner turned back.

Fold the third corner over in a similar manner.

Then turn pack round and remaining flap of paper is folded over and tucked under the two top folds.

Leave the corner projecting out.

When the pack is ready to be used pull the corner out and open. The OUTER WRAPPER is opened by a person who need not be 'scrubbed up'.

Plate VII   Illustration of the making of a sterile pack. *By courtesy of the Bowater-Scott Corporation Ltd.*

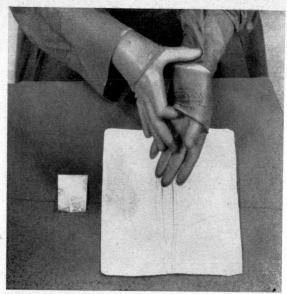

(a) Turning back first cuff.

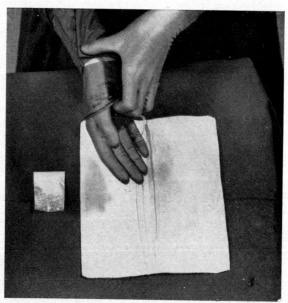

(b) Turning back second cuff.

Plate X   Showing correct method of putting on sterile gloves.   From *Operating Theatre Technique* (R. L. Brigden). *By courtesy of E. & S. Livingstone.*

(those which cause bowel infections) upon which it has no action. Benzalkonium chloride ('Roccal'), chlorhexidine ('Hibitane'), chlorhexidine with cetrimide ('Savlon'), and domiphen bromide ('Bradosol') are all antiseptic agents in current use.

Some of the older agents have certain aspects which make them difficult or not fully satisfactory to use. The mercurial salts are slow in action and are neutralized by proteins, and some of them sensitize the skin. Carbolic acid is a corrosive poison, so that care must be taken not to let it splash the skin. Although much less caustic, Lysol is capable of producing skin irritation, and all the cresol and phenol preparations even in weak dilution must be thought potentially dangerous.

Some of the preparations which have long been used to clean wounds (for example hypochlorite solutions) are now seen as possibly harmful because they may delay healing by damaging leucocytes and tissue cells, and may provide in the damaged tissues conditions which favour bacterial growth. In present practice for cleansing wounds these solutions are being replaced by preparations such as 'Bradosol' 0.05 per cent in saline, and 'Hibitane' 0.05 per cent in aqueous solution.

CENTRAL STERILE SUPPLY

The matters of prevention of infection in hospital and the practices of sterilization have been and are still the subject of research by various organizations. A current practice is the establishment of central sterile supply services—that is the provision of a central department which would supply the hospital with all that is needed in ready sterilized equipment. This removes from the wards and special departments such as the X-ray department the need to operate their own sterilizing systems.

There are obvious advantages in such an arrangement which make it worth the financial outlay on instruments, washing equipment, and other specialized apparatus. It is less liable to failure in efficiency than a system which relies on separate sterilization processes carried out in many different places by many different people with many demands on their time. This is not to accuse doctors, nurses, and radiographers of methods which are bad practice, and of lack of conscientious care; but we are all of us aware of the human element and know that it is wise to make this factor as small as possible in processes which it is wished to keep precise. A central department for sterilization where mechanization can be introduced and the efficacy of the whole system supervised must reduce the factor of human failure. The nurse is freed from the tasks of sterilizing equipment, and thus has more time to spend in the direct nursing care of patients.

In order to use the central supply system, the ward or department in the hospital assesses its daily requirements of sterile equipment and receives this in suitable packs—such as nylon film for trays and instruments, and metal cylinders for syringes—the equipment being then returned to the central supply after use.

The modern tendency is towards making disposable as much of the equipment as can be so made, and applications of many modern materials are sought for this purpose. Aluminium foil, plastic, and cellulose are typical examples. Aluminium foil bowls, gallipots, and trays, paper dressing towels, and disposable hypodermic needles, syringes, and forceps are available, to be used once and then discarded. These provide an obvious saving in time and labour and an increase in patient safety.

In recent times much medical attention has been given to a serious risk to hospital staff which syringes and hypodermic needles may represent as conveyors of the virus of serum hepatitis ('jaundice' to the layman). This is a grave condition, much more severe than the milder infectious hepatitis for which a closely related virus is responsible. Deaths from the serum variety have occurred among workers in hospital who are occupationally concerned with procedures involving blood, the virus being carried in the blood of any patient who may once have had the disease.

The availability of disposable equipment which is discarded as soon as it has been used does much to limit the risk but student radiographers and anyone who may have to handle syringes and needles should recognize the danger and exercise care to avoid being either pricked or possibly conveying the virus from their hands to their mouths. A wary approach is always desirable.

There are even disposable bedpans and urinals available. After use these are 'posted' into a special unit in the ward or X-ray department which pulverizes the vessel and its contents which are then consigned for disposal along the usual channels for sewage.

PREPARATION OF THE HANDS FOR ASEPTIC PROCEDURES

It has long been the practice of surgeons and nurses to prepare their hands by 'scrubbing up'—that is thorough washing and scrubbing of the hands with warm water, soap, and nail brush for a period of 5 to 10 minutes, usually with the use of a bacteriostatic soap or suitable antiseptic solution. It seems to be open to debate among surgeons as to whether this process renders the hands sterile or just clean, but the safest and most regular procedure is to consider that the hands are not in fact sterile and cannot be put in contact with sterilized materials. In any case, whichever view a particular surgeon may hold, his practice will be to enclose his hands in sterile rubber gloves before he handles sterilized instruments, and anyone who assists him and also directly handles sterilized materials will do the same. The correct technique for putting on sterile gloves is shown in Plates viii–x between pages 58 and 59. It is now being thought that it may be possible to replace the 'scrubbing up' process by a less time consuming technique of immersion of the hands in suitable solutions of cetrimide and chlorhexidine.

Certain procedures such as surgical dressings are carried out with what is called the 'no touch' technique, all the dressing requirements which are sterile being manipulated with sterile forceps and not touched by hand. In this technique it is unnecessary to try to achieve sterility of the hands, and it is a safe procedure just to wash the hands well in soap and water and dry them on a clean towel. In modern practice the towel is a paper one, used once and then discarded.

By way of summing up, it must again be stressed that continuous care is necessary in the handling of sterile equipment. This must be manipulated with sterile forceps, and kept in sterile containers in sterile conditions if it is to maintain its sterility. If any contamination, even the slightest, occurs the equipment must not then be used, but must be discarded and resterilized at whatever cost in time and effort may be necessary.

CHAPTER V

PREPARATION OF THE PATIENT

It is wise to regard nearly all X-ray examinations as requiring some preparation of the patient. In the strict sense of the term preparation of the patient has been made when merely a jacket or stocking is removed prior to the X-ray examination of a limb. This is a simple procedure. More elaborate preliminaries are required for many investigations with which the student will become familiar, for example, prior to radiography of the abdomen. Whether simple or manifold, both are equally important to the patient and each should receive from the radiographer its due measure of attention.

In the interests of the satisfactory conduct of any X-ray examination it is important to think first of what may be required in the way of preparation for it. This may be the local preparation of a part or it may be the general preparation of a system; the alimentary, the respiratory or other tracts. It may be undertaken immediately prior to the X-ray examination, as mentioned above, or it may extend over 2 or even 3 days and require the administration of certain medicines and drugs.

In relation to the appropriate preparation of patients who are to have X-ray examinations the responsibilities of the radiographer are broadly two-fold. In the first place it should be made clear to the patient what is required of him and, if he is to attend for the examination at a later date, this must include some indication of the length of time the procedure is likely to occupy.

Like ourselves many of our patients lead busy lives. The mother of a family may require to make special arrangements for the care of young children in her absence; the business man probably has a full schedule of engagements. It is most unfair to allow either of these to attend the X-ray department believing that it is a matter of no more than an hour, when in fact the significant procedure is more likely to occupy 2 or 3 hours or even most of the day. To the radiographer such features of any examination are so familiar that it is very easy to overlook their strangeness to the patient. The omission of that moment or two of sympathetic explanation may at the time seem trivial, but it is very upsetting for everyone when the patient who has just had a barium meal announces that he cannot return for the follow-through film 5 hours later since he is flying to Europe on an afternoon plane.

The responsibilities of the radiographer, if in the first place to the patient himself, are secondly to those others in the hospital who have patients in their immediate care. In an earlier chapter observation has been made of the close inter-relationship of members of the medical team. No department, no unit within the hospital can properly be considered as an isolated entity. We are all inter-dependent. We cannot provide our best service for the patient if others in the hospital do not know something of what we are trying to do or understand the way in which it may be done.

To this end it is clearly essential that we should keep ward and departmental sisters conversant with our requirements for the preparation of all patients. We should see that this information is given accurately and that it is kept up to date. The radiographer who assumes that the training of nursing staff must include some knowledge and experience of preparing patients for X-ray examination is, of course, correct. But such an assumption, if the matter is left at that, does not take either party far enough; neither understands fully the needs of the other and in the outcome it is the patient who suffers most, since another examination may be required if preparation on the first occasion has been incomplete.

Such preparation is not absolute and universal. It will vary in detail between hospitals, due to the individual methods and requirements of each consultant radiologist. Even in any one hospital, it will and should undergo variation in the course of time. All branches of medicine are continuously advancing; discoveries are made, a fresh conception arises and a new practice is introduced. We cannot wisely regard any part of our work as a finished chapter, something static and complete, with which all are so familiar that we are not required to give it further attention.

For these reasons it is clearly of first importance that those in wards and other departments of the hospital, who have patients in their charge and are required to supervise the preparation of these patients prior to X-ray examination, should know in detail our current requirements in this respect. To transmit this information verbally is neither sufficient nor satisfactory. In the course of time it then acquires the reliability of mere rumour or allegation. It is possible that owing to some emergency or other exigency of circumstance a staff nurse or sister may be temporarily in charge of a ward to which she is not accustomed. It is essential that she have available written information to which she can refer in case of doubt.

The best way of providing this is in a loose-leaf bound book which is an appropriate format for 'standing orders' on the ward and more enduring and less likely to be mislaid than a number of unattached sheets. It is possible to include in such a volume not only detailed instruction on patient-preparation but notes on any special after-care required and even on the nature of each procedure; the value of such additional information is in enabling a nurse to answer questions raised by a patient when he is anxious about a forthcoming examination.

In the absence of so complete a communication it is a straightforward matter in any X-ray department to have stencilled and duplicated a sheet of simple instructions relating to the preparation of patients for X-ray examination, whether these be special procedures or even plain investigations requiring only immediate preliminaries. All wards and departments can then be circularized with this information and in the same way notified of changes as these become necessary. It is important to keep all facts issued—in whatever form—fully up to date.

An efficient 'information service' on these lines will do much to prevent oversights. For example, unless staff are suitably informed, a patient who has rib injuries may have adhesive strapping applied to his chest *before* being sent to the X-ray department to confirm the presence of fracture. If the radiographs are to be of any value the radiographer is obliged to request the removal of such strapping since it may give rise to linear shadows simulating fracture lines. The reader should pause to consider what it is like to have strips of adhesive plaster removed from the skin, particularly over a fresh injury. It will be very clear then who suffers most when this sort of lack of co-operation occurs between departments.

GENERAL ABDOMINAL PREPARATION

Many X-ray examinations involve the visualization of abdominal organs, for example cholecystography, intravenous urography barium meal. Whatever may be the special preparation required for each procedure, they have in common the feature that difficulties of interpretation sometimes arise because of confusing shadows in the lower alimentary tract, due to the normal presence of faeces and intestinal gas. It is customary therefore to include in the preparation of the patient measures which will eliminate these as far as possible.

Use of Purgatives

Usually preparation begins with the administration of a purgative 48 to 36 hours or in some cases 24 hours before the examination. In certain conditions, however, the taking of any such drug is contra-indicated, for example in the presence of haemorrhage or obstruction. Due to this, it is the practice of some radiologists to forbid the use of a purgative in the preparation of any patient for X-ray examination. In the case of in-patients any drug to be used will be given under nursing supervision on the ward. However, where out-patients are concerned it is the radiographer's responsibility to ensure that the patient receives proper instruction.

Not all bowel evacuants are equally suitable for this purpose. So many varieties of these household remedies are generally available to everyone that student radiographers may feel confused not only about the appropriateness of each in this context but also about the terminology of the subject.

Uncertain distinctions have sometimes been made between the terms *laxative, aperient, purgative* and *cathartic* drugs on the basis of the intensity of the effect produced. As the results upon any individual are unpredictable to a degree, such categorizing is unsatisfactory: there seems good reason to employ the common-sense term *purgative* for any drug which is administered for the purpose of producing a bowel action and to regard all other names as synonymous.

If cathartic drugs are to be classified at all, it is more logical to consider, not results, but differences between them in the ways they act. They may be divided into three groups:

   (i) irritant purgatives;
  (ii) lubricant purgatives;
 (iii) bulk purgatives.

IRRITANT PURGATIVES

The method of action of the so-called irritant purgatives is not fully understood and the term 'irritant' is perhaps misleading: certainly it over-simplifies, since all the drugs in this group do not act in exactly the same way. The following substances are examples of irritant purgatives.

Bisacodyl ('*Dulcolax*') produces peristalsis (automatic wavelike contractions) of the gut—mainly the large bowel—on contact with the mucous membrane which lines it; the drug has an irritant effect upon the sensory nerve endings in the mucosa. Administration may be either oral, in tablet form, or by means of a suppository inserted in the anus: in many cases a combination of both is adopted. A typical regimen might be two tablets (10 mg) taken on the evening prior to examination and a suppository inserted on the following morning.

Senna and *cascara* are both vegetable purgatives and are similar in their action, which is thought to be direct stimulation of a plexus of autonomic nerves (Auerbach's plexus) between the muscular coats of the bowel. The dose range of senna is 14–28 mg and of cascara 130–260 mg.

Castor oil breaks down water in the small, rather than the large bowel and produces an oily acid. The normal absorption of fluid is prevented and the liquid content of the large bowel thus increased. The result is to encourage peristalsis and the breakdown and dispersal of faecal masses. The usual dose of castor oil is 5–15 ml.

LUBRICANT PURGATIVES

The operation of lubricant purgatives by softening faeces is easy to understand. The most commonly used of these drugs is *liquid paraffin*, of which the usual dose is 15–30 ml. Liquid paraffin must not be given to a patient who is receiving anti-coagulant therapy for vascular disease.

Also in this group is a substance with a difficult name: *dioctylsodium sulphosuccinate* which lubricates the faeces by lowering surface tension and permitting water to penetrate them: compare the function of a photographic wetting agent in promoting the effective action of developer upon a film emulsion. '*Normax*' is an example of a purgative which contains dioctylsodium sulphosuccinate as one of its active ingredients.

BULK PURGATIVES

Bulk purgatives achieve their purpose—generally in one to three hours after administration—by increasing the volume of intestinal contents: the result is to stretch the bowel wall and encourage normal peristaltic activity.

The drugs in this group obtain the same effect in one of two different ways:

(i) the important active ingredient is an indigestible plant material or vegetable fibre which absorbs water in the intestine and swells;

(ii) the active substance is an inorganic salt which is not absorbable and by a process of osmosis retains water in the lumen of the bowel. Osmosis is the tendency of fluids which are different in concentration and separated by a permeable membrane—in this case the bowel wall—to mix with each other, the solvent of the solution which is less in concentration passing into the solution of higher concentration.

'*Normacol X*' and '*Prepacol*' are examples of bulk-forming evacuants of the first type; Epsom salts (magnesium sulphate) is a well-known member of the saline group.

SIDE EFFECTS OF PURGATIVES

The side effects of purgatives are numerous and varied and occasionally have been fatal. Some, usually elderly people may dose themselves regularly with a purgative in large quantities and without any medical advice over a long period of time: they become in fact addicted and may suffer from such consequences as electrolyte deficiency and protein loss. Sometimes the indiscriminate self-administration of a purgative has masked a serious condition, such as acute appendicitis, with tragic results.

The occurrence of these situations has roused medical anxiety about the side effects of purgatives in the hands—or rather in the bowels—of the general public. These problems are not of direct concern to the student radiographer but it is well for us to remember, whenever we instruct a patient to take a laxative prior to X-ray examination, that we are giving him a potentially harmful drug.

Lower abdominal discomfort, flatulence and colic may not be particularly serious but are extremely common side effects of purgation. Their occurrence in a proportion of patients, when cathartic

F

drugs are used as a preparation for abdominal radiography, is difficult to avoid. Ideally such preparation should be made during a period of days by means of small doses: in practice results must often be obtained quickly, usually by increased dosage. Almost inevitably for some patients disagreeable side effects—of pain, spasm and even diarrhoea—will occur.

Because so many aperients are in some degree unpredictable and inconstant in action it is difficult to formulate an ideal preparation for abdominal radiography. Departmental routines are developed from the preferences of the radiologist in charge who will have selected in the course of his experience some one method from several which are reasonably satisfactory. It is the radiographer's responsibility to be familiar in detail with the method in departmental use and to ensure that the out-patient receives correct instruction in its application.

On this point of instruction of the patient some further observations should be made. Many patients attending hospital will accept incuriously and with unquestioning placidity anything which they are given and directed to take. If the radiographer is busy and suffering from the pressure of several other people who require attention, it is likely that the assumption will be made that the patient understands what he is receiving and—as he does not ask about it—that he knows the effect it will have. In many instances this is far from being the case.

No out-patient should be instructed to take an aperient given to him, without at the same time being informed of its nature. This is important in the administration of any drug, and not least in this procedure which may appear relatively insignificant to the busy radiographer. It is most undesirable, and even cruel, to issue a standard dose of some aperient to all patients. Obviously their individual needs in this respect will vary, and very often the patient himself is the best judge of the dose he should take.

Before he is given the medicine each patient should be questioned a little about his normal bowel habits. Those who say that they 'have always been a bit stubborn, miss,' probably need the maximum dose and can safely be given it. But to dose heavily someone who normally does not require or use a laxative is unnecessary and unforgivable in circumstances when a brief enquiry could easily have been made.

In some X-ray departments it is the practice not to issue the patient directly with the required evacuant in suitable form but simply to instruct him to take an aperient. In this case it is most important that the medicine or medicines should be specified, together with some indication of normal dosage. If the choice is left, without further information, to the patient's native wit he may simply take a larger than usual amount of his customary laxative or depend on the suggestions of his neighbours and friends. In either event the favoured aperient may not be particularly suitable and the result so far as the X-ray department is concerned is indeed unpredictable. It is sufficiently difficult to obtain a consistent and satisfactory preparation of the patient without adding the additional hazard of not knowing the precise form it may take.

Young patients require special consideration. If strong purgation is to be avoided in adults, it is particularly undesirable in the case of a child. Children under a year of age rarely should be given an aperient at all and some pediatricians may not regard with favour the routine preparation of their patients for X-ray examination. If a bowel evacuant is considered necessary it may be better to rely on whatever aperient the mother normally uses for the child when need arises. The suppository form of bisacodyl already mentioned is also useful as *one* can safely be given to a child over 12 months of age. It is small enough to be easily inserted even in a youngster.

Use of Enemata

The use of an enema to empty the large bowel of faeces is well known. For this purpose, soap and water, glycerin, and olive oil enemata are all described. More recently an enema consisting of a small quantity of mixed sodium phosphates has been found to be effective. This is available as a disposable pack which allows it in some cases to be self-administered. Its disposability, which obviates difficulties of sterilizing equipment, and the advantage of there being only a small volume of fluid to inject, are clearly features which favour its use domestically, either by a nurse or even by someone untrained in hospital practice. Such an enema pack, however, is relatively expensive compared with other methods.

Unless the radiological examination is specifically of the colon (by barium enema) the use of enemata as a general preparation for abdominal radiography is not widely recommended. There are several reasons for this, an important one being that the results obtained are not completely satisfactory. Residues of fluid and air may be present which will obscure radiological appearances. Unless the enema is properly given, it may be returned without having done much more than empty the rectum and in this event faecal residues also can lead to intrusive shadowing on the radiograph.

Further important disadvantages are those associated with the use of enemata on out-patients, who constitute the majority of cases examined in many X-ray departments. If they are to be successful they require expert administration by a nurse or other skilled person; they need simple but specialized equipment; they are a time-consuming procedure; in the home they inevitably create a certain amount of inconvenience. There may perhaps also be a local difficulty in organizing a sufficiency of visits by a district nurse if the home nursing service is already strained by the demands of more urgent work.

None of this applies to the treatment of in-patients. In these cases, if an enema is recommended, it may be preferable to give a high colonic washout, using plain water. Practice will be found to vary between hospitals depending on the wishes of the radiologist concerned.

Prevention of Intestinal Gas

It has been earlier stated that the presence of intestinal gas can seriously impair radiographic detail and may delay diagnosis. It is in fact often a more troublesome problem than faecal residues. For example, a common difficulty in cholecystography is the superimposition upon the opacified gall bladder of translucencies which may be either gall stones or pockets of gas in the small or large bowel. Technically the radiographer must—and usually can—elucidate this point in the end, but it often requires considerable extension of the examination to do so. Clearly it is to the advantage of the patient and of the X-ray department if this source of doubt can be eliminated in the first instance.

Some pathological conditions give rise to abnormal gas shadows on the radiograph. For example, air may be seen to have leaked outside the alimentary tract in the case of a perforated gastric ulcer; or gas may accumulate massively and distend the bowel proximal to the site of an intestinal obstruction. In these instances its appearance is helpful to diagnosis and indeed may considerably influence treatment.

If 'snap' radiographs could be taken of any random group of people, nearly all would be found to have gas present in greater or less degree in the stomach and in the lower alimentary tract. Certain circumstances favour its collection. Diet, for example, is a factor. The subject may be eating starchy foods (carbohydrates) or vegetables such as parsnips, peas or beans, which tend to produce gas during digestion: or he may be addicted to effervescent drinks. Again, he may be an 'air swallower', a nervous habit likely to become accentuated under the slight tension of a visit to hospital and an impending X-ray examination. Confinement to bed is also a significant factor, as during prolonged immobility intestinal gas is less readily absorbed or dispersed. Adequate preparation is aimed at reducing the amount likely to be present in any individual by avoiding, whenever possible, those circumstances which increase or are favourable to its formation.

To this end a very simple but important measure is to include in the department's instructions to nursing and other hospital staff a request that any patient who is sufficiently fit should be out of bed at least for part of the day prior to the X-ray examination, or even only for an hour or so immediately before coming to the X-ray department. However, in many cases it is impossible for the patient to be on his feet and then it may unfortunately be a matter of trying to effect the absorption of accumulated gas which the patient is unable to disperse. In this case there are certain recognized treatments which may be helpful. These include:

(i) the use of a flatus tube;

(ii) the giving of one or two charcoal biscuits to eat at bed-time on the night prior to the X-ray examination;

(iii) hypodermic injection of Pituitrin (posterior lobe pituitary extract) about half an hour before radiography is undertaken.

It is to be noted that the last mentioned is seldom used in Great Britain and never except on proper medical authority. It is a smooth muscle stimulant which acts not only on the plain muscles of the intestinal walls but also on blood vessels and the uterine muscle: its use is consequently strongly contra-indicated in such conditions as cardiac disease and pregnancy.

It is generally acknowledged that to secure for radiographic purposes the adequate dispersal of abdominal gas in a patient bed-ridden for some time can be a problem virtually insoluble in a particular case.

As has been noted, diet is also a significant factor and some attention should be paid to this during the 48 hours prior to examination. Medicines containing a heavy element—for example, bismuth preparations—should be withdrawn during this period as the ingestion of such substances will lead to their appearance as opacities on the radiograph. On the day prior to the examination the patient should take a low residue diet, avoiding green vegetables, cereals and whole-meal bread. On the morning of the examination itself, if this is to be a simple radiograph of the urinary or biliary tract, it is usual to allow the patient to take a light breakfast. Some radiologists prefer that nothing should be taken from the previous midnight and in this case it should be noted that if the patient is to come starving to the department special considerations apply to the diabetic subject. This will be more fully studied in the next chapter.

Once the X-ray examination has been completed many patients will be glad to be told that they may visit the hospital canteen before travelling home: or they may be advised beforehand to bring with them a few biscuits for their temporary sustenance at the appropriate time.

CLOTHING OF THE PATIENT

The subject covered under this heading may appear one relatively insignificant in the successful outcome of an X-ray examination. It is in fact an important part of patient-care and carelessness in this regard can cause the patient appreciable suffering and can waste an immoderate amount of the radiographer's time. Here, as in many other aspects of our work, attention to detail will be consistently repaid.

Reference has already been made to inter-departmental lack of liaison in respect of the application of radio-opaque dressings: the radiographer will readily bring to mind many extensions of this. As well as adhesive strapping, lead lotions, Kaolin poultices, plaster of Paris, jaconet, and oiled silk are all materials which interfere with the visualization of radiographic detail. Whenever possible their application should be deferred until after the X-ray examination has taken place.

Any patient who is allowed to enter the X-ray room unsuitably clothed suffers unnecessarily in the course of the examination. If the subject is reasonably fit there may be only a minor degree of inconvenience: for example, perhaps a male patient will be found to have retained an abdominal truss through lack of clear instruction when being told to undress. However, for a patient who is very infirm, in pain, or acutely ill, the X-ray examination becomes an unnecessarily traumatic experience if the radiographer has to struggle single-handed to remove, say, a long, buttoned nightdress which can only be taken over the head. This sort of difficulty can readily cause a helpless patient to dread further visits to the X-ray department.

A suitable plain linen gown, preferably having a wide neck opening and no fastenings of any kind, should be provided for all patients undergoing X-ray examinations of any part of the trunk. Patients coming to the department from a ward should be dressed in this beforehand, and if the examination is to be made in the erect position it is important that slippers also should be worn. Unless nursing staff are aware of this point, in some cases the patient will be found to arrive with bare feet simply tucked into a blanket for warmth.

Out-patients who have to undress in the X-ray department should receive clear instructions. This may seem a very simple matter, yet it is worth considerable emphasis. The radiographer may have told twenty patients already that morning to 'put on this gown, please,' and through repetition will have lost all appreciation of the words used: indeed they seem perfectly clear and intelligible to the speaker. Yet it constantly must be remembered that the patient is hearing them for the first time. He is in strange surroundings which appear to him not only strange but frightening: he is concerned about himself and in some degree or another doubtful about the outcome of his present experience; he cannot ever in these circumstances be at his best. In this, as in any other point of preparation, the wise radiographer will never readily assume that the patient understands. It requires only a moment's sympathy and a few extra seconds of time to make sure.

CHAPTER VI

THE GASTRO-INTESTINAL TRACT

Radiological investigations of the gastro-intestinal tract, by barium meal and barium enema, are very frequently performed. In any general X-ray department these procedures may constitute a large section of the week's work and occupy one or more X-ray rooms for a considerable part of any day or days set aside for the purpose. Since a fluoroscopic examination by a radiologist is an essential feature of these procedures it is usual to arrange for him to see a series of patients referred to him at one time: he will undertake a 'screening' session, in the same way as a surgeon works through an operating list, on a morning or afternoon suitable to him and to the department.

The number of cases likely to be examined during any one session will vary widely, depending on local features. The availability of radiological staff, the radiologist's own assessment of the number of patients he can properly examine at one time, the size of the department and the pressure of work on it, all are among significant factors in determining the number of appointments which may be made.

It is customary to divide each session into cases for examination by barium meal (including barium swallow) and those for examination by barium enema. Alternatively separate sessions may be set aside for each. This becomes practicable when:

    (i) the majority examined are out-patients,

    (ii) the department is large enough to command several X-ray rooms and possesses ample radiological staff, so that a greater number of fluoroscopic sessions can be more readily encompassed.

Whichever way it is done, the separation of the meal and enema bookings is important from the point of view of saving time and facilitating work. Each type of examination needs its own minor specialized equipment: for example, the trolley lay-out, the availability of films of the size generally used for the examination, fitting of compressors on the serial changer, and so on. All this requires

74

to be set ready only once for a run of similar cases. It is unnecessary and uneconomic of effort to have to 'chop and change' in this respect.

If it is properly used it is a recognized advantage of any appointment system that waiting time can be appreciably decreased. In 'block booking' patients for gastro-intestinal examination some attention should be paid to the length of time likely to be required for each case. It is not a proper use of the system if the last patient to be examined has been told to come at the same hour and minute as the first. This can lead only to a lack of faith which may have repercussion. It is not unknown for a patient who is late for his appointment to explain, 'Well, I know I usually have to wait, so I didn't think it would matter.'

An understandable reluctance in hospitals to keep medical staff waiting usually leads to block appointments being over-booked. A similar result is consequent upon many departments being currently overworked: when a waiting list becomes unduly long there is a natural tendency to attempt to 'fit in' patients at an earlier date. It is likely that the time allowed for each examination will be underestimated and perhaps the possibility of some patients' failing to attend may be assessed too high. All these of course are important considerations. Those responsible for the allocation of appointments should try to evaluate them reasonably and reach a balance which will be acceptable as a working system.

In this and in succeeding chapters each special radiological procedure will be discussed under three similar headings.

(i) Specific preparation of the patient.
(ii) Preparation of the trolley.
(iii) Care of the patient.

BARIUM MEAL: BARIUM SWALLOW

Preparation of the Patient

In the previous chapter reference has been made to some general points. These include:

(i) indication to the patient of the amount of time likely to be required for (*a*) the initial fluoroscopic examination, and (*b*) any follow-through series of films for which the need may be suggested on the request form or which may be customary in the department;

(ii) such instruction as is routine in the department in relation to general preparation for abdominal radiography.

In addition to the above, gastro-intestinal radiography requires certain specific and essential restrictions of diet, upon adherence to which much of the efficacy of the examination will depend. The alimentary tract is not inherently opaque to X rays and cannot therefore be directly examined. It becomes opaque upon the introduction of a suitable contrast agent, barium sulphate, which fills the lumen of the tract and thereby will reveal irregularities due to pathology: for example, ulceration, neoplasia, or constrictive lesions.

It will be appreciated readily by the student that on the administration of a barium (sulphate) meal the radiological appearances can be reliable only if the stomach is empty at the time the meal is taken. A misleading impression of deformity may be received if the barium pattern is distorted by the presence of food residues. It is a recognized truth that in a patient whose stomach is obstructed by disease and contains an accumulation of fluid, it may not be possible to make any adequate radiological examination of the pylorus and duodenum: barium is prevented by the large gastric residue from passing into the distal portions of the stomach. In this case aspiration of the gastric contents may prove helpful.

Because of these physical principles it is essential that no patient who is to have a barium meal should come to the X-ray department having recently taken either food or drink. It is important that instructions on this point should be specific: a patient told not to eat may well think that the restriction does not apply to a glass of milk or an early morning cup of tea. It is usual, if the X-ray examination is to be in the forenoon, to instruct the patient to take nothing by mouth after the evening meal on the previous night. This probably means that he has eaten last some 12 or 15 hours prior to taking the barium meal and of course this is a starvation period of more than adequate margin.

Difficulty with this regimen, which is a very useful one, however, will arise if the patient is working during the night or if the X-ray examination has to be arranged for the afternoon. Both circumstances oblige him to miss certainly two consecutive meals if he is to refrain from food after the middle hours of the evening. It is better in this case for him to be told specifically for how many hours he is required to starve.

On this point departmental routines vary to some extent. Some radiologists prefer to tell the patient to take nothing by mouth for 6 hours prior to examination. Others will forbid food or milk for 8 hours but will allow non-milky drinks up to 4 hours before giving a barium meal. The emptying rate of a normal stomach is generally accepted as being from 4 to 6 hours. It is obviously impossible to give any exact figure, since variations will arise from the nature and amount of the food taken and individual differences in the subject at the time.

THE DIABETIC PATIENT

In any preparation involving restriction of diet, special attention must be paid to the diabetic subject. Diabetes is relatively common and is the most common of the metabolic diseases: it is a disorder of the chemical processes of the body.

There are two types of diabetes.

(i) *Diabetes Mellitus*, which is due to deficiency of insulin secretion by the pancreas. There may be partial or complete failure of secretion.

(ii) *Diabetes Insipidus*, which arises from impaired function of the posterior lobe of the pituitary gland. This is a very rare condition.

The first is very much more common than the second and the patient who says he is a diabetic almost without exception will mean that he has *diabetes mellitus*.

Insulin is a secretion of the islets of Langerhans in the pancreas. Its function in the blood stream is to control the reserve of sugar which is stored in liver and muscle in the form of glycogen. A failure in supply of insulin immediately raises the level of blood sugar and this condition is known as *hyperglycaemia*. Sugar appears also in the urine and to its presence the student will see the term *glycosuria* applied.

A disturbance of sugar metabolism in the body is associated with impaired combustion of fats, as the one process assists the other. When the oxidation of fats is only partial, certain aceto-acetic acids or *ketones* are formed in the blood. This condition is known as *ketosis* and leads to diabetic coma in the untreated subject.

Diabetes is not curable and must be treated by:

(i) correct diet, maintaining a balance of carbohydrate and fat, and of proper calorific value;

(ii) insulin administration in all but a mild form of the disease in an elderly person.

With this treatment the blood sugar can be kept at normal level, the patient is free of glycosuria, and his diabetes is said to be stabilized. Once a proper balance has been found, it is clearly of some significance that there should be little interference with the diet. Anyone known to be a diabetic must receive proper instruction if it becomes necessary for him to omit or limit a normal meal.

Such a patient should be asked first if he is taking insulin. A patient who is not receiving insulin may postpone a meal for a short period. He should be told to omit breakfast, but he must be placed *first* on the morning's list for examination and the radiographer is responsible for ensuring that he in fact receives attention quickly. The diet kitchen should be warned in advance and will provide him with a suitable meal before he leaves the hospital. Alternatively the patient may if he wishes bring his own food with him and on completion of the X-ray examination should be allowed appropriate facilities for eating his meal, away from other patients and general departmental traffic.

However, the great majority of sufferers are on insulin treatment. These should be clearly warned that, as breakfast has to be omitted prior to the X-ray examination, it is most important that the insulin is not taken either. These patients too should be placed first on the morning's list for examination. Similar arrangements should be made to provide them with a meal and they must at the same time receive their normal injection of insulin. The co-operation of the sister in charge of the out-patient department will ensure that this is done. In general diabetics are well informed and thoroughly alive to their dangers: in these circumstances many will be discovered to have come to the X-ray department already equipped with their own supplies of insulin for injection and food.

DIABETIC AND INSULIN COMA

Two forms of unconsciousness are associated with diabetes:

(i) diabetic coma;

(ii) insulin coma.

The first occurs in a subject in whom the disease is untreated or from whom the correct dose of insulin has been for some reason withheld. It is due, as has been explained already, to the accumulation in the blood of aceto-acetic acids through faulty combustion of fats. It is of slow onset, taking as a rule a matter of days to develop.

Insulin coma, on the other hand, may occur in a patient who has received too much insulin. This may be because the dose has been wrongly given, or equally it may arise in a patient who has taken the correct amount of insulin but has not eaten food, so that he has little sugar on which the insulin can work. His blood sugar falls to an abnormally low level (*hypoglycaemia*) and unconsciousness results. It is of rapid onset and may develop within an hour of the patient's arrival at the hospital.

Should a diabetic subject become unconscious while in the X-ray department it may be of importance that the radiographer is able to recognize each type of coma. Rapidity of onset is a significant point: a diabetic patient, apparently normal on arrival, who subsequently becomes faint or unconscious, is almost certainly suffering from hypoglycaemia. The signs of both types of coma, however, are given below.

Diabetic Coma (Hyperglycaemia)
(i) Drowsiness and eventual unconsciousness.
(ii) Stertorous deep breathing. (The respiratory centre is stimulated and endeavours to restore via the lungs the normal chemical balance of the body.)
(iii) A sweet smell of acetone on the breath.
(iv) A dry skin.
    This patient requires insulin by hypodermic injection.

Insulin Coma (Hypoglycaemia)
(i) A sinking feeling, accompanied by hunger.
(ii) Faintness and eventual unconsciousness.
(iii) Quiet shallow breathing.
(iv) Absence of the characteristic breath odour.
(v) Sweating and moist clammy skin.
    This patient requires glucose. Its administration must be intravenous if unconsciousness is complete. In some cases an injection of glucagon or adrenaline may be made. Either of these releases the patient's own reserves of 'sugar' stored as glycogen in the liver. However, if the patient is able to take anything by mouth

two lumps of sugar should be given: indeed the first-aider is quite likely to find these in the pocket or handbag of the sufferer, and can make use of them before the arrival of medical assistance.

PREPARATION OF INFANTS

The procedure to be followed in the case of babies who are to have a barium meal requires some notice. Usually the child is being fed four hourly. The mother may give the customary meal at 6.0 a.m. but should not feed the child again until after completion of the X-ray examination. This will ensure firstly that the stomach is empty and secondly that the patient is hungry on arrival in the X-ray department, no small factor in the successful administration of an unusual drink in unusual surroundings. It is wise to give the mother a word of explanation as to the reason for the starvation; otherwise, if the baby becomes fretful and crying through hunger, she may be tempted to feed it before coming to the hospital. The X-ray examination should be timed for 10.0 a.m. or as near to that hour as possible.

It has sometimes been advocated that the barium sulphate mixture should be mixed in suitable quantity with the child's customary food and the two given in combination: the principle presumably is that the child will accept such a mixture more readily. However, the system has little to recommend it. The fat present in milk leads to flocculation of the barium sulphate and visualization of the alimentary tract is impaired. Secondly the combination of barium sulphate and water with the dried milk powder usually employed often seems to result in a thickly viscous consistency, more solid than fluid, which the patient cannot take.

A preferable method is to replace the child's ten o'clock feed with a normally prepared barium drink administered in a feeding bottle of conventional type. A baby who is hungry will generally show little reluctance to take it.

The most difficult patient is the toddler who has to be persuaded to drink from a cup an unusual drink which, even if he is hungry, he will probably find that he does not like. His mother or father, if present, may or may not prove an asset to the radiographer. Sometimes in these circumstances children are found to respond better to the ministrations of a stranger with whom there is no emotional link, but it is as well for the radiographer to discover from his parents as much as possible about the child.

The correct use of his name or nickname is an obvious beginning. If he enjoys drinking through a straw, to allow him to take the barium in this way may be adequate encouragement. If he is averse to milk, the appearance of the barium sulphate will be off-putting at the start, and in this case a suitable colouring agent might well be added.

In the case of babies and young children cleanliness in the preparation of the meal is particularly important. After use, feeding bottles should be rinsed in cold water, washed with warm soapy water, rinsed well and finally boiled. If there is no sterilizer in the X-ray department they may have to be done elsewhere. Teats also should be well washed, using a soft brush; they should be rinsed likewise in cold water, boiled and then stored in a covered jar. Common salt rubbed inside and over the outside of each teat after the initial washing is said to be a helpful cleansing agent.

Preparation of the Trolley

Before the beginning of each fluoroscopic list a 'barium trolley' should be made ready containing all that will be needed for the complete session of 'meals'. A 'barium preparation' room is a feature of many departments. Here the 'meal' is mixed in accordance with the requirements of the radiologist concerned and poured ready for use into the appropriate number of beakers or tumblers set ready on a tray.

In general use at the present time are proprietary preparations of barium sulphate in suspension form. These require further dilution with water in accordance with the wishes of the radiologist or—as the case may be—the manufacturers' instructions. Radiologists' requirements vary. Some find most satisfactory a 'half and half' mixture: others prefer a dilution of the barium preparation 1 part in 3 parts of water. A small quantity of the 'neat' solution also may be needed, as this provides the best visualization of the oesophageal and gastric mucosa. In some departments it is the practice to administer such an 'aperitif' to every patient for barium meal examination and in this case the required number of 'short drinks' should also be made ready beforehand.

Required, too, is a suitable supply of barium sulphate paste for examination of the oesophagus. Barium in this thickened form is usually given to patients in whom the oesophagus is the point of clinical interest and this will be indicated on the X-ray requisition by the expression 'Barium swallow'. Its advantage is that the paste travels down the gullet less rapidly than fluid and thus facilitates its radiological study in detail. A further asset is that when the main bolus has passed into the stomach, the pattern of the oesophageal mucosa remains well outlined by a thin coating of the barium paste.

In addition to the prepared barium sulphate the trolley for the screening room should contain the following further items.

(i) A box of tissues.

No patient should leave the department with visible traces about the mouth of having recently taken a barium drink. Spills in the screening room are not infrequent.

(ii) One or two receivers in case of vomiting and for the reception of soiled articles and disposable containers for dentures, which some patients may wish to remove.

(iii) A box of drinking straws of the type which can be flexed at right angles.

These are useful to allow a patient to drink from a cup or beaker while lying down.

(iv) One or two dessert spoons or large teaspoons.

Thin solutions of barium sulphate may form a sediment after standing for some while and require stirring before being handed to the patient. Barium sulphate paste is best given a mouthful at a time from a spoon.

(v) A small jug of water and a spare cup or two.

(vi) A little cotton wool.

This may be required for the demonstration of impacted foreign bodies in the upper alimentary tract.

It is to be noted that the barium trolley is not required to be sterile, but it must be socially clean. After use, all barium containers and other utensils should be thoroughly washed with soap and hot water and stacked to dry in a clean dust-free atmosphere. If plastic beakers are used it is possible to obtain these in a material which will withstand sterilization by boiling and this should be done at regular intervals or after use by any patient with a communicable disease. The provision and use of disposable paper cups in all cases are strongly recommended. They are hygienic and save much time in cleaning operations. Barium being a heavy material, the cup should be of strong waxed paper and is best used with a plastic holder which has a suitable handle. The trolley top should be washed with soap and water and dried thoroughly after the barium session. In addition to the preparation and care of the trolley it is the radiographer's responsibility to have ready for the radiologist the requisition form and any previous X-ray films and reports relating to each patient. A check also should be made on the correct functioning and readiness of the X-ray equipment and its accessories.

Care of the Patient

The barium meal or barium swallow examination will include fluoroscopy and the taking of a number of immediate films. Before the patient leaves the department these are generally processed and checked for quality by either the examining radiologist or a senior radiographer. In many cases this completes the examination and the patient is free to go.

However, it may be that a 'follow-through' series is required; that is, a number of radiographs are taken at later intervals to show the process of the 'meal' through the small bowel and perhaps the remainder of the alimentary tract. During this procedure the patient may be required to refrain from eating for a further period.

At present 'accelerators' are often employed to hasten the progress of the contrast agent from the stomach and through the small bowel. Without the aid of such a substance, which results in mild acceleration of normal peristaltic movements, the patient must expect to spend the greater part of a day in the X-ray department. For example, he might be examined at 30-minute intervals—by means either of a single abdominal radiograph or of further fluoroscopy accompanied by radiography—during a period of 2 hours. This could be followed by subsequent hourly radiographs and fluoroscopy when necessary up to 5, 6 or even 8 hours after the original ingestion of the barium sulphate meal. A 24-hour film would be required if examination of the colon were included.

The administration of a suitable drug to increase the normal peristaltic rate is advantageous firstly in saving the patient's time and secondly in enabling the radiologist concerned to complete a follow-through examination under fluoroscopic control during the course of a normal morning's screening session, that is in a total period of about 2 hours. This gives a more satisfactory examination and greater flexibility to the day's timetable of both patient and

G

radiologist. In some instances a consultant radiologist who is in one hospital during the morning is required to be in another during the afternoon, while the patient's commitments are various and unknown.

Drugs which increase the normal rate of peristalsis of course are not new. Magnesium sulphate (Epsom salts) is a typical example. However, all are not appropriate to radiological use, since any accompanying effect—such as dilatation of the bowel—which would alter the normal radiographic intestinal patterns is to be avoided: it could be misleading to diagnosis.

A modern accelerator without such undesirable effects is perhaps best known to student radiographers in the United Kingdom by its proprietary trade name of 'Maxolon'. Its full chemical name runs to a line or more and even the approved shortened version is somewhat polysyllabic: it is metaclopramide monohydrochloride.

The operation of 'Maxolon' in increasing intestinal peristalsis is not completely understood but it is thought that its effect is on the area of the brain—the hypothalamus—which controls visceral activity; in particular that part which influences the spontaneous movements of the stomach and bowel.

'Maxolon' may be given by mouth in syrup or tablet form or by intravenous or intramuscular injection. If oral administration is preferred, 20 ml of the syrup (containing 20 mg metaclopramide) should be given 30 minutes before the barium meal; tablets are too slowly absorbed to be useful prior to radiography since they would entail a long wait for the patient while they took effect. If the drug is to be administered by injection 10 mg (in a 2 ml ampoule) should be given, either 15 minutes before the barium meal if the approach is intramuscular, or 10 minutes beforehand if the more rapid intravenous route is selected.

It is the radiographer's responsibility prior to a barium session to study the X-ray requisition forms and note those patients who are for a follow-through examination. Radiological advice should then be obtained about the preparation of each patient and provision made for the administration of the accelerator if one is to be used. If it is to be given by injection, this will be a matter of preparing a simple tray or trolley as described on page 213 in Chapter XVI.

If the drug is to be given orally, the patient is still entitled to a measure of privacy. It is undesirable to approach a patient in the semi-public area of the department's general waiting space and require him there and then to swallow your strange concoction—familiar though it may be to you. He will be the more reluctant to comply with your instructions since he knows neither what the proffered cup may hold nor the effect upon him of its contents. He is also afraid of being judged a fool by his audience and consequently will not ask you anything about it but he will not enjoy the difficult position into which he has been put nor remember his visit to the X-ray department with any sensation of gratitude.

At the end of each patient's fluoroscopic examination the radiographer should ascertain whether or not the procedure is complete and in the latter event know the timing of the further series. This information should be given accurately to the patient, together with advice as to when he may have a meal. He is entitled also to a word of simple explanation as to what will happen during the remainder of the procedure. It is common to meet with the horrified question, 'Have I got to take any more of that stuff?'—a concern in the circumstances wholly understandable.

Following this examination it is wise to inform patients of the sometimes aggravating effect of barium sulphate on constipation. A mild dose of an aperient on the following two or three nights should be helpful.

Barium sulphate is insoluble and unabsorbable and these features make it unsuitable for oral administration to certain patients. One of the functions of the colon is to absorb fluid and in the large bowel the barium sulphate mixture becomes denser, solid rather than liquid in character. One patient's account of the after-effects of his barium meal was that he thought he had had 'a load of concrete' and this is not altogether an inappropriate description of colonic events. There is a risk that a patient who has a partial intestinal obstruction and to whom a barium meal is given may afterwards become completely obstructed and require immediate surgery. Such patients—if radiological examination of the gastro-intestinal tract is necessary—should have 'Gastrografin' (see p. 44 Chapter III) which is a water-soluble contrast agent and safely excreted by the kidneys.

The other category of patients to whom barium sulphate should not be given by mouth are those suspected of having a gastric leak. This may be from a perforated peptic ulcer or occur because certain joins made during surgery on the stomach break down postoperatively. In either case barium finds its way into the peritoneal cavity and is difficult to remove by suction or other mechanical means which are the only methods possible. For these patients, too, a 'Gastrografin' meal is the preferable procedure.

BARIUM ENEMA

During a barium enema the large bowel is examined fluoroscopically and radiographs are taken while a suitable barium sulphate mixture is allowed to fill the bowel per rectum. The physical principles of the procedure are identical with those applying to the X-ray examination of other parts of the alimentary tract: it is the filling with radio-opaque fluid of a body cavity which—if the information obtained is to be diagnostically reliable—must in theory be empty. Ideal preparation of the patient has been achieved when the selected cavity in fact *is* empty.

Preparation of the Patient

Allusion has been made earlier to the difficulties inherent in preparing patients for abdominal X-ray examination. When the radiological investigation is to be specifically of the large bowel by barium enema the aim can be simply stated—the colon should be free of all faeces at the time of the examination. Given sufficient care this condition can be achieved; yet a number of patients attending for barium enema have not been sufficiently prepared, for one reason or another.

During the 48 hours prior to examination the patient should take as far as possible a low residue diet: eggs, fish, chicken, rusks or crisp-bread, butter, fruit, milk. It may be wise to omit the previous evening meal but take breakfast, when the X-ray examination is to occur in the morning; and omit breakfast but take a light lunch if the appointment is for the afternoon.

On the evening before the barium enema, a simple enema should be given and this should be followed on the succeeding morning by a high colon wash-out, 2 to 4 hours before the X-ray examination. It is important that the wash-out be properly administered. It may require considerable patience to continue the procedure until the returning fluid really is clear of faecal matter, but attention to detail in this respect is most significant in successful preparation.

Mention has been made in the last chapter of some of the difficulties of obtaining this satisfactory level of preparation in the homes of out-patients. In their case the foregoing procedures may have to be replaced by the administration of a suitable oral bowel evacuant and perhaps the use of a suppository on the morning of the X-ray examination, an hour or so beforehand.

In some X-ray departments—at present a minority in this country—facilities are available to administer a colonic wash-out to every out-patient attending the department for barium enema examination. Clearly it requires extra space and extra nursing or other suitably qualified staff, both of which the hospital service is already strained to provide in adequate degree in many areas. However, when such an arrangement is practicable it offers an ideal method of final preparation and has everything to recommend it, both radiologically and from the point of view of simplicity to the patient himself.

It should be noted that there are two classes of patients who generally should not be prepared prior to barium examination. These are cases of ulcerative colitis or of megacolon.

Use of Castor Oil

Some radiologists recommend the administration of castor oil during the afternoon previous to the X-ray examination, as a preliminary to the preparation just described. It should be given at 3.0 p.m. approximately.

Castor oil does not have any direct action on the large bowel itself and is thus considered suitable for administration to many patients in whom the colon is to be radiologically investigated for the presence of a lesion. Of course there are certain strong contra-indications to its use: for example, inflammation of the appendix with possible abscess formation, or obstruction of the bowel. Perhaps for these reasons it is a form of preparation not widely followed in this country, though under controlled use in knowledgeable hands the prescription may be thoroughly satisfactory and of proven value.

Preparation of the Trolley

The Enema Solution

It should be a firm rule in the X-ray department that the preparation of barium enemata, or indeed other barium mixtures, is undertaken only by suitably qualified persons—a radiographer or member of the nursing staff—and never by auxiliaries, such as a darkroom-technician or porter. Mishaps have been known to occur, with tragic and even fatal results in some instances.

In preparing a barium enema, an important difference is that the solution is more dilute for injection per rectum, than when it is to be taken by mouth. A thinner solution (*a*) fills the bowel more readily, (*b*) as it is less radio-opaque, owing to the smaller quantity of barium per volume, allows for better visualizations of super-imposed loops of gut: it is often the case that one part of the bowel lies behind another and may not be distinguishable radiographically if the density of the injected medium is high.

The exact dilution of the barium sulphate mixture again will depend much upon the preference of the examining radiologist, or the manufacturers' instructions may be followed. A certain recom-mended practice is to make the solution to a specific gravity of 1150 and this has the advantage of precision and simplicity.

Another important point is the temperature of the enema. Nursing text-books will be found to state that the temperature of enemata should be 37°C (100°F). To inject a hot solution per rectum is obviously dangerous, and in no circumstances should a warm enema be administered to a patient without a careful check of its temperature being made immediately beforehand. If a warm solution is prepared and has to stand for some while before being used, it is customary to make arrangements to maintain its tempera-ture: for instance, the container may be partly immersed in a bowl of hot water which is frequently renewed.

It is often stated that it is equally undesirable to inject per rectum any solution which is appreciably below blood heat, on the ground that discomfort at least will be caused and, in some instances, even shock. However, in relation to barium enemata there is a con-siderable body of opinion at present in favour of giving the barium at refrigerated temperatures.

The reason for this is that warm solutions produce greater activity of the bowel mucosa, resulting in increased secretion of mucus which may impair its visualization radiographically. When the barium enema can be given chilled, finer detail in the mucosal pattern of the bowel is seen. In regard to the possible effects of low temperature, the patient in many instances seems almost un-aware that the solution *is* cold and no unfavourable outcome has been reported—even a literal one in the quick return of the offending mixture.

In some cases, in addition to barium sulphate and water, the enema may contain a bowel evacuant. The presence of an activator assists in the subsequent evacuation of the enema and leads to the remnant barium sulphate appearing as a fine coating over the bowel mucosa, a circumstance of marked diagnostic value when taking the post-evacuation radiographs.

The total volume of prepared enema solution should be on the basis of 2 litres being required per patient. If more than one patient is to be examined at the time it is more economical in every way to make up sufficient for the full requirement, if this is possible. The solution can be suitably mixed in a large jug, from which it may be dispensed into the appropriate enema container prior to injection. A surplus of the mixture remaining at the end of the screening session must be discarded at once. To retain solutions, in the expectation of their use on some future occasion, comes from a misguided sense of economy and is a thoroughly dangerous practice.

THE RECTAL CATHETER

For the administration of barium enemata, several devices have been described and are in general use. The simplest is a plain rectal or oesophageal tube of soft rubber, which can very easily be inserted through the anal orifice to a distance of about 7–10 cm. Its major disadvantage is that as it is easy to insert it is equally easy to extrude.

During the fluoroscopic and radiographic examinations the patient will be required to change considerably his position on the X-ray table. Even if a close surveillance of the catheter is made during these manœuvres, experience shows that it is quite likely to escape from the rectum. These considerations make the administration of a barium enema rather different from enemata of other types and in view of them some variety of self-retaining catheter or cannula has much to recommend it.

Examples of these are the 'Banbury Cannula' and the 'Enema Tip'. The first is a short aluminium cannula of which the end for insertion into the rectum is approximately triangular in section, similar indeed to a blunted barb. This design gives the instrument a well defined neck which in most cases can be firmly gripped by the internal sphincter muscle, and prevents it from being readily dislodged in the absence of a deliberate effort to expel it. It is well made, the metal being thoroughly polished and having smooth rounded sides. These features provide for easy insertion and lessen discomfort when the instrument is in place.

The 'Enema Tip' operates on a similar principle. This cannula is of a firm plastic material and bears a perforated olive-shaped expansion at its distal end. It has a certain advantage in that it is re-

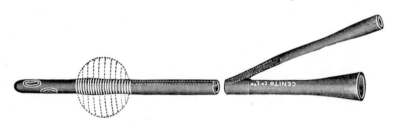

Fig. 6. Foley catheter. *By courtesy of the Genito-Urinary Manufacturing Co. Ltd.*

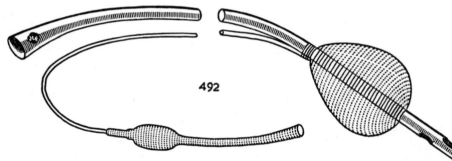

Fig. 7. Franklin rectal barium catheter. *By courtesy of J. G. Franklin & Sons Ltd.*

garded as being disposable and consequently does not require cleaning after use.

For those who prefer a soft catheter, the Foley variety is serviceable. This is a rubber catheter which near its distal end passes centrally through a small rubber balloon, capable of inflation by means of a separate narrow tube. The catheter is inserted through the anus until the balloon lies completely within the rectum, behind the internal sphincter muscle. Expansion of the balloon by means of a syringe prevents the catheter from passing back through the internal sphincter unless the patient is deliberately attempting to expel it. On completion of the examination, deflation of the balloon allows the catheter to be as easily withdrawn as it was easily inserted.

These catheters are available in different sizes according to their gauge and the capacity of the balloon. The Franklin rectal barium catheter is essentially a variant of the Foley but has a larger balloon. The use of these rubber catheters is often preferred to a rigid cannula, in case careless insertion of the latter should lead to perforation of the rectal wall.

Disposable barium enema kits have been available in the U.S.A. for a long time and in the United Kingdom more recently. They are self-contained, ideally hygienic and easy to handle. They avoid troublesome and unpleasant cleaning operations and thus economize on time and energy in the X-ray department. They do not economize on cash and their use adds considerably to the costs of a barium enema examination.

The kit consists largely of a bag, usually of a strong translucent material, which has a capacity of the order of 3 litres and may be graduated in order to indicate the volume of solution present at any time. The bag may be supplied already containing an appropriate quantity of barium sulphate powder, for example 500–750 g.

A filler hole and cap near the top of the bag allow the enema solution to be made to the desired concentration and a colonic activator can be included if wished. The bag is then shaken briskly to mix the solution well.

At the other end of the bag is an outlet tube equipped with (a) a simple ball valve to prevent leakage of the bag's contents before use and during the preparation of the enema; (b) a clip which can be varied in position and is employed to control the flow of the enema. The outlet tubing is of a firm, transparent plastic material. It has a diameter of about 80 mm and should be of adequate length, that is about 1.5 metres. A rectal cannula or flexible catheter—whichever is preferred—can be easily fitted to the distal end of this tubing.

In use the bag is suspended from its upper end on a stand in the way customary for the injection of the enema. During this process it may be an advantage to keep the filler cap open since normal air pressure is then maintained, faster delivery insured and the flow of the enema more precisely controlled.

When it is desired to obtain evacuation of the enema, the bag—

with its filler cap safely closed—is removed from the stand and simply lowered to a position below the level of the X-ray table when the barium mixture should flow back into it. Evacuation thus takes place under maintained fluoroscopic control and the post-evacuation films can be easily and expeditiously exposed. When the procedure is completed the enema bag is clipped off and the whole arrangement discarded as it is.

From the point of view of the patient and the radiographer who gives the enema the use of such a disposable kit has every practical advantage. It may be that the degree of evacuation obtained with it is sometimes less complete than when the patient leaves the X-ray room and achieves it by himself: this difference may be sufficient to make the post-evacuation films less than satisfactory. Furthermore, the kit requires some modification if a two-channel system, permitting either barium *or* air to be injected, is required. However such an adaptation should not be difficult to provide.

OTHER EQUIPMENT

In preparing the enema trolley, certain other equipment is required. None of this needs to be kept sterile, but catheters and receivers used by the patient should be thoroughly washed afterwards. For a patient who has a known communicable disease, the use of disposable equipment is preferable and essential if means are not available for the sterilization of instruments afterwards.

The barium enema may be given either through a funnel or from a container such as a Valentine glass jar suitably suspended, perhaps by a pulley from the ceiling or by an adjustable metal stand such as is used during intravenous infusions. It is very important that at no stage in the administration of the enema should the container be raised to a great height above the table. To do this is directly to increase the pressure at which the enema is given. Such pressure can be dangerous should the bowel wall be thinned and delicate, as it is in the presence of ulcerative colitis, and in any case makes retention of the enema difficult and unlikely.

Whatever form of container is used, a length of rubber or polythene tubing will be needed to join it to the rectal catheter; a glass or translucent plastic connector is placed at this point to allow for inspection of the solution's flow and easy disconnection of the catheter. A rather more elaborate and useful arrangement is provided by a T or Y shaped three-way connector and a suitable tap

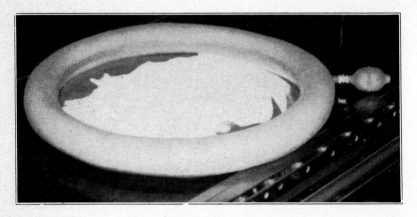

Plate XI   The ' Victoria ' Enema Ring.   *By courtesy of Macarthy's
(Wholesale Chemists) Ltd.*

or clips, to allow the in-flow to be simply exchanged for out-flow during withdrawal of the enema.

Other items required are listed below.

(i) A Victoria Enema Ring.

This is a useful accessory since it restricts the spread of a flood of barium in the advent of the patient's being unable to retain the enema. It consists of a small circular rubber sheet, attached to the periphery of which is an inflatable rubber ring—placed beneath the patient's buttocks when the device is in use. The arrangement rather resembles a miniature of those inflatable paddling pools obtainable as garden toys for children. Should leakage of the enema occur, it is contained within the ring and its disposal is subsequently easy and complete. The device is quite radiolucent and does not seriously interfere with fluoroscopic or radiographic detail. Since it offers rather a cold surface to the patient's skin, the enema ring should be made more comfortable in cold weather by the insertion of a circle of gauze, lint, or cellulose wadding. Devices serving the same purpose as a Victoria enema ring but of disposable material are also available.

(ii) A suitable lubricant to ease insertion of the catheter. One which is water-soluble, such as glycerin, has advantages, as it does not readily block the catheter and is easily removed from it during washing.

(iii) One or two receivers.

(iv) Plenty of tow or cellulose wadding.

(v) A bedpan and cover.

(vi) A pail, partly filled with a suitable antiseptic, will be needed if the enema is to be removed by siphoning.

(vii) A Higginson's syringe may also be required.

Care of the Patient

While the patient is being made ready for barium enema examination, it is kind to give some explanation of what is about to happen. Points which should receive attention are the following.

(i) The darkness of the room, if conventional fluoroscopy is to be the method of examination.

(ii) The enema injection.

(iii) Movements of the patient which will be necessary during fluoroscopy, with an affirmation that he will not be allowed to fall off the table.

As an immediate preliminary to the examination and during its course, reassurance should be given to the patient in the event of his being unable to retain the enema for as long as we wish. A positive outlook should be encouraged by an explanation that the enema mixture is not irritant to the bowel and that it is not designed or intended to produce evacuation; it may also be useful to refer to the feature of fluoroscopy which allows us 'to see exactly what is happening inside' and thus prevent discomfort. A patient who has a colostomy (an artificial opening into the colon through the abdominal wall) needs special notice and this will be found on page 95.

However, inevitably there are some patients who prove unable to retain the enema with success, particularly perhaps the elderly in whom the anal sphincter may have become lax. When this happens, almost all experience feelings of distress and even shame, residual memories of childhood's guilt over such lapses.

We have a responsibility here to reassure the patient that he is neither a nuisance nor the cause of censure. We should tell him with a smile how well accustomed we are to this minor difficulty, which is a recognized and may be a frequent feature of this examination. Mopping-up operations should be conducted expeditiously and without comment, and the patient gently encouraged to do his best to allow the examination to continue.

On completion of the immediate examination, it is usual to take at least a postero-anterior radiograph following evacuation of the enema. This radiograph may have to be repeated after an interval, if the first attempt removes only part of the barium mixture. In this case a satisfactory result is often obtained if the patient is sent away for a while, with the advice to take something to eat and a cup of tea or coffee. A patient who is not fit enough to walk to the lavatory or to reach it with assistance must be given a bedpan for this part of the procedure (see Chapter XVI).

Following this the examination may be extended in many instances, if an 'air study' is thought to be necessary. This refers to the introduction of a suitable quantity of air per rectum which will distend the lumen of the bowel and throw into sharp relief the barium-coated pattern of the mucosa. It is a valuable procedure in cases of unexplained rectal haemorrhage, since it may lead to the demonstration of small polypi which are otherwise not readily detected. It is, however, an uncomfortable procedure which the majority of patients find more distressing than the original barium enema. A similar double contrast—though less brilliant—can be obtained from the administration of plain water instead of air, and this is more acceptable to the recipient and quicker to use.

It will be appreciated, however, that the double contrast study adds something to the length of the examination and the possibility of this should be kept in mind when making appointments and advising a patient of the length of time likely to be required. It is probably better to over-estimate than to give the impression that the examination necessarily can be completed within a few minutes.

Following a barium enema, it is a significant point that no patient should be allowed to dress and leave the department without *first* going to the lavatory. In some cases, particularly if the enema has been partially removed by siphoning during the fluoroscopic examination, little discomfort is felt and the patient may be firm in his belief that he has no immediate need to evacuate further. He departs eagerly to get dressed, glad to put on his clothes and assume again responsibility for himself. If the radiographer has failed to give warning and has allowed this situation to occur, it has been known that the hospital was afterwards obliged to settle an account for the cost of cleaning a suit.

Elderly patients, or those in a weakened condition, should not be dispatched to the lavatory and left unattended for any length of time. In a few instances the patient may become suddenly shocked and faint. It is far better that we should many times give supervision more often than is necessary to the comparatively fit, than that we should once fail to be near at hand when the patient's need was real.

THE PATIENT WITH A COLOSTOMY

A colostomy is a surgical procedure in which the colon is opened on to the surface of the abdomen. This is done so as to provide an artificial outlet for the faecal contents of the colon, the patient's bowel motions being discharged through this opening and not through the anus from the rectum in the normal way. Colostomy is undertaken for two main reasons: (i) to construct a permanent 'artificial anus' when the rectum is to be surgically removed because it is diseased; (ii) to construct a temporary diversion route for the faecal contents when it is thought advisable for the distal part of the colon not to function for a time. So a temporary colostomy may be established as part of a treatment plan when the distal colon is obstructed or inflamed or perforated or is to be the subject of difficult surgery.

A permanent colostomy is what is known as a terminal or end colostomy. Distal to the colostomy there is no bowel remaining, the colostomy opening being the end of the line (if we make an analogy with the railway track). The rectum is surgically removed and the sigmoid colon is brought out as a colostomy opening on the anterior abdominal wall; a favoured site is the left iliac fossa. In the case of a temporary arangement planned to stop the distal colon functioning a loop of transverse colon is used to construct the colostomy. The siting of a transverse colostomy of this kind is often to the right of the midline in the upper quadrant of the abdomen (that is, between the umbilicus and the lower costal margin). In this type of colostomy there is bowel remaining distal to the abdominal opening and usually there is still an anal orifice at the extreme distal end of the bowel.

Radiographers are confronted with either type of colostomy in patients coming to the X-ray department. When a patient with a terminal colostomy presents himself for a radiological contrast enema, the only possibility for giving it is through the colostomy opening. If the colostomy is temporary there are usually two routes of access: via the colostomy or via the anus. Selection of route for a particular examination depends on why it is being made, which part of the colon it is wished to study and whether the anus provides a satisfactory opening (it may be narrowed or obstructed or damaged as a result of a disease process). If the anus is used for entry point when an enema is given to a patient with a colostomy the enema solution of course will shortly appear through the colostomy opening.

In the case of a baby born with an imperforate anus there is no anal opening at all. Temporary colostomy may then be done on the new-born and at a later stage, when the child is bigger and stronger, surgery to construct an anal canal may be planned. The child may be X-rayed at that stage with a view to finding out how much colon there is distal to the colostomy opening. Clearly then the contrast enema must be given into the distal colon through the colostomy opening as there is no other way in.

Temporary colostomy often has a double-barrelled construction in which two entrance points present themselves at the colostomy opening. The two openings are separated by a spur of tissue which has been organized to prevent the faecal contents of the bowel passing over from the one opening to the other. Of the two openings, the one further to the patient's right is the active one through which the bowel discharges its contents in its action. A catheter inserted in this opening can be used to fill with contrast agent that part of the colon which is proximal to the colostomy. The other opening (the one further to the patient's left) leads to the inactive remaining bowel. If a catheter is inserted here the distal part of the colon is filled. When an enema is given to a patient with a colostomy, the solution must be delivered at a low pressure and the container must not be raised too high.

By whatever route an enema is injected, the patient has no voluntary control over evacuation through a colostomy. So it is a bewildering waste of effort for us to tell him that he must try to retain the enema as if we were instructing a patient whose evacuation arrangements were normal and who has the anal sphincter at his command to relax or keep firm. This patient has no sphincters for his colostomy at his own or anyone else's command for there are no muscles of this type around the opening. Radiographers dealing with colostomy patients must be prepared for various approaches in regard to giving the enema; lack of control of evacuation through a colostomy is, however, a constant feature to be understood. We must be ready in advance for mopping up procedures.

Management of a Colostomy

The patient with a permanent colostomy has to learn to live with a new arrangement for defaecation. He will receive help and advice for this while he is in hospital for the operation and as time goes by he will learn management of the colostomy. As we have seen, he is never able to *control* it but the bowel adjusts itself. The colostomy actions become less frequent than in the immediately postoperative period and eventually the patient will find that the colostomy behaves in a predictable way, acting at regular times in the day (such as after a main meal) perhaps only once, perhaps twice or more.

It is easy to see that the patient will manage best when the motions are firm, are not too frequent and are predictable. Aid in achieving this state of affairs can be found by attention to diet and if necessary by the use of certain medicines. Another technique of management is to teach the patient to wash out the large bowel through the colostomy each morning. This is time-consuming if the washout is to be performed properly and preferably it requires a combined bathroom and lavatory. As a hazard there is the risk of damage to the bowel if the washout is given with insufficient care. The advantage of the daily washout is that the colostomy should not work again and during the day the patient will not have to deal further with his colostomy. In the United Kingdom most surgeons prefer not to recommend a washout routine to their patients. On the other hand it is a favoured technique in the United States—perhaps because more people have bigger bathrooms!

Colostomy Appliances. Various appliances are available for management of a colostomy. The commonest practice now is for the patient to wear a disposable plastic bag over the opening. When the colostomy functions, the results are held securely in the bag until the patient can attend to it, dispose of the used bag and fit another. Patients with colostomies will be found to carry with them spare plastic bags and cleaning materials to enable them to make changes while away from home. It is not a bad idea for the X-ray department to include among its stores some spare colostomy bags.

The plastic bags which are used come in two main types: (i) those which are adherent and stick directly on to the patient's skin around the colostomy; (ii) those which are non-adherent and are held on to the patient over the opening by some type of belt or corset. The non-adherent type of bag attaches to a rigid or semi-rigid plastic ring or flange which fits over the colostomy opening and is kept in position by the colostomy belt.

One of the disadvantages of using adherent bags is that the patient's skin may become sore, especially if removal and renewal of the bags must be done two or three times in the course of 24 hours. There is a Danish appliance which avoids both the encumbrance of a belt and the necessity for frequent changing of an adherent bag. This is achieved by means of a rigid plastic flange which has an adhesive square on its back surface. The flange is thereby stuck directly to the skin around the colostomy opening. It can be left in place for two or three days and a new bag is simply fitted to the free rim of the flange as often as is necessary.

A patient with his colostomy so well regulated that he is confident of no action during the day may be found to wear very little in the way of an appliance—perhaps a small dressing of cellulose wadding held in place by a belt of light elasticated fabric.

Before the era of disposables and plastic bags, an older type of colostomy appliance was a belt that held a cup over the opening. The cup was filled with a wool pad. This, however, was not such a leak-proof arrangement as the modern plastic bag when it is properly applied.

CHAPTER VII

THE RENAL TRACT

Plain radiographs of the renal tract are taken but they do not constitute the most useful procedure unless there are present known radio-opaque calculi, the progress of which it is desired to assess. A plain film of the abdomen will generally indicate the size, shape, and position of each kidney but a proportion of all urinary stones are translucent to X rays; their degree of opacity depends entirely on the salts of which they are composed. Those containing a high content of calcium carbonate are in fact markedly radio-opaque and show well on a plain radiograph.

However, other calcium salts such as calcium oxylate and calcium phosphate are commonly present. Some urinary calculi may prove wholly translucent and incapable of plain radiographic demonstration against the tissues which normally surround them. In this case a radiological report which states that 'There is no evidence of a renal calculus', or that 'No abnormality is detected', cannot be taken to mean that no stone is present, or that all is necessarily well with this patient. Such information is clearly of limited value.

These considerations usually make it preferable to undertake X-ray investigations of the renal tract which incorporate the introduction of a contrast medium and from which the presence and site of a radioparent stone may be inferred by its effect on the functioning and the appearance of the system. Since a plain 'scout' film is always taken at the beginning of these special investigations, any radio-opaque stones will be identified from this; the subsequent procedure can further assist in their localization, should there be any doubt of the shadows being due to the presence of calcified mesenteric glands.

INTRAVENOUS UROGRAPHY

Intravenous urography is the most frequently performed of the special investigations relating to the urinary tract. It has several advantages.

(i) It is a simple procedure for the patient which does not involve the passing of instruments or the induction of anaesthesia.

(ii) It gives information on the efficacy of renal function and is the only examination to do this.

(iii) Providing there is adequate function of the kidneys, satisfactory detail of the structure of the renal system can be obtained which may lead to the diagnosis of other lesions than calculi; for example renal tuberculosis.

The procedure of intravenous urography (sometimes termed *excretion urography, descending urography or I.V.P.* for intravenous pyelography) implies the injection into a vein—usually in the antecubital fossa at the elbow—of a suitable contrast agent which is rapidly excreted by the kidneys. It will normally appear in the renal tract in a matter of minutes and delineate the whole renal system in a series of radiographs taken at short intervals following injection.

Preparation of the Patient

When making the appointment the patient should be warned that the examination is likely to occupy an hour to an hour and a half. It is questionable whether or not he should be told also that he will be given a simple injection of a 'dye' which will assist in obtaining better X-ray films. Many people have a disproportionate dislike of injections. They view this procedure with an irrational nervousness which can scarcely be related to the momentary and usually trivial pain of the needle's insertion: indeed such sufferers often accept stoically physical pangs far more severe.

Such a patient, when told long in advance of what is going to happen, inevitably has considerable time in which to dread the event, and this may be considered an unnecessary infliction of mental distress. On the other hand, if nothing is said on the subject, it has been known for the patient to refuse the injection—admittedly not a frequent occurrence but when it happens at the last minute very wasteful of time and effort both by the X-ray department and the patient himself. Then, too, many people prefer to know something of what is ahead of them.

Experienced radiographers can be found defending both sides of this argument, and indeed it is true that each contains a measure of right and good sense. Whatever decision may be made on the main issue, it is most important that when the patient *is* told of the coming injection, he should receive the additional information that it should not affect him in any way. Understandably enough, many people believe that they are being given some form of anaesthetic, from which they will afterwards have to recover and a patient can easily wonder in these circumstances if he will be fit to drive a car away from the hospital. In any case information about the nature of the procedure should be given to the patient during the preliminaries of the examination.

Physical preparation of the patient often consists of the form of general abdominal preparation current in the department (Chapter v), together with some restriction of the patient's intake of fluid. The reason for this is to obtain concentration of the contrast medium in the renal pelves and therefore visualization of radiographic detail. If the patient has taken much to drink immediately prior to intravenous urography this will of course be reflected in the renal drainage system by increased urinary excretion. Dilution of the radio-opaque agent with urine may lead to fainter contrast and consequently loss of perception of radiographic detail in the pyelogram.

The extent of the restriction actually imposed on the patient will vary between departments, depending on the wishes of the radiologist in charge. In some cases, for instance, fluid intake may be limited to 1 pint on the day before the examination, with total abstinence only during the last 8 or even 2 hours prior to examination. Others prefer that the patient should take no fluids at all for 12 to 14 hours before intravenous urography, though he may—if he wishes —drink up to a moderate amount until that time. However, too severe a regimen of dehydration may defeat its own ends as in these circumstances renal function may be much reduced: in effect the factory closes down for lack of materials. A specific optimum period of dehydration has not been established and, provided that the contrast agent can be given in an adequate amount, a satisfactory result will be obtained in a patient who has received no special preparation at all.

An alternative procedure to the usual intravenous injection is to give the contrast agent in the form of an intravenous infusion drip. This is done only when the standard examination proves unsatisfactory and it requires preliminary hydration of the patient.

For the purpose again of preventing dilution of the contrast agent, it is of considerable importance that the bladder should be empty when intravenous urography is performed. If this is not so, radio-graphic visualization will be impaired when the medium enters the bladder and its detail may never be adequately demonstrated. Attention should be paid to this when the patient is making ready for the examination: he should be requested to visit the lavatory immediately before undressing.

When intravenous urography is performed as an emergency procedure no long-term preparation of the patient is possible and the emptying of the bladder is the only essential preliminary.

A child or infant who is to have an intravenous urogram should not be prepared with a laxative and must not be subjected to a lengthy period of dehydration: 2 hours may be considered appropriate.

Preparation of the Trolley

When any hypodermic injection is given the rules of asepsis must be strictly observed. Infection can very easily follow if practice is allowed to become lax in this respect. The technique of intra-venous urography is simple. It is at the same time so frequently performed in many departments as to become a commonplace of every day's work: perhaps there is some danger that its risks—if it receive only a careless attention—may be overlooked or disregarded. We have all of us a real responsibility in this respect and should maintain continuous vigilance in the preparing and handling of any sterile equipment, however trivial, however familiar may seem the procedure for which it is to be used. Whether we are newcomers to the X-ray department, or senior members of its staff, the obligation is equal for us all. Preparation of the trolley (see Chapter xvi) is considered below under two headings for sterile and non-sterile items.

Sterile (upper shelf)
One 20 ml and one 50 ml syringe.

F𝚒𝚐. 8. 20 ml syringe with eccentric nozzle. *By courtesy of Down Bros. and Mayer & Phelps Ltd.*

These should have an eccentric (side) nozzle.

Needles to fit the above syringes and suitable for intravenous injection: for example Nos. 1 and 2.

One small dressing bowl or covered dish for gauze or wool swabs and a towel.

One kidney dish or closed container in which to place the syringes and needles.

It is probable that all of this equipment will be obtained pre-sterilized and packed from the central sterile supply department.

One pair of plain dissecting forceps.

One cannula for filling the syringe.

Fɪɢ. 9. Dissecting forceps. *By courtesy of Down Bros. and Mayer & Phelps Ltd.*

The student may note the omission of the gallipot sometimes used to contain surgical spirit for cleansing of the skin. If the spirit is not in an aerosol, the correct technique is to tip the fluid directly from its bottle on to a swab held in the fingers, avoiding contact between the glass and the gauze or wool. This procedure is perfectly clean and avoids the risk of having an open container of spirit on any trolley prepared for intravenous or intra-arterial injections. On such a trolley there should be no material directly accessible which would be harmful were it accidentally introduced into the blood stream. A small quantity of surgical spirit in a bright steel gallipot may appear nearly colourless, as is the contrast medium itself which is to be introduced into the vascular system. Their similarity constitutes some risk of confusion occurring at a vital moment, particularly during the more complex examinations, when strain and tension may be present.

Non-sterile (lower shelf)

Ampoules of the contrast agent: for example 'Urovison' in a 25 ml ampoule or a 50 ml phial; 'Conray 280' or 'Conray 420' in a 20 ml ampoule or a 50 ml phial. A wide range of dosage for intravenous urograms is now accepted and in some departments more than 40 ml are routinely given. The trolley should be prepared accordingly. The ampoules or phials should stand in a container of warm water (37°C).

A file for opening the ampoules if necessary.

A sphygmomanometer or tourniquet.

A bottle of surgical spirit (industrial methylated 70 per cent) or other skin cleanser: for example 'Hibitane' 0.5 per cent in spirit. An alternative presentation of surgical spirit for the purpose of skin cleansing is an aerosol spray. This is exceptionally hygienic, quick and simple to use.

A small sandbag or pad for support of the arm.

THE EMERGENCY PACK

The student will know from an earlier chapter (Chapter III) that many radiological contrast agents contain iodine and that some individuals are sensitive to this element. Such people may rapidly develop unpleasant and possibly dangerous reactions if they have to take any substance containing iodine, particularly—and this is a significant point—if it is introduced directly into the blood stream by way of an artery or vein. In any X-ray room where such procedures are undertaken there should be permanently available a sufficiency of equipment for the administration of restorative drugs and other measures. This equipment is considered in detail in Chapter XVII.

Care of the Patient

During the preliminaries for intravenous urography some explanation of the procedure should be given to the patient. As we have said, the technique becomes familiar to us, simple, and so ordinary in its routine that we may easily fail to realize how it strikes the eye of the uninitiated. Our patient not only may be seeing for the first time the ritual of preparation for intravenous injection, but is well aware that it is he who in some way will be at the receiving end of a syringe which looks at first glimpse more suitable in size to a horse than a man. A little sympathetic reassurance may be comforting beyond our knowledge.

It should be mentioned that apart from the needle's prick little else will be felt from the injection. Certainly in skilled hands and providing the needle is sharp—literally and figuratively, this is a very important point—many patients may be hardly aware that the injection has been given, perhaps particularly those who are nervous beforehand.

It is a mistake to attempt to quiet an alarmed child by saying 'It will not hurt'. Within a very short time this is manifestly proved an untruth and that child will not readily trust us again. We can fairly say that 'it will hurt a little', but that if he is brave this part will be over quickly and that all we have to do then is to take a few pictures of him.

A word with his mother or the ward sister may allow us to extend to him the expectation of some little treat afterwards—perhaps 'a ride on the swings in the park', or an ice-cream or similar tit-bit. As far as possible all preparations for the injection and the instruments to be used should be kept out of sight of the child. He should be spoken to cheerfully and encouraged to look away while the injection is made.

The injection should be given only by a qualified medical officer. Following it the patient should not be left alone for at least 15 or 20 minutes.

Here again it is worth bearing in mind that our attitude may easily become conditioned by the familiarity and general safety of the procedure. If the patient does experience adverse effects from the contrast agent, they may appear at any subsequent time but most probably they will occur during this quarter of an hour.

It is true of course that such an emergency is a rarity. It may not happen within the working experience of any one radiographer, and because of this we find ourselves believing that it will not happen at all. Usually we are right. Many times we may leave the patient for a few moments but in these circumstances we can never do so in safety. The risk remains that on some occasion on returning to the room we shall find the patient extremely ill; it is no over-statement that in this event a few minutes' earlier attention could have altered the balance between death and life.

The reactions which may occur are well defined in type.

(1) *Sneezing or coughing, vomiting*
This sequence of events is produced in a normal subject if the injection is made too rapidly. It arises from stimulation of the vomiting reflex: that is, it occurs only when the drug has circulated from the site of injection through the heart and lungs and has reached the

brain. The sneezing or coughing may or may not be the prelude to actual sickness, but they indicate essentially stimulus of the same reflex. The patient may experience feelings of warmth and flushing of the skin which are thought to be due to a high concentration of the organic substance in the blood stream. Occasionally there is a rigor and rise of temperature. None of these are dangerous in effect and if they occur at all are usually transient. Reassurance, a warm covering, and a receiver in case of vomiting are adequate measures of help.

(2) *Allergy (angioneurotic oedema, bronchospasm, iodism)*
The conditions in the brackets are all examples of an allergic response. Allergy is an altered reaction of the tissues of some individuals on exposure to substances which in similar quantities are innocuous to most people. More simply we can say that the person concerned has a peculiar sensitivity to the substance.

An agent which produces allergy is known as an *allergen* or *antigen*. Almost any substance is capable of exciting a reaction of this kind: it may be a food such as fish or strawberries; it may be an inhalant such as the pollen of some plants or chemical fumes; it may be a drug.

It is unusual for an allergic subject to be sensitive to only one allergen. Multiple sensitivities are the rule. In any person there is a very slight potential risk that a radiological contrast agent containing iodine, particularly one introduced into the bloodstream intravenously or intra-arterially, will result in allergy. The risk obviously is increased if the subject is known to be sensitive to other antigens.

For this reason, before embarking on a procedure which requires direct injection of one of the organic iodine compounds into a blood vessel, the examining radiologist should take a careful history from the patient to establish that he is not an allergic subject; the patient may be asked, for example, whether he has ever suffered from hay fever or asthma since each of these conditions is a manifestation of allergy. A specific enquiry should be made as to whether he has ever been told that he is allergic to anything. Typical of a mild allergic reaction are soreness and running of the eyes and the appearance of an urticarial rash over the body: this may be a faint patchy blush or may be very pronounced, the patient becoming heavily covered with large, red, irritating weals.

In more serious cases bronchospasm can occur, or laryngeal oedema (swelling of the mucous membrane) may be so marked as vitally to impair breathing. If the respiratory disturbance is sufficiently severe, *tracheostomy* may be necessary: this is a means of creating an artificial airway through an incision in the front of the neck, the opening being kept patent for as long as required by the insertion of a tracheostomy tube.

Medical assistance should be sought immediately on the appearance of the early signs of allergic reaction, because of the potential danger of a rapid involvement of the respiratory system, although as a rule this kind of reaction does not become serious. To suppress an allergic state the most effective drugs are the corticosteroids which—given intravenously—act in about 30 minutes. Adrenaline may be used for an acute condition as it obtains results much more rapidly (in 2 or 3 minutes). The anti-histamine preparations (for example Phenergan) are more appropriate for preventing a reaction than for treating it.

Sometimes to guard against allergy in a patient, particularly one who gives a history of having had asthma, some form of a test dose of the contrast agent is given beforehand. Various methods have been described: for example, the placing of one or two drops in the eye is said to lead to its engorgement if the patient is sensitive. However, the most reliable form of test is undoubtedly a *slow* intravenous injection of 1 to 2 ml of the medium, followed by observation of the patient for 10 to 20 minutes. The development of any untoward effect is a directive to discontinue at once both the immediate trial injection and any further procedure. For the purpose of performing such a test, it will be noticed that some manufacturers of radiological contrast agents supply small ampoules of their product together with those containing the full dose.

(3) Circulatory collapse

This is by far the most serious of the reactions known to occur since it is the most lethal. No prior indication is received of the subject who may be prone to it; nor would a previous test, subcutaneously or in the eye, reveal susceptibility. Following intravenous injection of the contrast agent the patient experiences a profound circulatory collapse. His blood pressure falls rapidly and cataclysmically; his pulses become undetectable; he presents the desperate picture of extreme shock. On rare occasions breathing may stop (respiratory arrest) and cessation of the heart's beat (cardiac arrest) can occur.

Every member of the X-ray staff should know what to do in the event of an emergency of this kind. This is described in detail in the first section of Chapter XVII.

Any patient who experiences a marked reaction following urography will naturally remain under close medical observation in the department for a period. His admission to hospital for at least 24 hours may be considered advisable, particularly in the case of the severe vaso-motor collapse just described.

RETROGRADE PYELOGRAPHY

In this examination the renal pelvi-calyceal system and usually at least the proximal portion of the affected ureter are outlined by the direct injection of a radio-opaque contrast agent. The injection is made through a catheter inserted into the ureter from the bladder by means of a cystoscope. The term *ascending pyelography* is sometimes applied to this procedure, for reasons which are clear enough on consideration of the direction of flow of the contrast medium.

It is evident that this is simply a mechanical filling of the upper urinary tract. The radiographs obtained will delineate certain structural features—deformities due to pathology, pressure effects or other congenital or acquired anomalies. It does not give any indication of renal function and of course is not dependent on function. For this reason the examination often follows an intravenous urogram which has shown that one kidney has poor or absent function. By retrograde filling of its pelvis and ureter, the condition of this kidney can be more fully investigated.

FIG. 10. Ureteric catheter. *By courtesy of the Genito-Urinary Manufacturing Co. Ltd.*

Following delineation of the pelvi-calyceal system, the ureteric catheter may be withdrawn until its tip is just within the ureter at the uretero-vesical orifice, when a further injection will outline the ureter itself. The position of radio-opaque ureteric stones may be localized by their relationship to the catheter, this being of a material which also is radio-opaque.

Retrograde pyelography may be confined to one side only or it may be bi-lateral. In the latter event it is usual to complete the radiographic examination of one kidney and its ureter before injection of the other is begun.

Preparation of the Patient

The placing of the ureteric catheter or catheters for retrograde pyelography is performed through a cystoscope, an instrument which permits visual inspection of the interior of the bladder and the ureteric orifices. Cystoscopy is an operative procedure, requiring temporary admission of the subject. It can be satisfactorily performed under local anaesthesia in both sexes; for convenience, however, a general anaesthetic is sometimes given.

Because of its surgical nature the preparation of patients for this radiological investigation is not primarily a responsibility of the X-ray department but rests as a rule with the ward concerned in preparing cases for the urological theatre. Apart from the department's usual preliminaries to general abdominal radiography (Chapter v), the immediate preparation is related to surgical requirements. It is customary for the anaesthetist to indicate the premedication which he wishes the patient to have and normal preoperative routines will be followed by the nursing staff.

Preparation of the Trolley

Very often the preparation of equipment for retrograde pyelography is carried out in the urological theatre, and the patient arriving in the X-ray department for this examination will be accompanied by a tray containing the necessary items, ready for use. In some cases their preparation will be the radiographer's responsibility. In either event it is clearly important that the radiographer knows what will be required. The following should be considered necessary.

Sterile (upper shelf)
One 20 ml record syringe.

A cannula used for withdrawal of the contrast agent from its ampoule.

Needles (Nos. 1 and 2) for insertion at the distal end of the catheter, the nozzle of the syringe being usually too coarse to place directly within the catheter.

A pair of plain dissecting forceps.

One small dressing bowl containing gauze swabs and a towel.

A kidney dish or covered container in which to place the syringe and other instruments.

All of this equipment is normally obtainable in pre-sterilized packs from the central sterile supply department.

Non-sterile (lower shelf)

Surgical spirit (industrial methylated 70 per cent) or other skin cleanser: for example, 'Hibitane' 0.5 per cent in spirit.

The ampoule of contrast agent in a bowl of warm water (37°C).

The agent used may be any of the water soluble iodine compounds applicable to urography. In some instances these are available in a lower concentration particularly for this procedure (for example Retro-Conray) or the medium may be diluted with distilled water. Distilled water suitable for injection is available in sterile ampoules.

A receiver for soiled swabs.

Care of the Patient

Comparable with certain other procedures which we have considered, retrograde pyelography can be truly informative only when complete filling of the renal pelvis is obtained. The amount of contrast agent required for this can vary considerably, depending on the condition of the urinary tract: for example, a ureteric calculus which is causing obstruction can grossly dilate the portion of the system above it (*hydro-ureter* and *hydronephrosis*), due to pressure effects from the blocked urinary flow. In this case a much greater volume of contrast medium will be required to outline fully the enlarged renal pelvis and ureter.

It is difficult to make any prior assessment of the correct amount: it may be as little as 5 ml or as much as 20 ml. On the other hand there is some risk to the patient if the tract becomes distended from the injection of too great a quantity of contrast fluid.

To prevent this occurrence the best guide during the procedure is simply the patient himself, since he will generally experience some discomfort or pain in the back or loin when filling of the renal drainage system is complete. It is customary to warn him not to endure this with silent fortitude but to complain of it immediately he feels it.

Since the best conduct of the examination is thus dependent upon the patient's co-operation, it is not usual to undertake retrograde pyelography on an unconscious subject. It sometimes happens that a patient may reach the X-ray department insufficiently recovered from a general anaesthetic. When this occurs he should not be left waiting unattended on a trolley in the corridor outside the X-ray room. If a suitable recovery room is available in the department, this can be used, but a nurse or other qualified person must remain with the patient. Alternatively he can be returned to the ward until such time as consciousness is restored at least sufficiently to allow him to understand and reply to questions put to him.

On arrival in the X-ray room the patient should be correctly lifted from the trolley (Chapter II) by an adequate number of assistants and placed in the supine position on the X-ray table. A folded blanket should be placed across the trunk and another across the legs, so that the pubic region may be exposed without its being necessary completely to strip the patient. During the intervals in the radiographic procedure, when films are being processed and assessed, the upper blanket may be replaced in position for warmth and comfort. It is, however, essential not to impair the sterility of the operative field by careless movements.

The free end of the ureteric catheter will usually have been placed within a test-tube strapped to the upper thigh. Both the tube and its contents should be handled with care and put in some place of safety during the examination, as the urine collected from the affected kidney will be required for laboratory tests. It should be ascertained that the tube is correctly marked 'Right' or 'Left': this is particularly important when the examination is to be bi-lateral and a ureteric catheter is in place on each side. On completion of the pyelogram, when the patient is returning to the ward, the radiographer should check that he is accompanied by his case notes and that the properly labelled specimens are either dispatched with him, or sent directly to the pathological laboratory with the appropriate requisition form.

CYSTOGRAPHY: CYSTO-URETHROGRAPHY

These terms refer to the radiographic investigation of the lower urinary tract following the injection of suitable contrast agents. *Cystography* implies that the bladder alone is examined. It is useful in a limited number of conditions, but of much wider application is the complete investigation of both bladder and urethra denoted by the expression *cysto-urethrography*. Cysto-urethrography includes *micturating cystography* (in which the urethra is visualized radiologically during micturition) and *ascending urethrography* (when the male urethra is filled with a contrast agent by means of a distal injection).

The student will find that the radiographic technique to be followed, and even the contrast agent to be used, show a marked variation which is dependent mainly upon the reasons for the investigation and in part on the individual wishes of urologist and radiologist. Given below are some instances of pathology or defects, in relation to which these examinations might be expected to be helpful.

(1) Bladder diverticula. (Cystography.)

(2) Tumours of the bladder. Diagnosis, and localization of treatment fields for radiotherapy of malignant growths. (Cystography.)

(3) Congenital or acquired lesions in children: narrowing of the bladder neck: in boys, obstructive lesions in the posterior urethra due to anomalous folds of membrane (posterior urethral valves). In these cases an intravenous urogram may appear normal, since it does not indicate vesico-urethral function.

(4) Urethral strictures or calculi in adult males.

(5) Stress incontinence in women; in this condition importance is attached to the demonstration of changes in the vesico-urethral angle when the intra-abdominal pressure is raised during micturition or by other muscular strain, such as coughing.

It will be seen that cysto-urethrography is scarcely a single examination but more truly should be regarded as a group of some four or five specialized procedures, each having particular requirements in respect of the contrast medium used, the equipment necessary, and the radiographic technique to be employed in its course. For these reasons it is difficult to make a summary along general lines which would be of use to the student radiographer. However, certain principles should have become apparent to the student at this stage of the course, and from these guidance may be obtained.

Preparation of the Patient

Points to be noted include the following.

(1) Some of these investigations are not usually performed on out-patients. Children may require prior sedation to secure placidity and co-operation.

(2) Application of routine abdominal preparation.

(3) Explanation of the procedure and reassurance of the patient.

(4) Emptying of the bladder immediately prior to the examination.

(5) Insertion of the catheter or urethral cannula under strictly sterile conditions. In some instances the patient may come to the X-ray room with the catheter in place.

(6) Withdrawal of residual urine into a suitable receiver. In some cases its measurement may be necessary.

Preparation of the Trolley

The trolley should be made ready in sterile and non-sterile sections along the lines previously indicated. (Chapter xvi for preparation of a sterile trolley.) The specialized equipment required must vary depending on the examination. However, the following observations may be helpful.

(1) For cystography a large capacity syringe (50 to 100 ml) is necessary. For urethral filling a 40 ml record or Luer syringe may be attached to the cannula of a Knutson's clamp. These of course must be sterile.

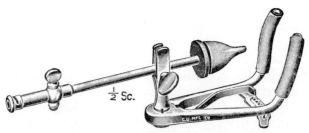

$\frac{1}{2}$ Sc.

Fig. 11. Knutson's clamp, and cannula for male urethrography. *By courtesy of the Genito-Urinary Manufacturing Co. Ltd.*

(2) All catheters, tubing and cannulae to be used must also be sterile.

(3) A suitable local anaesthetic will be required for the male patient. Usually this is in the form of a jelly containing a surface anaesthetic. It is supplied ready packed in a tube with a small nozzle through which it may be introduced into the urethra, or in some cases the surface anaesthetic may be actually combined with the contrast medium in a gel packed in a 40 ml tube sufficient for a single examination. This type of pack obviates possible difficulties in maintaining sterility.

(4) A relatively large number of contrast agents are in use for these examinations: for example, 'Steripaque', a sterile barium sulphate preparation, sometimes combined in practice with the introduction of carbon dioxide for the demonstration of bladder tumours; 'Umbradil Viscous', a water-soluble iodine complex available in different viscosities for 'ascending' and 'descending' urethrography.

(5) Micturating studies require the provision of a suitable receiver.

Care of the Patient

This will follow general principles of comfort and reassurance during these rather exacting procedures. The provision of reasonable privacy is a significant factor which will mean much to the sensitive patient, and may indeed mark the difference between a successful and an unsatisfactory examination. To this end, the coming and going through the X-ray room of staff not directly concerned in the procedure is to be avoided and the number of people present should, whenever possible, not be more than is necessary to its proper conduct. Students attending for instructional purposes should be confined to a small group.

In regard to young children, there may be some difficulty in obtaining the radiographs during micturition, owing to the child's reluctance or inability to initiate the act to order. External stimuli can be utilized. The suggestive effect of a running tap is well known, or local warmth may be applied to the lower abdomen. However, in many instances the personality of the radiographer and the relationship of confidence and kindness which has been created are without doubt operative factors in swinging the balance from failure to success.

I

CHAPTER VIII

THE BILIARY TRACT

A correctly exposed radiograph of the abdomen will reveal the outline of the liver, but the extra-hepatic parts of the biliary system are not normally demonstrated without the introduction of a contrast agent. On such a radiograph a common abnormality may be the appearance of gall stones, and it is to exclude or confirm the presence of these that the biliary tract is most frequently submitted to X-ray examination.

However, the radio-opacity of these stones, in a manner comparable with calculi in other anatomical systems, is related to the substances which compose them. Some gall stones contain a high proportion of calcium and these are readily detected on a plain radiograph. The student will soon appreciate, however, that they can vary signally in appearance. In some cases, even to an inexperienced eye they are easily recognizable as 'stones': they are large and circular or probably faceted in outline. Frequently their centres are radiolucent in relation to the outer border and the impression of a hollow core or cavity is obtained. These stones may be so numerous as to fill more or less completely the entire gall bladder sac, and in this case the classic anatomical description of a 'pear shaped organ' comes to life on the radiograph. It is indeed apparent that we are looking at the gall bladder and that it contains a number of calculi. We need go no further for the diagnosis.

However, not all gall stones can be so readily identified from a plain film. If opaque, they may appear only as flecks or isolated spots of calcium in the right hypochondrium; they may overlie the renal outline, or be situated close to the lower ribs. In this case determination must be made that the opacities are in fact related to the gall bladder, and are not either renal calculi or calcified areas in costal cartilage.

Again, many gall stones do not contain calcium and are formed of cholesterol only. This substance is transparent to X rays and such stones will not be apparent on a plain radiograph. In this circumstance too, a further procedure is necessary to exclude or confirm their presence: this procedure is the introduction of a contrast agent into the biliary tract.

ORAL CHOLECYSTOGRAPHY

Oral cholecystography is a contrast examination of the gall bladder which is very frequently performed: it far outnumbers the taking of plain radiographs, from which the information to be obtained is limited for the reasons just discussed. We may say that the gall bladder is always examined by oral cholecystography in the first instance, unless a condition is present which makes it advisable to confine the investigation to a plain film: for example, if the patient is jaundiced.

The student will have deduced from the term *oral* cholecystography that the contrast medium is taken by the mouth. It is therefore a simple procedure readily performed on out-patients. However, it requires a stringent preparation if it is to be fully successful and a considerable amount of time to complete all its stages. The examination has three sections, radiographs being exposed at the following intervals:

(i) before administration of the contrast agent (the preliminary radiograph);

(ii) 12 to 16 hours (sometimes 3 to 5 hours) after taking the contrast agent (the repletion radiographs);

(iii) 8 to 30 minutes after a meal containing fat (the emptying radiographs).

Preparation of the Patient

Each stage of the examination requires the patient to submit to certain preliminaries. His preparation will be considered with reference to the first two of these stages and their particular features.

The Preliminary Radiograph

When making the appointment for this the patient should be told something of the full examination, particularly the facts that it will necessitate his visiting the department on 2 consecutive days and that the demand on his time will be markedly greater on the second day than on the first. In some instances a visit on a third morning may be necessary. The preparation for the preliminary radiograph is usually the department's routine for abdominal X-ray examination which—with some of its difficulties—has been discussed in Chapter v.

For cholecystography good preparation is particularly desirable. Its absence frequently increases to a great degree the time required to complete the examination satisfactorily. The reason for this is that intestinal gas shadows can simulate transparent (cholesterol) stones if they happen to overlie the image of the opacified gall bladder. On the radiograph taken following ingestion of the contrast medium both entities appear as rounded dark areas. To make the differential diagnosis it is necessary to obtain at least one radiograph in which the gall bladder is seen to lie clear of any intestinal shadows.

Evidently this may involve considerable extension of the examination while various radiographic projections are applied, with consequent loss of time for the patient and increased demand upon the department. If it can be avoided by adequate measures in the first place, it is in everyone's interest—our own not least—to make the initial preparation of the patient as efficient as possible.

It is recognized, however, that it is not always possible to obtain the ideal. In the case of in-patients it is not difficult to repeat the process of preparation, should the first radiograph reveal accumulations of abdominal gas. Where out-patients are concerned it is less easy to arrange further preparation and renewed attendance in the department, and because of this it is usual to accept the first result, unless conditions are seen to be really extremely unsatisfactory. As an alternative to repeating the examination use is sometimes made of a gas-dispersing agent called methylpolysiloxane (Polycrol). This is a silicone and effective by coalescing small bubbles to form large pockets of gas which the patient may more easily dispel. It is presented as a fluid for oral administration and should produce results within 20 to 30 minutes after a dose of 2×5 ml spoonfuls.

Even in those instances when the preliminary radiograph is reassuringly clear, this cannot be taken as a guarantee of the appearances some 24 hours later.

THE REPLETION RADIOGRAPH

Once a satisfactory preliminary radiograph has been obtained, the patient receives instructions in taking the contrast agent. Various media for oral cholecystography are currently available and in general use. At present the form most widely encountered is probably a tablet or capsule, of which the patient is required to take a number varying from six to twelve at one time. One product is available also as powder which is taken as a suspension in fluid. Apart from any clinical features, this may present certain advantages to a patient who—as many people are—is a poor swallower of tablets. In any department the choice of medium to be generally used is a matter of radiological opinion, based on experience of clinical results.

A variety of practice is seen in the distribution of dose. The following techniques are currently employed in administering contrast agents for oral cholecystography.

(i) A single dose, some 12 to 16 hours before attending for examination. Six tablets or capsules are taken, which may be increased to nine in some cases if the patient is very heavy.

(ii) A double dose. (Twelve capsules 3 to 5 hours before examination.)

(iii) A fractionated dose. (Six capsules on the night before and a further 6 at 6.0 a.m. on the morning of the examination, or some variant of this.)

A further version of (iii) is the administration of repeated doses of the agent over a period of 4 days, but this is not customary unless more usual methods have failed to produce adequate filling of the biliary passages.

A meal is usually taken prior to the ingestion of the contrast agent and there is current a difference of procedure in regard to this. Two lines of thought are expressed in statements diametrically opposed to each other. They may appear thus curiously incompatible elements to be part of one and the same process, but there is a rationale for each.

(i) The meal should contain fat. This will contract the gall bladder and empty it of bile in readiness for the reception of the contrast medium.

(ii) The meal should be free of fat. This will allow the radiological agent to mix readily with the normal bile content of the system.

Of the two regimens the second is perhaps the more commonly practised. Their relative advantages are scarcely germane to this present discussion, of which the really significant point is that whether the meal in question contains fat or is free of fat, our responsibility is to give the patient specific information about it.

The second (fat free) category of meal is the more likely of the two to cause confusion. It is not enough to give the patient merely the negative instruction, 'You must not eat anything containing fat'. He may not be sufficiently educated in dietetics to recognize that milk contains fat, and will almost certainly rely on the favoured cup of tea or coffee to sustain him through his strange experiences.

It is much better to amplify the instruction to avoid fat with positive details of what food he is allowed to eat. The following suggestions may be made.

> Any lean meat.
> White fish (steamed).
> Smoked haddock.
> Fresh or grilled tomatoes.
> Garden peas, though these perhaps are better avoided as they tend to produce gas during digestion.
> Boiled potatoes.
> Fruit of any kind, stewed or fresh according to taste.
> Fruit drinks.
> Tea or coffee must be taken black or with *skimmed* milk only: they are probably better avoided.

It is a misfortune of many patients referred for cholecystography that their complaint includes some intolerance of fats. If the departmental preparation for this examination requires a meal containing fat to be taken, it is wise to exercise some dietary discretion. Fried foods or full cream are likely to have distressing results for such a patient. He will view with greater equanimity the request to take some bread and butter with a milky drink.

TAKING THE CONTRAST MEDIUM

The most usual timing of the repletion radiographs is to bring the patient to the X-ray department between nine and ten in the morning, some 12 to 15 hours following ingestion of the contrast agent: that is, he will have taken a light evening meal of the appropriate kind at possibly 6 or 7 o'clock, followed by the specified medium at 8.0 to 9.0 p.m. Tablets or capsules should be swallowed whole and one at a time with a draught of water. If the contrast medium is in powder form, its container should be filled with water and shaken until a suspension is formed. This should then be swallowed in one or two gulps, followed by a glass of fruit squash or water.

After this the patient must fast until the X-ray examination on the following morning. If he is thirsty, he may have a fruit drink or water according to his taste. In some instances, particularly when frying is the method of cooking, merely the smell of food has been thought to cause contraction and emptying of the gall bladder, with consequent failure of the examination. However though taste and smell have a stimulating effect on the gall bladder, in themselves they do not lead to evacuation of bile. Some radiologists prefer the patient to abstain from smoking during this period.

Where it is departmental practice to take the repletion radiographs a little later in the day, or where a special arrangement is made to suit some individual convenience, appropriate adjustments to the whole scheme of events of course will be needed. However, it should be kept in mind when making any particular alterations that it is hardly a suitable arrangement which would require the patient to take the contrast medium in the middle of the night. Consequently any appointments for the afternoon should be carefully considered.

Once familiarity with it is attained, the departmental routine becomes simple and we may again make the point that we sometimes underestimate its demand upon the patient. To him it all seems very complicated indeed. He must in fairness receive detailed written instructions and not a mere word of mouth account of what he should or should not do.

Care of the Patient

On his second visit to the department for the repletion series of radiographs, it is the responsibility of the radiographer to discover from the patient whether any untoward effects have resulted from taking the contrast agent. In the media used for cholecystography the opacity is due to iodine. The student should be already familiar with the radio-opaque nature of this element and will know how often it is employed to obtain radiographic contrast in a large number of procedures. In the previous chapter reference has been made to the sensitivity of certain individuals to this substance, and occasionally in the course of cholecystography the allergic type of reaction is encountered. However, it is rather unusual and when it does occur is seldom worse than an uncomfortable urticaria and perhaps a general malaise of a few hours' duration.

Much more common are gastro-intestinal disturbances which essentially are reactions, not to the iodine content of the preparation, but to the complex salt which 'carries' the iodine molecule. The patient may experience nausea and vomiting, or diarrhoea, sometimes to a prostrating degree. In this regard, however, the modern contrast agents for cholecystography are generally much better tolerated than were their forerunners.

These reactions, when they occur, may prevent concentration of the agent in the gall bladder and lead to the impression that dysfunction is present. It is therefore important to ask the patient specifically about any ill results, since if he has experienced only a slight upset he may think that to mention a trivial ailment is to appear to complain unnecessarily, and will say nothing of it, unless questioned. It is surprising, too, how many patients believe that the purpose of the contrast agent was to induce bowel action and that their diarrhoea was intended to occur. In those cases when the patient has suffered from diarrhoea after taking the medium and no filling of the gall bladder is detected on the repletion series of radiographs, it is the practice in some departments to repeat the examination using tincture of opium to control the diarrhoea. However, because it is spasmodic and has been thought to provoke biliary colic, this drug is not employed by many radiologists. It is more usual to repeat the examination on the following day with the use of another oral cholecystographic agent. The patient should remain on a fat-free menu until after completion of this further examination.

The object of the repletion radiographs is twofold:

(i) to obtain a firm diagnosis of the presence of gall stones;

(ii) to assess function of the gall bladder—that is, its ability to concentrate and store bile.

On these radiographs opaque calculi will remain in constant relation to the opacified gall bladder. Cholesterol stones, which cannot be detected on the plain film owing to their radiolucency, will now appear as dark areas (negative shadows) superimposed on the image of the gall bladder: sometimes, if they are numerous and small, they adopt a characteristic string formation when a radiograph is taken in the erect posture. Reference has already been made to the possibility of confusing intestinal gas with these cholesterol stones and to the significance of good preparation of the patient in this connection.

THE FATTY MEAL

When the second part of the examination has been satisfactorily performed, the final stage completes the assessment of gall bladder function. It may obtain visualization of the common bile duct if this has not been apparent on the earlier series, and will show calculi maintaining their relation to the now contracted and diminished gall bladder shadow.

As a preliminary to this last stage of cholecystography, the patient must take a meal containing fat. In most cases, for convenience' sake, this 'meal' is actually a synthetic product containing fat in a concentrated form given as a drink.

One of these is a fluid of milky appearance and is not unattractive to the eye as when poured from the container it develops a slight frothy 'head'. Another has the appearance of *café au lait* and a taste suggestive of coffee. The average subject should not find either nauseous to take in a small quantity. It must be borne in mind, however, that many patients undergoing cholecystography are readily sickened by fat and there is a definite psychological advantage in presenting this draught as attractively as possible. Perhaps not much can be done to make a disposable paper cup very pleasing but at least a tray, a paper napkin and a holder for the cup might be used. These details may appear trivial, but are important factors in sustaining morale and even a sense of physical well-being.

Alternatively to the use of the synthetic product, the diet kitchen may be asked to supply an appropriate light meal. In this case the choice of food can be important. A glass of milk and some buttered toast are likely to prove more appetizing than fried fare of any kind. In some instances the patient may prefer to go out for a meal, but this is not usually so convenient an arrangement if radiographs are to be taken within 10 minutes of the ingestion of fats. When the patient is given a meal in the department he should be provided with peaceful and relatively private surroundings in which to take it.

INTRAVENOUS CHOLANGIOGRAPHY

In this radiological investigation a contrast medium ('Biligrafin') is introduced intravenously to the biliary tract. Its subsequent appearance in the biliary system is not dependent—as oral cholecystography generally is—upon a functioning gall bladder, but upon excretory function of the liver. It is therefore suitable for examination of the hepatic ducts in subjects in whom the gall bladder has been removed; or for visualization of the gall bladder itself, when oral cholecystography has failed to produce or has shown inadequate radiological evidence of function.

Preparation of the Patient

Considerations which apply to the preparation of patients for intravenous cholangiography are closely similar to those already discussed in relation to oral cholecystography. This examination of course can be completed during one visit to the department, since following the intravenous injection the biliary passages are usually well visualized within 25 minutes, and filling of the gall bladder is obtained in a period varying from 45 minutes to 3 hours. The patient should be given some indication that he is likely to be retained in the department throughout the morning or afternoon.

Apart from the general principles discussed in Chapter v, some diversity of opinion exists as to the best preparation for intravenous cholangiography. A typical preparation might be:

(i) a meal rich in fat on the evening prior to the procedure, followed by

(ii) a period of fasting until completion of the X-ray examination on the following day.

In some departments, however, it is the practice to omit (i), and indeed intravenous cholangiography has been successfully undertaken without any specialized preparation of the patient at all in many instances. During the course of the examination itself, nothing either to eat or drink should be given, nor should the patient smoke after the injection has been made.

In some cases preparation of the patient may include the use of certain drugs to modify the activity of the sphincter of Oddi. For example, 20 to 50 mg pethidine given intravenously will cause immediate contraction of the sphincter and thus retention of bile within the biliary system. This should result in improved radio-opacity of the gall bladder on the introduction of the contrast agent.

Preparation of the Trolley

This procedure is very similar to intravenous urography and reference may be made here to the corresponding section in Chapter VII (see also Chapter XVI). The trolley should be laid in sterile and non-sterile areas with the following items.

Sterile (upper shelf)

One 20 ml or one 50 ml syringe. These should have the nozzle eccentrically placed; one or other is selected, depending on the dose to be given.

Needles to fit the syringes and suitable for intravenous injection: for example, Nos. 1 and 2.

One small dressing bowl for gauze or wool swabs and a towel.

One kidney dish or closed container in which to place the syringe and needles.

A pair of plain dissecting forceps.

A cannula for filling the syringe.

Non-sterile (lower shelf)

Two 20 ml ampoules of 'Biligrafin' or one 20 ml ampoule of 'Biligrafin Forte'.

A skin cleanser: for example, industrial methylated spirit 70 per cent or 'Hibitane' 0.5 per cent in spirit.

A sphygmomanometer or tourniquet.

A file for opening the ampoules if necessary.

A small sand-bag or pad for support of the arm.

All of this equipment is normally obtainable in pre-sterilized packs from the central sterile supply department.

Care of the Patient

The intravenous injection will be given by either a radiologist or some other medically qualified person. 'Biligrafin' is available in two forms; the standard strength contains 3 g iodine in 20 ml of a 30 per cent solution; 'Biligrafin Forte' is a more concentrated preparation containing 5 g iodine in 20 ml of a 50 per cent solution.

The use of 'Biligrafin Forte' is recommended if the patient is very heavy or has had a cholecystectomy, as the higher content of iodine improves the contrast obtainable. However, some radiologists prefer to give a double dose (40 ml) of the standard preparation: it is less viscous, consequently easier to inject intravenously, and appears to be better tolerated by some subjects.

At this stage of the procedure, the patient should have received a brief explanation of what the examination involves. Reassurance should be given as to its ease and simplicity. In the previous chapter reference has been made to reactions which may appear following the administration of radiological contrast agents containing iodine. The possibility of these exists, whatever may be the procedure concerned and—should ill effects occur—naturally they will prove more severe if the iodine content of the medium is high.

In this investigation the trouble most likely to be encountered arises from too rapid an injection of the medium and is therefore easily avoidable in experienced hands. A minimum of 3 minutes is recommended for the injection of 20 ml of 'Biligrafin', or 4 minutes if 'Biligrafin Forte' is used. These must appear rather lengthy periods of time relative to that required in general medicine for many hypodermic injections, but they are indeed critical. If the introduction of the dye is hurried to any degree, nausea very readily results and it is likely that retching and vomiting will follow.

Generally this is quite transient and passes off within a few minutes; sometimes the disturbance may be more prolonged. In any event the patient can be reassured that his malaise will be of short duration, that it is not an uncommon trouble, and is of no significance. A nauseated patient who is retching can be helped if he is encouraged to breathe deeply and slowly through the nose. If vomiting occurs, a receiver and tissues should be provided and the patient's shoulders may be supported by the radiographer or with pillows during the bout. He should not be left until it is certain that the upset has passed, and in any circumstance the radiographer should remain in the room for 15 minutes following the injection.

In cases where the gall bladder has not previously been removed, the final stage of this examination may follow lines similar to an oral cholecystogram: a fatty meal will be given and further radiographs exposed at suitable intervals to show contraction of the gall bladder and emptying of the biliary system into the duodenum. The student is referred for completeness to the section on page 123, headed 'The Fatty Meal'.

OPERATIVE AND POST-OPERATIVE CHOLANGIOGRAPHY

These and the following investigation are included here in order to complete the survey of the biliary tract. However, they are essentially very different procedures from either oral cholecystography or intravenous cholangiography and it is scarcely possible to consider them under the headings previously used. This being so, they perhaps are not strictly within the scope of the present subject.

Operative and post-operative cholangiography imply the direct injection of the common bile duct with a suitable contrast agent: for example, a sterile solution of barium sulphate or one of the water-soluble urographic media. This may be done either at operation (operative cholangiography) or within a short period following surgery by means of a drainage tube left in the common bile duct during the cholecystectomy (T-tube cholangiography). The result and the aim are one whichever method is used: to demonstrate radiographically the biliary passages remaining after removal of the gall bladder, and to ascertain that they do not contain small residual calculi which subsequently might cause a recurrence of trouble.

It will be clear to the student that in both cases the procedure is simply the mechanical filling of an anatomical tract. In regard to operative cholangiography the student is referred to Chapter xiv for general guidance on conduct and technique when undertaking radiographic procedures in the operating theatre.

T-tube cholangiography is usually performed about 10 days after cholecystectomy, just prior to the removal of the drainage tube. It may be necessary in the X-ray department to make ready a simple sterile trolley on principles already indicated in relation to other procedures (see, for example, Retrograde Pyelography on page 109 and also Chapter xvi), bearing in mind that 20 ml of the contrast agent may be employed. A suitable syringe of this size should be available, the injection being made directly into the catheter communicating with the T-tube.

Preparation of the patient directly for cholangiography is scarcely practicable in view of over-riding surgical considerations. Care of the patient is on general lines required in the course of any X-ray examination and discussed elsewhere in this book.

PERCUTANEOUS TRANSHEPATIC
CHOLANGIOGRAPHY

During operative and post-operative cholangiography direct injection of the contrast agent is made when the common bile duct
has become accessible as a result of surgery. Transhepatic cholangiography also is a technique for introducing contrast into the biliary
passages by direct injection and is again to be distinguished from
the physiological oral or intravenous methods earlier considered.

In this difficult procedure the biliary system is entered through
one of the ducts in the liver itself which is penetrated by a needle
inserted through the abdominal wall; often although not invariably
at a site 1–2 cm below and to the right of the xiphisternum.

Many radiologists prefer to use a needle-catheter, which is
potentially a safer instrument. This is a short length of polythene
tubing about 1.5 mm in diameter which is tailored to suit the needle,
one end being tapered to a close fit. The other extremity is flanged
and carries a collar and adaptor with a tap, similar to the arrangements required by the Seldinger technique for aortography. The
length of the catheter is a little less than that of the needle, which is
of the order of 12–15 cm.

The needle is first passed down the catheter and the composite
tool used to enter the liver. As soon as this has occurred the needle
is at once withdrawn, leaving the catheter alone in place. The
operator then pulls gently on the catheter at the same time as he
applies suction at its free end by means of an attached syringe,
until he sees by entry of bile into the syringe that the catheter tip is
lying within a bile duct. After this the injection of contrast (for example 20–50 ml of 45 per cent Hypaque) is made under fluoroscopic control and films are taken as needed. For this, as for any
fluoroscopic examination which involves a surgical procedure, the
use of an image intensifier offers marked advantages.

Preparation of the sterile trolley for percutaneous transhepatic
cholangiography would require the inclusion of one or two of the
above needle-catheters and adaptors; a lay-out similar to that
described in Chapter XI for spleno-portal venography would be
suitable.

This procedure would be employed when other methods of investigation of the biliary system have failed or have been equivocal

in result. It is likely to be undertaken to give surgical guidance within a few hours of operation and the impending surgery must largely influence the patient's preparation. The X-ray examination is likely to be made under a local anaesthetic. Premedication would be given on the lines described in Chapter XI. It is usual also to arrange beforehand to check and if necessary correct the blood-clotting time, since patients suffering from jaundice are often deficient in this power.

In caring for the patient during percutaneous transhepatic cholangiography it is to be remembered that he is likely to have had a disabling illness for some time. He will most probably have a long-standing jaundice due either to duct obstruction or to damage of the liver cells. It is in the hope of making this differential diagnosis that the radiological procedure is undertaken.

CHAPTER IX

THE RESPIRATORY TRACT

BRONCHOGRAPHY

This examination is a special X-ray investigation of the lungs. When a plain radiograph of the chest is taken, the detail apparent in the lung fields is due to their blood vessels. In certain conditions useful additional information will be gained if the bronchi are filled with a radio-opaque medium and thereby delineated radiographically: like other organs which we have discussed earlier they are hollow structures, not themselves radio-opaque in relation to their surroundings.

A number of methods are available for introducing the contrast agent into the trachea, from where it may be tipped by gravity into different parts of the lung through appropriate positioning of the patient. With care a complete outline of each bronchial tree can be obtained—the reference is not inapt, since a well filled bronchogram has indeed the attractive likeness of the branches of a tree bright with snow.

The route into the trachea may be:

(i) by direct injection, a suitable needle being used to penetrate the crico-thyroid membrane;

(ii) through a catheter inserted down the trachea, generally from the nose;

(iii) through a cannula inserted by way of the mouth into the larynx, the contrast medium being allowed to drip over the back of the tongue;

(iv) through a catheter placed in position in the course of bronchoscopy (visual inspection of the bronchi through an instrument known as a bronchoscope, a procedure helpful in locating tumours or inhaled foreign bodies).

The first two methods are more generally used. The third approach has the inherent disadvantage that frequently some of the medium is swallowed and appears in the oesophagus. In regard to the last, not every patient for bronchography requires bronchoscopy and no one would embark on this procedure, which needs general anaesthesia, simply to place a catheter.

Crico-thyroid penetration has certain drawbacks. The needle may slip out of place during movements of the patient, or may damage the trachea if coughing or vomiting should occur. Some operators feel that the possibilities of trauma and the surgical nature of the method do not justify its use when other means are available. However, it is at least as widely followed as that employing the nasal catheter, and curiously enough appears to be the more popular with the patient.

Preparation of the Patient

Bronchography may be readily performed on out-patients provided that proper preparation can be given. Details are found to vary between different departments and hospitals but good preparation is likely to include all or some of the following four points.

(i) *For 3 days prior to the examination the patient should take 600 mg potassium iodide three times daily.*
To obtain this, he must at the time the appointment is made receive a suitable prescription, signed by a qualified medical officer.

Some radiologists or chest physicians may prefer to omit this part of the preparation. However, when used, the purpose of the drug is two-fold.

(*a*) It increases expectoration; accumulations of mucus in the bronchi are removed during coughing and when the contrast agent is introduced better filling of the bronchial tree is obtained.

(*b*) It will indicate whether the patient is sensitive to iodine.
An earlier chapter (Chapter VII) has stressed that the latter is a point of some importance. We know that a patient allergic to this substance may develop an alarmingly fierce reaction if it is unwittingly given to him in any considerable quantity. In common with many others employed throughout a wide range of X-ray examinations, the contrast agents used in bronchography contain iodine. Although in this instance the agent is not injected directly into the blood stream and afterwards may be largely removed by suction or coughing, the possibility of an unpleasant reaction remains.

K

(ii) *In addition to the administration of potassium iodide, the patient should receive instruction in postural drainage and should undertake this three times a day during the 3 days prior to bronchography.*

Postural drainage consists of tipping the patient into various positions so that gravity will encourage accumulated mucus to drain from the lungs.

A number of such positions are described and used depending on the area which it is desired to clear. They are related to the converse performance, in which correct positioning of the patient can lead to the filling of different lung segments in the course of bronchography itself. However, from the point of view of securing some drainage, a general simple procedure can be usefully followed: the patient should lie across his bed with shoulders and head supported at a lower level. The physiotherapy department will give instruction to the patient in carrying out postural drainage for himself and it is usual to request the superintendent physiotherapist to arrange this. In the case of in-patients, the necessary tipping will be done on the ward by a physiotherapist.

(iii) *0.6 to 1 mg atropine may be given by subcutaneous injection half an hour before bronchography is performed.* The action of this drug is to reduce the bronchial secretions so that adequate filling of the passages by the radio-opaque agent will more readily occur.

(iv) *The patient should take a light diet on the day of the examination and should be advised to take nothing by mouth for 4 hours prior to bronchography.*

It will be clear to the student that three of the measures above described have the common aim of rendering the airways as clean and dry as possible, before any attempt is made to introduce the contrast agent. Should a small bronchus be fortuitously blocked by a plug of mucus and the opaque medium be prevented from entering it, part of the examination is invalidated. This segment of the lung cannot be visualized and the impression may be received that the obstruction is a pathological entity. The student will recognize the similarity between the respiratory and alimentary tracts in regard to their correct preparation for X-ray investigation by contrast agents.

Preparation of the Trolley

In a thoracic unit, where bronchography is undertaken very frequently, it may be helpful to have permanently available one or more sterile packs containing the required equipment. Such a pack can be made suitable for all three methods of introduction of the contrast medium: by transcricoid penetration, by intubation of the trachea, or by direct instillation into the larynx.

Alternatively, if one method is known to be preferred by the radiologist or other doctor who will perform the majority of the examinations, that alone may be prepared. In the list given below, against items particular to each of the approach routes indication is made of the one to which it is applicable. By whatever way the contrast agent is introduced into the trachea, the procedure requires asepsis. The trolley must be prepared in sterile and non-sterile sections (Chapters IV and XVI).

Sterile (upper shelf)
One 20 ml syringe for the contrast agent. This should preferably

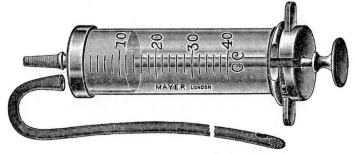

FIG. 12. Bronchography syringe (40 ml) and catheter. *By courtesy of Down Bros. and Mayer & Phelps Ltd.*

have a screw cap and finger grips. A bayonet junction on the needle is helpful if transcricoid injection is to be made: a Luer Lok fitting may be used with a laryngeal cannula. However, neither is suitable for use with a catheter.
One 2 ml and one 5 ml syringe (cricothyroid route).
These are for use during local anaesthesia of the skin and of the trachea; for the latter a Luer Lok fitting on the syringe may be helpful.

Needles for use with the above syringes (cricothyroid route).
   Sizes 1, 2, 12, and 16 would be suitable.
Two stout, wide-bore needles for injection of the contrast agent
   (cricothyroid route). These should be about an inch long and
   have a short bevel. In place of these needles, a Field's inter-
   cricothyroid needle might be used. This is a curved trocar and
   cannula which has a shield at the proximal end so that it can be
   left in place as long as is necessary to complete a bi-lateral ex-
   amination; essentially it is a small tracheotomy tube once the
   trocar is withdrawn.
A tongue depressor (laryngeal instillation or tracheal intubation).
Jacques' catheters or fine rubber tubing (tracheal intubation).
A long, curved, laryngeal cannula (laryngeal instillation). A Luer
   Lok fitting may be helpful, but note that in this case the fitting on
   the contrast syringe must match it.
A pair of dissecting forceps.
A gallipot.
One or two small dressing bowls containing wool and gauze swabs
   and a dressing towel.

Non-sterile (lower shelf)
A bottle of local anaesthetic, for example xylocaine hydrochloride
   2 per cent (cricothyroid route).
A lubricant, for example glycerin, sometimes combined with a
   local anaesthetic, for example lignocaine ointment (tracheal
   intubation).
A De Vilbiss throat spray containing local anaesthetic (laryngeal
   instillation or nasal catheter).
A receiver for soiled swabs.
A receiver containing a small quantity of antiseptic ('Miltherex')
   into which the patient may expectorate.
Methylated spirit for cleansing of the skin.
Zinc oxide strapping or small prepared dressings.
A pair of scissors.
The contrast medium: for example 'Dionosil Oily' or 'Dionosil
   Aqueous'.
   It is sometimes recommended that the contrast agent should be
   warmed by standing in hot water, but this statement really re-
   quires qualification. If the medium is very cold on introduction
   into the chest coughing will more readily occur. However, if it is

warmed to a fluid condition, it is sometimes found that peripheral (formerly termed 'alveolar') flooding results. This is a common and often unpredictable occurrence in which the medium fills the respiratory bronchioles and satisfactory visualization of the smaller bronchi is prevented. It would appear to be sounder practice to allow the contrast medium merely to stand in the warmth of the room, since the best temperature for injection is seemingly rather less than blood heat.

Care of the Patient

It is extremely important for the success of bronchography that the full co-operation of the patient be obtained. For this reason young children referred for this investigation are usually examined under general anaesthesia. At best the procedure must entail some minor discomfort and strain, of which the worst feature is the necessity for the patient to refrain from coughing. Adequate anaesthesia of the trachea is designed to suppress the cough reflex, yet it must be expected that every patient is likely to experience some desire to cough, even if only to a minor extent. Coughing, in addition to expectoration of the contrast medium, favours the fine peripheral spread to which reference has already been made and can spoil the whole examination.

The forbearance and co-operation of the patient, so essential to success, can be enlisted in the first place only if he is given an acceptable explanation of what the examination will be like and of what he himself must do towards its effective accomplishment. This does not mean that he need receive an alarming account of its redoubtable features, such as will convince him that he is about to experience all the sensations of drowning except its wetness. This is what will happen if he is summarily told, 'We are going to fill up your lungs with oil and you mustn't cough while we do it.'

It is possible to explain the procedure rather less tersely, yet suc-cinctly and reassuringly. The patient should be told that he will still have plenty of space in his lungs with which to breathe easily but that he may feel a desire to cough and to this he must make every effort not to yield, until the X-ray films have been taken.

We have a narrow way to walk here if our patient is unfortun-ately so suggestible that immediately on our mention of the word 'cough' he has the impulse to do so. However, much can be done by encouragement during the examination, by frequent reassurance that he is doing well, by audible expressions of satisfaction over progress, by giving him repeated evidence of our own confidence that we can do our job properly and that he is in good hands.

The bronchogram may be of one side only or it may be bi-lateral. In the latter event it is usual to finish the examination of one lung before injection of the other is begun. In either case when the requisite radiographs have been exposed, processed, and viewed, and the bronchogram is considered to be satisfactorily completed, the patient is advised to cough up as much of the contrast medium as he can. If he is an in-patient, further postural drainage can readily be carried out by a physiotherapist on his return to the ward. Out-patients should be retained in the X-ray department for a short while and encouraged to cough freely.

'Dionosil', the medium most likely to be used in bronchography at present, is rapidly absorbed and excreted by the kidneys and consequently does not remain in the lungs, even if the patient proves unable to expectorate the full amount. In this it is to be distinguished from the older iodized oils ('Lipiodol' and 'Neo-Hydriol') which are not capable of excretion by the urinary system and can be removed only along the same avenues as they entered—that is, through expectoration or direct suction. The latter, by means of a simple 'sucker' apparatus, is often applied to a child who has had bronchography performed under a general anaesthetic. Most children at best do not find it easy to cough up mucus or other material in their lower respiratory tract: nor in this difficulty is the period of recovery from anaesthesia likely to be of assistance.

However much he may feel in need of immediate refreshment, even the prevailing solace of that 'nice cup of tea', it is most important that no patient should take anything at all by mouth for at least 3 hours after bronchography. Until the tracheal anaesthetic has worn off, he is quite likely to inhale what he attempts to swallow. He must be firmly and clearly warned of the danger of food or a drink 'going the wrong way'. He can, however, be assured that when the prescribed hours have elapsed he may freely take a good sustaining meal.

CHAPTER X
GYNAECOLOGY

HYSTEROSALPINGOGRAPHY

Hysterosalpingography (uterosalpingography) is the demonstration of the uterine cavity and the uterine tubes by the introduction of a radiological contrast agent. In most cases the purpose of the procedure is to determine whether a tubal obstruction is the cause of sterility. However, evidence is also obtainable of abnormalities of the uterus itself and of its form and position. The examination is sometimes undertaken for reasons opposite to those first mentioned, in order to confirm that surgical ligation of the tubes—with the intention of preventing pregnancy—has been successful. Hysterosalpingography usually is conducted under fluoroscopic control by either a radiologist or gynaecologist.

Preparation of the Patient

Hysterosalpingography is not a major procedure. It should not cause undue disturbance and consequently very often is undertaken upon out-patients.

Hysterosalpingography is contra-indicated in certain circumstances:

(i) if the patient is pregnant;

(ii) in the presence of acute infection of the genital tract;

(iii) during the week preceding and the week following menstruation.

The reasons for the first prohibition are obvious and the risk in the second situation is that of ascending infection. The explanation of the third may be less immediately evident to the student and is partly related to the fact that the oily structure of certain contrast agents used for hysterosalpingography sometimes resulted in the formation of an oil embolus. An embolism is the sudden blocking of a blood vessel by a clot or other obstruction which has been carried to it by the blood current; it is an undesirable and potentially very serious complication.

There is a higher risk of oil emboli entering the circulation in the course of hysterosalpingography when the uterine mucosa is highly vascularized and thickened—as it is just prior to menstruation—or is denuded of tissue by the processes of menstruation. Because of this increased risk the argument for limiting hysterosalpingography to the quiescent phase of the endometrium was strong.

At present, however, water-soluble contrast agents have largely replaced those which were oil-based and—provided only *they* are employed—the danger of embolism is removed. Menstruation in itself is not now considered to be a physiological contra-indication to hysterosalpingography. However, the timing of the procedure continues to be important if the possibility of the existence of an early pregnancy is to be avoided.

Ovulation normally occurs half-way through the menstrual cycle and when hysterosalpingography is limited to the period prior to it then the absence of pregnancy can be practically guaranteed This makes the second week of the cycle the most usual time for the examination but probably not later than the 11th to 12th day after the onset of the previous menstrual period. There is some evidence that tubal filling occurs more readily *at* ovulation but routine timing of hysterosalpingography for the day of ovulation would be too inconvenient for many X-ray departments to be practicable. However, it might be appropriate in a special case if an earlier similar investigation had been uncertain in outcome.

It is customary to undertake a pre-arranged number of these examinations during one fluoroscopic session and usually it is the responsibility of the department of gynaecology to arrange with their patients suitable dates and appointment times and to provide the X-ray department with a list in advance of their attendance. On the arrival of the patient the radiologist may take a clinical history and will enquire especially into the menstrual history: a period which is irregular in time or of very short duration may suggest the existence of an early pregnancy.

Premedication of the patient is not necessarily indicated and some gynaecologists normally dispense with it in most cases. A common cause of pain during the procedure is tubal spasm; factors leading to it may be both physical (arising from the pressure of the injection) and psychological (due to emotional tension in the patient).

To avoid these possibilities, some practitioners routinely administer a sedative and anti-spasmodic drug; local anaesthesia of the uterine mucous membrane may or may not be used.

Sedation of this kind generally will be given to the patient shortly before the procedure is begun. Its use is a matter of clinical opinion and for clinical decision, but where it is the custom to employ it, departmental preparations for the procedure obviously must include provision of the appropriate drugs and the means to give them. It may be noted that the form of administration can vary. For example, several drugs may be combined in a *suppository* which is applied an hour before the examination: or a capsule of amyl nitrite may be *inhaled* during the procedure if spasm is seen to occur: sedatives may be given by *mouth* or by *injection*.

It is of some importance that the bladder and rectum be empty during hysterosalpingography because of the close relationship of the uterus to these structures, and the possibility of distorted appearances occurring should either be distended. Because of this the preparation of in-patients may include the administration of a simple enema on the morning of the examination and out-patients may be advised to take a laxative on the night before. Every patient should empty her bladder immediately before entering the X-ray room.

Preparation of the Trolley

The trolley should be prepared in sterile and non-sterile sections, as described elsewhere (Chapter xvi). If several hysterosalpingograms are to be undertaken the trolley must be laid anew for each patient with freshly sterilized instruments and equipment. Clearly the items required must be at least duplicated, unless a great deal of time is to be lost between examinations, and it is far better if a sufficiency of instruments can be prepared in advance for, say, three or four examinations. The following will be required for each patient:

Sterile (upper shelf)
A Cusco's vaginal speculum.
A pair of sponge-holding forceps.
A pair of tissue forceps.
A pair of vulsellum forceps.

A uterine sound.

Dilators, for example, sizes 5 to 8.

One 10 ml syringe: this should have finger grips and a screw cap; a bayonet junction or similar non-slip mount for the needle is also useful. A Green-Armytage syringe for hysterosalpingography has a screw type of plunger designed to eject 1 ml of the syringe's contents for every complete turn. This makes the quantity of the injection easy to control.

A uterine cannula. Various types of cannula are available. The Green-Armytage cannula has a rubber cone which is placed near its tip and plugs the internal os, thus preventing reflux of the contrast agent. Another, called the vacuum uterine (M.W.) cannula, has a glass cup which fits over the cervix and is held there by suction: it is associated with a small hand-operated vacuum pump which has a pressure gauge to record the degree of the partial vacuum created and a screw valve to release the vacuum.

Two small dressing bowls, one to receive sterile swabs and the other for cleansing lotion.

Two sterile towels and a supply of swabs.

A pair of sterile rubber gloves of appropriate size.

Non-sterile (lower shelf)

A jar of obstetric cream (for example, 'Hibitane' 1 per cent).

A cleansing lotion for the outer vaginal area (for example, chlorhexidine gluconate 0.1 per cent in aqueous solution).

The contrast agent (for example, 'Urografin' 76 per cent, 'Salpix').

A small mackintosh sheet.

A box of face masks; the disposable variety are satisfactory.

Also available should be a good light (for example, a standard 'Anglepoise' lamp) and a bin for soiled swabs.

Care of the Patient

It is inherent in the nature of hysterosalpingography that those referred for it are fit young women; they do not suffer from disabling diseases nor such infirmity as to require much physical assistance in the course of the examination. However, we need to remember that associated with every condition of the body there may be—indeed are—psychological factors which often influence to a marked extent our physical reactions.

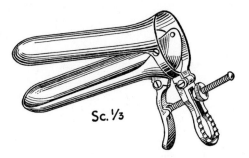

Sc. ⅓

FIG. 13. Vaginal speculum. *By courtesy of Charles F. Thackray Ltd.*

FIG. 14. Sponge-holding forceps. *By courtesy of the Genito-Urinary Manufacturing Co. Ltd.*

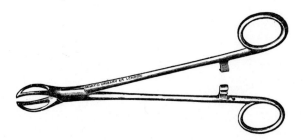

FIG. 15. Tissue forceps. *By courtesy of the Genito-Urinary Manufacturing Co. Ltd.*

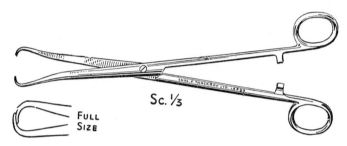

Fig. 16. Vulsellum forceps. *By courtesy of Charles F. Thackray Ltd.*

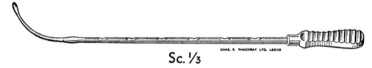

Fig. 17. Uterine sound. *By courtesy of Charles F. Thackray Ltd.*

Fig. 18. Uterine dilator. *By courtesy of Charles F. Thackray Ltd.*

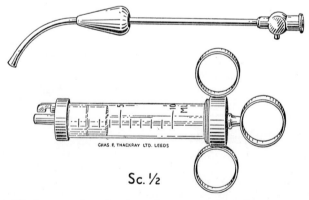

Fig. 19. Uterine cannula and syringe. *By courtesy of Charles F. Thackray Ltd.*

With this examination there is often (if the purpose of the investigation is to establish the cause of infertility) a highly charged emotional background. These women are anxious for children: their hopes of pregnancy have not been rewarded, no doubt over a period of several years, and every month must carry for them renewed insistence that time is fruitlessly passing. When eventually they reach the X-ray department their infertility will have become a considerable force in their emotional make-up. Inevitably there is some tension associated with the result of the examination: they are very eager to know that they are 'all right'. In addition to this psychological overlay, many of them are genuinely apprehensive about the procedure itself; they are wondering what is actually going to happen to them and whether it will hurt very much.

It is the experience of many who regularly perform hysterosalpingography that whatever contrast medium is used its commonest side effect is pain, and that there is a remarkably wide variation in the degree and even the type of pain experienced. Apart from the effect of the contrast agent, some patients suffer considerable pain from the necessary passage of instruments into the uterus; while in others the discomfort is so slight and so transient as not to receive mention. More than one authority has referred to a link between tension, apprehensiveness, and the subsequent pain of the procedure. We are perhaps too late to remedy the emotional build-up; certainly we can allay fear, and this is an end worth achievement if we can mitigate for any patient the physical distress which she may experience.

In most instances even fairly severe pain resulting from the examination will have passed off within an hour. The patient should be allowed to lie down for a while and a suitable analgesic may be given, such as two pentazocine hydrochloride tablets ('Fortral'). A cup of tea and a hot water bottle are other simple comforts which will be welcome and probably of some benefit. In the majority of cases no other treatment or drug is necessary, though all these patients should be seen again by the radiologist before leaving the department. Delayed abdominal pain, which may occur several hours later, and bleeding are potentially much more serious complications and the patient should be considered for admission.

While the fact may have little to do with our responsibilities in caring for the patient, the student perhaps will find interest in knowing that this diagnostic investigation appears from time to time to have a therapeutic value. A significant proportion of women investigated for infertility are found to become pregnant shortly after hysterosalpingography has been performed, perhaps due to the removal of some occlusion of the uterine tubes by the introduction of the contrast agent or possibly to some bacteriostatic action. Various attempts have been made to clarify the reasons for this phenomenon; but whether or not the causes for it are well understood, it is certainly pleasant for the radiographer to meet some of these patients again at the ante-natal clinic!

CHAPTER XI

THE CARDIOVASCULAR SYSTEM

ANGIOGRAPHY

To obtain radiographic contrast it is necessary for there to be some difference in opacity to X rays between the structure it is desired to examine and the tissue surrounding it. The student is already familiar with this principle and is aware of the use of radiological contrast agents to provide the opacity within the organ or structure.

In the systemic circulatory system blood vessels are not normally demonstrated on a plain radiograph, because their 'density' is similar to that of the tissues which enclose them. We may detect radiographically the course of a blood vessel in certain instances.

(1) If there are deposits of calcium within its walls.

This is an expected finding in many elderly subjects. Radiographs of the pelvis, abdomen, or lower leg, taken for reasons unrelated to any circulatory troubles, quite frequently demonstrate some part of the iliac arteries, the abdominal aorta, or the arteries of the leg, owing to calcific deposits within them.

(2) Following the introduction of some suitable radiological contrast agent in sufficient concentration to render the lumina of a group of vessels temporarily opaque in relation to their surroundings.

(3) We may note as a third instance the special case of the vessels in the pulmonary circulation. Since the lungs normally contain air they are more radiolucent than other tissue and provide a natural radiographic contrast. The vessels supplying them appear dense by comparison and are visible on a plain radiograph. It is in fact these vessels which constitute the major part of the pattern of the lung fields radiologically.

However, there is a significant difference between the pulmonary vessels (and cardiac shadow) as they are seen on a plain radiograph, and their visualization following the introduction of a radio-opaque contrast agent (as in (2) above). In the first instance we are seeing the external contours of the vessels (or in the case of the heart, the profile of the cardiac chambers). In the second, a contrast medium is present within a vessel or cavity: we see revealed its *internal* outlines and consequently the information obtained is in a different category. The procedures are complementary, and in certain conditions both plain radiographs and contrast studies may be necessary for diagnosis.

To the introduction of a radio-opaque agent the term *angiography* is applied, being usually qualified to indicate the region examined: for example, *cerebral angiography* relates to a contrast examination of the vessels of the brain, *angiocardiography* to the chambers and circulation of the heart, and *peripheral angiography* to the vessels of the limbs.

These examinations technically are not easy. The problems associated with them essentially are twofold.

(1) A relatively large quantity of contrast agent (10 to 50 ml) must be introduced *quickly* into the vessels under examination, so as to create an appreciable concentration of radio-opaque blood within them. Injection of the contrast agent in a thin, gradual stream—as occurs in the usual form of intravenous injection—fails altogether to fill the lumen of the vessel which is penetrated and is therefore useless in demonstrating any pathology.

The medium, while appearing fluid in solution, has in fact enough viscosity to offer resistance in the syringe. It is relatively difficult to introduce in sufficient volume and at sufficient speed by hand alone. Some means of manipulating the plunger mechanically at higher pressures is often employed in examinations relating to the larger vessels.

(2) Films must be *rapidly* exposed to visualize the filled vessels. In the large arteries particularly the rate of blood flow is considerable: it approximates to 50 cm per second. The time required for the complete circuit from the heart to the heart again is less than half a minute. To obtain radiographs demonstrating in sequence phases of the blood flow through a group of vessels, films must be changed successively within seconds—or less—of each other: for example, during angiography of the abdominal aorta and its branches, the arterial phase of filling persists literally only for 1 to 2 seconds following injection.

An automatic changer or one providing at least semi-mechanical assistance is necessary, since the series of films cannot be manœuvred conventionally by hand with sufficient rapidity. Associated with this, the switching of the X-ray unit must be of a type which allows making and breaking of electrical circuits several times a second—again no mean technical achievement.

The methods available by which these technical difficulties may be met are not our present concern. However, some appreciation of the problem is necessary if the student is to understand that angiography in any form is a complex procedure, requiring careful preparation and in some instances well synchronized team work by two or three radiographers. It is in fact fundamental to the success of this work that the examining radiologist has a practised team upon whom he can rely and that each should recognize his own personal responsibility for its effective outcome. Even a momentary failure in co-operation, a brief carelessness on anyone's part, can result in the necessity to repeat an entire examination. This not only is an unwarranted addition to the department's work, but carries for the patient—if young especially—certain risks inherent in increased radiation dosage, and the universal danger of heavy administration of a radio-opaque agent containing iodine. The responsibility of repeating such an examination is consequently not light, and it should never become necessary because of some trivial error in procedure.

Preparation of the Patient

Angiography is not as a rule undertaken upon out-patients; admission for at least 24 hours is generally advisable to ensure satisfactory preparation and adequate after-care.

For this reason the preparation of the patient is not usually the immediate concern of the X-ray staff, though clearly there is a departmental responsibility to provide the ward sister with detailed information of what is required. Preparations will vary depending on a number of factors.

(i) Whether or not the examination is to be made under a general or a local anaesthetic.

(ii) The preference for a particular premedication of the responsible anaesthetist in the first instance, or in the second of the radiologist who will perform the examination.

(iii) The type of vascular study to be undertaken.

Within the scope of the present work only the most general observations can be made. However, it is hoped to give the student some indication of the lines which preparation of the patient for

L

these examinations is likely to follow, and so assist in familiarization with a particular departmental practice in any case.

General Preparation for Abdominal X-ray Examination

This is advisable if angiography of the abdominal vessels is to be performed: for example *renal aortography* or *arteriography* (investigation of the renal arteries) or *spleno-portal venography* (examination of the portal circulation). The subject of general preparation has been fully discussed in an earlier chapter (Chapter v) and scarcely requires reiteration here. The importance of obtaining adequate bowel clearance with at the same time an avoidance of strong purging may again be usefully noted.

General Anaesthesia

Medical and nursing staff will be aware of the usual measures in patient-care prior to taking a general anaesthetic. These include:

(i) routine examination of the chest and urine;

(ii) the obtaining of written consent to the administration of an anaesthetic;

(iii) the removal of make-up from women patients, since artificial colouring on the face and nails might prevent the detection of cyanosis during anaesthesia;

(iv) the removal of any denture and jewellery, including a watch.

Prior to the procedure some restriction of diet is necessary. Nothing should be taken by mouth for at least 4 hours previously, or longer if the anaesthetist so orders. A heavy meal of any kind must be avoided.

Thirty minutes before the examination the patient will receive the appropriate premedication which the anaesthetist will order. This will be given by hypodermic injection. The trip to the X-ray department must be made on a stretcher or in a bed. The patient should be suitably dressed in an operating gown and comfortably covered with blankets.

During the course of the procedure, the trolley or bed upon which the patient was brought should remain at hand in the X-ray department, to facilitate his removal and return to the ward as soon as possible afterwards. These indeed should be general rules of patient-care during any major radiological procedure of this kind, whether or not general anaesthesia is employed.

Local Anaesthesia

Many vascular radiological examinations can be done under a local anaesthetic, provided that the patient is adequately sedated beforehand. A radiologist may prefer this who considers that the giving of a general anaesthetic adds to the complexity and risk of the procedure and converts what may be a relatively simple examination into a major one. There may also be practical difficulties associated with obtaining the services of an anaesthetist at the time when the X-ray department needs them.

In certain instances general anaesthesia is indisputably indicated.

(1) In the case of children up to about 14 years of age (babies shortly after birth may be best examined under local anaesthesia).

(2) For a patient unable from any cause to understand what is happening to him and to give reasonable co-operation.

However, it is probably more common practice to give a general anaesthetic for most angiographic examinations than not to do so. There are several reasons for this.

(1) They are all procedures which need a high degree of co-operation and forbearance from the patient.

(2) Each requires a surgical lay-out, entails blood-letting and imposes discomfort on the subject: all these features naturally tend to alarm and distress any patient. However successful he may be in concealing these emotions from us we must recognize that they are certainly present, admittedly to a varying extent.

(3) During some angiographic examinations, special control of the patient's respiration is helpful and the anaesthetist can provide this: for example, respiration may be safely and surely arrested or the patient may be hyperventilated during certain film sequences.

When the procedure is to be done under a local anaesthetic the significant feature is to secure adequate tranquillity of the subject by sufficient premedication. Upon the introduction of the contrast agent the patient will experience local warmth and discomfort, even perhaps pain: for example, in the eye, throat and head during cerebral angiography, or in the abdominal region during renal aortography. He should receive enough drugs to make him pleasantly drowsy; he will be capable of answering questions and will understand what is said to him, but apparently does not mind very much what actually happens during the procedure.

The choice of drugs to induce this happy condition of indifference is a matter for medical decision and is the concern of the radiologist who is to perform the examination.

It is important for the radiographer to know the radiologist's choice of premedication and when and where it will be given, in order that the appropriate drugs, together with suitable syringes and needles, may be made ready beforehand in the department or that ward staff may be suitably advised. It is bad organization to wait to find out about this until the patient is actually in the department.

TESTS FOR SENSITIVITY

In some cases it will be known that the patient has had previously another contrast radiological examination: for example, many subjects for renal arteriography will already have had intravenous urography performed. Where this is not so, a trial injection of a small quantity of the contrast agent should be made. This can be done on the ward on the previous day if desired, or it may be given by the anaesthetist during the preliminary stages of the procedure.

Some hospitals use an 'allergy form'. This must be completed by the doctor who refers a patient for arteriography and it is sent to the X-ray department before the procedure. The form puts specific questions regarding any history of allergy. It may seek information also about drugs with which the patient might be under treatment and which could have significant effect during arteriography. These are anticoagulant drugs which inhibit blood clotting and vasodilator drugs which expand blood vessels, each being relevant to the treatment of peripheral vascular disease.

Premedication of the patient often includes the administration of an antihistamine drug, such as Phenergan (which is both sedative and prophylactic against an allergic reaction). This may be given by intravenous injection immediately prior to the X-ray examination.

The radiological contrast agents in use for vascular examination at the present time in general are well tolerated and few untoward reactions occur as a result of their use, even should the procedure require several injections of the medium. Those applicable are the water-soluble iodine compounds used in urography, in certain cases in greater strength: for example, 'Conray 480' or 'Cardio-Conray'.

PREPARATION OF THE SKIN

Preparation of the skin prior to surgery is often stringent. The introduction of an arterial catheter or cannula must be regarded as a surgical procedure, requiring strict observation of asepsis. Some preparation of the skin may be necessary during the time that the patient is on the ward: for example, if the femoral artery is to be punctured in the groin the pubic hair is often shaved. The skin should be washed over a wide area and should be generally clean.

Whether or not any further preparation is undertaken by ward staff, cleansing of the skin with an antiseptic (for example, industrial methylated spirit 70 per cent; 'Hibitane' 0.5 per cent in spirit; tincture of iodine 2.5 per cent) will be a necessary and immediate preliminary to puncture of the vessel.

Preparation of the Trolley

The equipment prepared will vary in detail, depending both on the nature of the examination and the technique to be employed. An exhaustive list of what might be required for every angiographic procedure can be of little profit to the student at this stage. In so specialized a subject it is possible here to give only broad guidance. What follows is intended rather as general aid than as an absolute statement of what will be done in every department.

In a department undertaking many angiographic examinations it is likely that a senior radiographer—or in some cases a qualified nurse who is seconded to the X-ray staff—will be responsible for the care and organization of the specialized surgical equipment which they require. The time needed for its preparation and disposal can be considerable when many such examinations are made.

METHODS OF STERILIZATION

This subject has been discussed in full in an earlier chapter (Chapter IV). It may be noted that though much of this equipment (for example, special trocars and cannulae, syringes, guide wires and stilettes) may be sterilized in an autoclave, some catheters are not suitable for this treatment. Certain grades of nylon can be safely autoclaved, but polythene (including the opaque 'Kifa' catheters) cannot. In their case, chemical sterilization must be employed.

Later in this chapter is listed the sterile lay-out for a small number of angiographic examinations. In most cases the non-sterile section of the trolleys will be similar and will contain the following.

Non-sterile (lower shelf)

A skin cleanser: for example, industrial methylated spirit, 70 per cent.

A local anaesthetic (for example, Xylocaine Hydrochloride 2 per cent; Lignocaine Hydrochloride 2 per cent), unless general anaesthesia is to be used.

A file for opening ampoules.

A flask of sterile normal saline solution for injection.

Certain anti-coagulant and anti-spasmodic drugs (for example, Heparin and Priscol) may be required.

The contrast agent warmed to blood heat (37° C) by immersion in warm water; two or three ampoules may be necessary for each examination. The substance used will be one of the organic iodine compounds, its choice being determined by the procedure, for example 'Hypaque' 45 per cent for cerebral angiography.

A pair of scissors.

A roll of 'Elastoplast'. This is a more satisfactory form of strapping than the plain zinc oxide tape, since it can be applied to maintain firmer pressure over a wound.

It is usual during these examinations for the radiologist and his 'scrubbed' assistant—either a radiographer or a qualified nurse—to wear sterile clothing as a guard against contamination of a length of catheter or guide wire, should it accidentally 'whip' against some part of the body during handling. Consequently a sufficient supply of masks, sterile gloves of the appropriate size, and gowns should be provided. The disposable type of face mask, if it is changed for each examination, is quite satisfactory.

AORTOGRAPHY (Seldinger Technique)

Sterile lay-out

Two towels.

A small mackintosh sheet.

A stainless steel rule about 30 cm in length.

A Seldinger arterial trocar and cannula or Sutton needle of appropriate size.

A Seldinger guide wire or stilette of the same size and appropriate length.

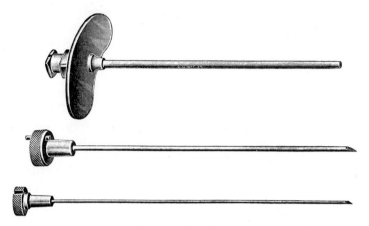

FIG. 20. Seldinger trocar and cannula. *By courtesy of the Genito-Urinary Manufacturing Co. Ltd.*

FIG. 21. Adaptor for Seldinger catheter. *By courtesy of the Genito-Urinary Manufacturing Co. Ltd.*

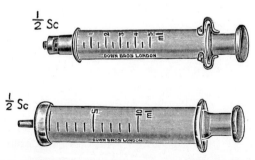

FIG. 22. (a) Syringe with Luer Lok fitting. (b) Syringe with Luer fitting. *By courtesy of Down Bros. and Mayer & Phelps Ltd.*

Catheters of suitable size and length: for example, 'Kifa' radio-opaque (Ödman) catheters; autoclavable nylon; polythene.

A threaded connector to fit the catheter used. This screws into an adaptor, combining a tap and a 'female' Luer Lok connection for the syringes.

A 50 ml and a 25 ml syringe for injection of the contrast agent. These should have a 'male' Luer Lok fitting, and if mechanical injection is to be employed should be all metal in construction.

Two 20 ml syringes, Luer fitting, for injection of normal saline.

Two 2 ml syringes and suitable needles (for example, Nos. 1, 2 and 12) for administration of any premedication which has to be given and local anaesthetic, if this is to be used. The syringes for the saline injection and for use in premedicating the patient may be of the disposable type and pre-packed.

A small dressings bowl.

A gallipot.

A scalpel handle—Swann Morton or equivalent, No. 3, small.

One blade, No. 15.

Gauze swabs.

The above can be regarded only as a minimum lay-out of essential instruments. A more flexible and satisfactory approach would cater for likely variations in technique which might arise during any examination by the inclusion of a full assortment of syringes, Seldinger trocars, wires, translumbar needles, and connectors.

In certain cases where the radial or brachial artery is catheterized using an 'open' technique, it may be necessary afterwards to suture the vessel, and this again will require suitable instruments to be at hand: suture needles, needle holder, and sutures.

CEREBRAL ANGIOGRAPHY

Sterile lay-out

A sterile towel.

A small mackintosh sheet.

One or two $3\frac{1}{2}$ inch angiography needles (Lindgren type), Luer Lok fitting, for carotid or vertebral injection.

A 10 ml syringe for injection of the contrast agent. This should be of the Luer type and may have a 'male' Luer Lok fitting. Depending on the preferences of the radiologist, the syringe may or may not be of the ordinary disposable type.

Two 20 ml syringes, Luer fitting, for injection of normal saline.

Two 2 ml syringes and suitable needles (for example, Nos. 1, 2 and 12) for administration of the local anaesthetic (unless the procedure is to be performed under general anaesthesia).

These last four syringes can be the disposable kind normally supplied by the central sterile department.

Polythene tubing in a suitable length (about 20 cm). This should have a suitable adaptor at either end; that for the needle should be a 'male' Luer Lok fitting; the other should be of the 'female' Luer (or Luer Lok) type for connection to the syringe.

FIG. 23. (a) Connector, polythene tubing to male Luer Lok. (b) Connector, polythene tubing to female Luer Lok. *By courtesy of the Genito-Urinary Manufacturing Co. Ltd.*

A small dressings bowl.
A gallipot.
Gauze swabs.
One Spencer Wells (or equivalent) straight artery forceps.
One Moynihan's large cutting needle.

During the procedure it is necessary to keep the tubing/needle system patent between contrast injections by irrigating it with a solution of normal saline. Some radiologists, preferring not to withdraw and recharge syringes repeatedly for this purpose, set up drip infusion equipment and provide irrigation from this. In such cases the trolley must include a two-way tap as additional sterile equipment and a pre-sterilized drip infusion set (see page 182).

SPLENO-PORTAL VENOGRAPHY

Sterile lay-out
Two sterile towels.
Two 2 ml syringes and suitable needles (Nos. 1, 14, 16 and 20) for any premedication and for administration of local anaesthetic.

These syringes and needles can be of the usual disposable kind.

Two 50 ml syringes, for injection of contrast agent and normal saline.

Two exploring needles with stilettes (size 14 Standard Wire Gauge), 7–9 cm long and having a short bevel. Alternatively a needle-catheter of the shorter length (7 cm) might be used; this instrument is described in the last section of Chapter VIII.

A large receiver.

A gallipot.

Portex vinyl tubing in a suitable length, with adaptors of the Luer Lok type, as previously described, to provide a flexible connection between the needle and syringe, or between the catheter and syringe.

If intrasplenic pressure is to be measured, a saline manometer with connections.

Care of the Patient

When a general anaesthetic has been given care of the patient must include those specialized aspects applicable to the unconscious subject which were discussed in an earlier chapter (Chapter II). To summarize this, two main factors require continuous attention.

(1) The maintenance of an unobstructed airway.

(2) Care in handling or moving the patient to avoid damage to limbs because of some improper position.

Under the second heading, certain circumstances may require special attention. For instance a patient referred for femoral arteriography is likely to suffer from impaired circulation in the lower leg and will be particularly susceptible to injury, even from trivial trauma. Gangrene of the toes, if not actually present in such a case, is a likely eventuality. In manœuvring such patients in an unconscious condition on the X-ray table, particularly in turning them into the prone position, it is important to provide adequate support for the ankles, so that prolonged pressure on the toes is avoided.

Care in moving the legs is always necessary, and the experienced radiographer in handling these patients should be sufficiently alert to appreciate the possibility of a gangrenous limb, even if coverings on the patient's feet prevent its immediate recognition.

Possible complications of any angiographic procedure are haemorrhage and the formation of haematoma (extravasation of blood into the tissues). This is unlikely to follow a clean arterial puncture, provided adequate compression is applied at the site of penetration following the withdrawal of the catheter or needle. Patience is required here; in some cases it may be necessary to compress the artery for 20 minutes or more before the patient is allowed to leave the department. A firm pressure dressing is applied after the manual compression ceases.

Following his return to the ward, the patient may be put on a 15 minute pulse chart and the condition of the dressing checked at the same intervals for 3 hours. Less frequent inspections should be made during the succeeding 24 to 48 hours, and at the end of this time, if all is well, the patient can safely be discharged.

It is understood that in any room where angiography is undertaken emergency equipment for resuscitation, including cardiac massage, must be readily to hand. In these examinations, particularly if a general anaesthetic is given, perilous situations can arise with great rapidity. It cannot be too often emphasized that the infrequency of trouble must not induce carelessness in providing for it. Minutes spent in fetching some needed item from a distant part of the hospital might be the ones which will cost the patient his life.

CHAPTER XII

THE LYMPHATIC SYSTEM

Lymphangiography

Like blood vessels, lymph vessels are not normally apparent on a plain radiograph. A suitable radiological contrast agent must be introduced to the lymphatic system before the courses of its numerous vessels can be followed. This procedure is called *lymphangiography*.

In medicine the prefix *angio-* or *angi-* implies relationship to a vessel, being derived from the Greek word for this. Usually it refers, as we saw in the previous chapter, to a blood vessel but here it is combined with the words *lymph* and *grapho-* to indicate that what we are doing is to record the avenues of the lymphatic system. The term *lymphography* is also in use for the same procedure.

The purpose of lymphangiography is often to determine the extent of a malignant process in the body. It is characteristic of cancer that in time cancerous cells may be carried to parts which are remote from the original sites of trouble. The lymph vessels are well recognized pathways which often convey the disease. By means of lymphangiography those glands which have become affected— particularly those which are difficult to palpate—can be discovered and treatment (radiotherapy) given. A patient who has a breast cancer, for example, may have malignant lymph nodes in the axilla; the abdominal and even mediastinal glands may be involved in a man who has a tumour of his testis. Other malignant processes of the lymphatic system are diseases of lymphoid tissue and arise in the nodes themselves. These conditions are called the malignant *reticuloses*.

Lymphangiography can be used in these cases in several ways:
  (a) to explore the extent of the disease;
  (b) to guide the radiotherapist in planning the location of treatment fields;
  (c) to facilitate therapy by the introduction of a radioisotope (colloidal gold) into the lymphatic system so that it may be carried by the lymph stream itself to affected nodes.

The investigation of certain benign conditions, too, is advanced by lymphangiography. The procedure would be justified in any of the following cases:

(i) traumatic lesions of the thoracic duct;

(ii) congenital lymphoedema (swelling of the extremities owing to inadequate lymph drainage);

(iii) chyluria (presence of chyle in the urine which is sometimes due to a tropical infection from a parasite).

Lymphangiography depends on putting a fine cannula into a lymph vessel in order to feed the radiological contrast agent into the system. This is the difficult part of the procedure. Once a suitable duct has been cannulated and filled there is nothing about the radiographic aspects of the examination to be noted apart from two special features.

(i) If the chosen medium is one of the water-soluble urographic agents, radiographs must be taken *quickly*. Several exposures are necessary, working upwards along the limb, and these are usually followed by films of the pelvis, abdomen and thorax as appropriate. Use of an oily contrast agent allows more time for radiography, although in both cases the necessity to repeat radiographs is undesirable since diffusion of the contrast substance—whether rapid or gradual—causes blurring of the lymphatic images. It is consequently important that everything should be ready beforehand so that the required films are taken without delay or mishap.

(ii) The patient may have to return 24 hours later for further radiographs which will show the contrast agent lying within— and thus demonstrate the structure of—the lymph nodes; these are like little lakes collecting streams of lymph from various parts. Some of the contrast agent may be retained in the lymph nodes for as long as a year.

Preparation of the Patient

Lymphangiography can be performed under local anaesthesia and is considered a suitable out-patient procedure by some radiologists and surgeons. Others prefer to have the patient admitted and this would be essential if preliminary treatment of any infection or of oedema of a limb were required; such treatment might continue over a period of several days.

Preparation of the patient is naturally influenced by whether or not the patient is admitted and also by the anaesthesia, whether local or general. Any of the following points may be significant.

(i) Premedication for general anaesthesia is at the discretion of the anaesthetist concerned.

(ii) If local anaesthesia is to be used, in-patients may be sedated half an hour beforehand (see Chapter XI, p. 149).

(iii) The limb to be cannulated may be shaved and the skin cleansed for surgery (see Chapter XI, p. 150). Such preparation should extend from the knee to the toes for lymphangiography of a lower limb and from the elbow to the fingers of an upper limb.

(iv) The patient should have no food or fluids by mouth for 4 hours before the examination.

(v) The bladder should be emptied immediately before the examination.

In addition to the physical preliminaries of his investigation the patient should have information. He is entitled to it and in the event it is as important a part of his preparation as any practical nursing measure.

Before introduction of the radiological contrast agent can be made the operator must inject into the subcutaneous tissues, at certain sites on the foot and ankle or in the interdigital spaces of the hand, a suitable diffusible dye (patent blue violet) which is taken up by the lymphatics and renders them visible. The later effects of this are exotic and rather alarming to the patient—and indeed for his relatives—unless previous warning has been given. The patient should therefore be advised of the following aspects of the procedure.

(i) Following the examination he will be generally blue in colour and will see through a light blue veil owing to the circulating dye. The skin discoloration will persist overall for up to 2 days and at the sites of injection for longer; it should disappear completely in about a week.

(ii) The urine will be green in colour for approximately 48 hours.

(iii) If a local anaesthetic is used and the radiological contrast agent is water-soluble, the patient will experience with the injection a fleeting burning sensation travelling along the limb. Despite this disturbance the patient should remain lying perfectly still until he is told he may move.

(iv) The examination is usually very lengthy, requiring 2 or more hours for each limb injected.

Preparation of the Trolley

Sterile (upper shelf)

Two 10 ml syringes.

One of these is for injection of the PBV dye and the other for the radiological contrast agent.

One 5 ml syringe for the local anaesthetic, if used.

Needles: No. 19 (fine) for injection of the PBV dye and No. 21G 1½ for use in giving the local anaesthetic. The syringes and needles may be of the pre-sterilized disposable type.

Gallipot.

One small dressings bowl.

3 to 4 towels.

One pair of gloves for the patient's forefoot or hand, as appropriate.

Swabs.

Several lymphatic cannulae.

Various ways of making these cannulae from needles and nylon or polyethylene tubing have been described but complete disposable lymphangiogram sets are also available. One example is the St Thomas' Hospital pattern. This consists of fine tubing, 90 cm (36 in.) long, already attached to a small 30 SWG needle and having a Luer fitting at its other end for the syringe. It is pre-sterilized and ready for use. If such equipment is not available sterilization should be by chemical means (for example, 12 hours' immersion in a 5 per cent solution of formaldehyde) and should be followed by thorough rinsing with normal saline before use.

00 plain catgut
No. 1 braided silk } for sutures.

One cut-down set.

This should normally be supplied complete from the central sterile supply department. Typically the pack might contain the following items but the student will meet minor variations.

CONTENTS OF CUT-DOWN PACK

One pair 5 in. Spencer Wells artery forceps.

3 pairs 5 in. mosquito artery forceps, curved on the flat.

One No. 3 Bard-Parker handle and No. 15 blade.

One pair vein scissors.

One pair Gillies' toothed dissecting forceps.

One pair McIndoe's non-toothed dissecting forceps.

One single hook, blunt.
One fine needle holder.
One aneurysm needle, large.
One aneurysm needle, small.
One gallipot.
5 wool balls.
5 four-inch gauze swabs.
One small tissue dressing towel.
One water-repellent towel, small.
One water-repellent sheet, small.

In addition to the sterile layout on the trolley sterile packs of gloves and gowns, together with a box of face masks, should be provided for the radiologist or surgeon and his scrubbed assistant, if any.

Non-sterile (lower shelf)
A local anaesthetic if used.
Patent blue violet.

This is already made up into an 11 per cent solution which is sterile and ready for use.

Normal saline, one bottle or ampoules.

This is required in order to dilute the PBV dye, for rinsing of the cannula and for flushing the lymphatic vessels on completion of the procedure.

The contrast agent.

This should be warmed by immersion of the phials in warm water until opened for use.

'Neo-Hydriol Fluid' or 'Lipiodol Ultra-fluid' in ampoules: alternatively ampoules of 65 per cent 'Hypaque' or its equivalent.

A skin cleanser; for example 'Hibitane' 0.5 per cent in spirit.

Other equipment in the room should include the special injection apparatus (see p. 163) and a good adjustable spot lamp. A pair of loupe glasses might also be helpful.

Care of the Patient

CARE DURING LYMPHANGIOGRAPHY

Patients for lymphangiography are usually adults. Very young children are excluded by the impracticability of cannulating their very small lymph vessels, the exercise being difficult enough even in a full-sized subject.

A high degree of co-operation and forbearance is required from the patient, particularly if an oily contrast agent is used. In this case —owing to the viscosity of the oil and the necessarily small calibre of the needle and tubing employed—the injection must be made at high pressure and can be given only very slowly if rupture of the lymphatic vessels is to be avoided, or at least minimized. A mechanical means of injection is essential and the equipment should be adjusted to deliver 7–12 ml at a rate of 8 ml per hour.

Various methods of automatic injection have been described. A typical device consists of a supporting metal frame which can hold a conventional 10 ml syringe in a vertical position, together with one or more weights. These ride on top of the plunger of the syringe in a slipway and maintain a continuous gravity-induced pressure on the plunger. By varying the amount of the weights in the apparatus the rate of the injection can be controlled.

Another suitable piece of equipment for this purpose is an electrically driven infusion pump in which a slowly rotating screw drives the plunger of the injection syringe. Such a motor may operate two syringes simultaneously over a wide range of flow rates. Students may see devices in their departments which work on either of these principles.

Lymphangiography is a lengthy procedure. It has several stages and to clarify these we list each of them below, together with an estimate of the length of time required for the successful performance of each one.

(i) Subcutaneous injection of the patent blue dye into one or more sites, followed by local massage and passive movements of associated joints to aid the dispersal of the dye along the limb.
10 min.

(ii) Cannulation of the selected lymphatics. This requires (a) the operator to mask, scrub and put on sterile clothing; (b) a skin incision and careful exposure of each vessel to be cannulated; (c) the introduction of stay sutures beneath the vessel and the introduction and securing of the cannula itself. **30–45 min.**

(iii) The injection of the radiological contrast agent. **60–90 min. if oil is used.**

(iv) The immediate radiographic series, taken on completion of the injection in as expeditious a sequence as possible. **5–10 min.**

Thus we can appreciate that lymphangiography is a protracted exacting investigation, requiring much patience from both the

M

performer and the subject. In view of the length of time for which he must occupy the X-ray table it is essential to make the patient as comfortable as possible, especially as—once the vessels are cannulated—he must remain reasonably still throughout the long period of injection of an oily contrast agent. The use at least of a standard radioparent foam mattress is desirable and some radiologists advocate a lightweight plastic air-mattress instead as a better form of support which does not interfere with radiographic quality.

Tilting of the table to lower the head about 30 degrees may be required during dissection of the lymphatic vessels, in order to keep the field of operation bloodless for maximum visibility of these fine structures. The patient should be advised in advance of this necessity and shoulder rests should be already in position on the X-ray table to prevent him from sliding from it.

The co-operation and tranquillity of the patient are more likely to endure if communication is effectively maintained between him and those conducting the examination. The radiographer can do much to strengthen the patient by frequent cheerful encouragement, by telling him from time to time what is happening, by taking care that he is not left lying alone with his intimidating attachments for long periods of time.

After-Care of the Patient

When the required radiographs have been satisfactorily obtained, the lymphatic cannulae are removed, each skin incision is lightly sutured and a dressing applied. A crepe bandage may be put round the limb, from the toes to the knee or from fingers to elbow as appropriate. The limb should be kept elevated for the following 24 hours and the patient should avoid using it for 3 or 4 days if a large incision has been made. Normally he should return a week after the examination for removal of the skin sutures.

CHAPTER XIII

THE CENTRAL NERVOUS SYSTEM

MYELOGRAPHY

In this procedure a radiological contrast agent is introduced into the subarachnoid space of the spinal canal in order to investigate certain lesions causing distortion of the normal channel and interference with nerve roots: for example, tumours of the cord or a prolapsed intervertebral disc.

The contrast medium is injected usually in the lumbar region. The patient is then turned to the prone position on the X-ray table and, under close fluoroscopic control, the flow of the medium along the whole spinal canal can be observed by suitable tilting of the table. Films can be exposed serially at points of diagnostic interest, or a cinematic record be made on film or video-tape, as the examining radiologist requires. Encroachment on the subarachnoid channel by a space-occupying lesion will be apparent when the passage of the contrast agent becomes obstructed or deflected at some site. An outline of any filling defect can usually be obtained if sufficient time is taken to allow the medium to flow past it under gravity. This may require the exercise of some persistence by the radiological team and an even stronger combination of endurance and patience by the subject. The complete procedure is exacting for the radiologist undertaking it and can make a heavy demand on the department's time.

Preparation of the Patient

Myelography is not an examination to be performed on out-patients. Usually it is one of several investigations which have to be made to obtain the diagnosis of a spinal lesion and these require admission to hospital for a period. Consequently it is the immediate responsibility of nursing staff to prepare the patient; though manifestly there is an equal charge on the X-ray department to ensure that the ward sister knows of the radiologist's requirements in this respect.

165

Four to 6 hours' starvation prior to the examination is probably advisable in case vomiting of a nervous origin should occur during its course. Sedatives may be given depending on the wishes of the radiologist who will conduct the examination and on the patient's condition.

The patient should arrive in the X-ray department suitably clothed in a plain cotton gown which should open at the back and in woollen socks. He should not be allowed to become cold during this probably lengthy examination.

Preparation of the Trolley

In many instances injection of the contrast agent may take place in the ward and the patient on reaching the X-ray department will be ready for immediate fluoroscopy. From our point of view this simplifies and shortens the procedure to a considerable extent. The care of a patient, who on arrival in the department has already been injected with the contrast agent, requires attention to certain points; these will be discussed in the next section.

Whether or not the injection is to be made in the X-ray department, it is quite likely that nursing staff will provide a suitable tray, which will accompany the patient if the lumbar puncture is to be performed elsewhere than in the ward. In some cases, however, it may be the responsibility of X-ray staff to prepare for the examination. The trolley should contain the following items.

Sterile (upper shelf)
A glass manometer.
A small piece of rubber or polythene tubing and adaptor.
   (These two items will be required if the pressure of the cerebro-spinal fluid is to be measured.)
Three or four lumbar puncture needles.
   These may be either of a plain (Harris) type or of the Greenfield pattern which has a side-piece and tap; the latter are necessary for use with the manometer.
A pair of sponge forceps.
Two dressing towels.
Towel clips.
A small mackintosh sheet.
A gallipot.

FIG. 24. Lumbar puncture needles. (a) Harris type. (b) Greenfield pattern.
By courtesy of Down Bros. and Mayer & Phelps Ltd.

A small dressings bowl.

A pair of dissecting forceps.

A pair of scissors.

One 10 ml syringe for the contrast agent.

One 5 ml syringe for the local anaesthetic.

Hypodermic needles suitable for local anaesthesia: for example, Nos. 1, 2, 12 and 16.

Some test-tubes or specimen jars.

These may be required for collection of specimens of the cerebro-spinal fluid for pathological examination. This is not essentially any part of myelography but is often done for convenience' sake at the time of the lumbar puncture which the procedure necessitates.

Gauze or wool swabs.

A pair of rubber gloves in an appropriate size.

Non-sterile (lower shelf)

Face masks. (The disposable type are satisfactory.)

A bottle of local anaesthetic: for example, Lignocaine Hydrochloride 2 per cent.

A skin cleanser: for example, tincture of iodine, 2.5 per cent.

(This is more penetrating on a dry skin than other skin paints.)

Two ampoules of the contrast agent.

At the present time in this country 'Myodil' (ampoules of 3 ml) is in general use.

Collodion to seal the skin.

A roll of adhesive plaster or some prepared dressings.

If prior to myelography specimens of cerebro-spinal fluid are collected for examination, great care of the test-tubes must be taken. They should be stoppered immediately with sterile wool and kept upright, so that there is no risk that the fluid will come in contact with the wool plug.

Emphasis must also be laid on the importance of observing strict asepsis during the procedure of lumbar puncture. If infection of the tract should occur there is a risk of meningitis. The risks of infection if the injection is made in a general X-ray room at the end of an out-patient list may be considered unacceptable. If the patient cannot be injected before he reaches the X-ray department, the procedure should be carried out in a 'clean' radiographic or clinical room.

Care of the Patient

From the patient's point of view myelography is a trying examination. Most subjects for it have suffered for a period, and in all likelihood are still suffering considerable pain from the condition under investigation. Since many movements of the body involve the spinal column, the patient is able to do little that does not aggravate his distress.

Reassurance should be given that it is the intention to make the examination as easy as possible and this should include an explanation of what it entails. The patient should be warned that he will be required to lie prone for some while and that he will be tilted head downwards as well as heels downwards at various times. In some cases he may be virtually upside down for a period. He should be shown the shoulder supports and handgrips or other forms of brace in position on the table and instructed in their use. It is important to give any patient sustained reassurance that he will not be allowed to fall, no matter in what way it may be necessary to tilt him.

The radiographer who fits the myelographic attachments to the X-ray table prior to the examination is responsible for seeing that they are correctly in place and in good order. Serious accidents have occurred because of faulty use of such equipment. During the procedure attention must be given *immediately* to a patient who says he is slipping or insecure; he may be right!

It is understood that the X-ray room will have been fully prepared before the patient's arrival. As far as possible other examinations should be scheduled to avoid any overlap, so that sufficient time may be given to adequate organization of technical equipment and the patient kept waiting as little as possible, either to enter the room or while various needed items are made ready. This is good practice in respect of any major radiological procedure requiring the use of specialized apparatus.

Once the injection of the contrast agent has been made, it is important not to allow the patient's head to lie at a lower level than his trunk; from the time of injection it should be kept propped up slightly until the completion of the examination. The purpose of this is to prevent the medium from entering the basal cisternae. It is questionable whether or not this results in any real harm to the patient. The point of immediate significance is that once the contrast agent has entered the cranium, it is difficult to recover from there to the spinal portion of the subarachnoid space.

These considerations must influence handling and moving of the patient in the X-ray department both during and after the procedure and even before it, should the introduction of the contrast agent have been made in the ward. In practice this requires an assistant to be responsible solely for support of the patient's head during any times when it may be necessary to move him: the head should be maintained gently as upright as possible. In the prone position the patient should be asked to keep his neck slightly extended, and if necessary assisted to do so. When he must lie thus for some time, the head should be turned sideways and adequate support with firm pillows provided for the cheek; if only one pillow is available it is often advantageous to fold this double. In turning the patient into the lateral decubitus, the head can usually be kept at a higher level than the body by applying gentle lateral flexion to the neck in the appropriate upward direction.

During the examination the patient should be given frequent encouragement. He will suffer it the more readily if he can be told from time to time that he is doing well and that the examination is proceeding satisfactorily. Upon its completion an attempt is sometimes made to remove as much as possible of the opaque medium; it is accepted general practice in the U.S.A. This is done by aspiration through the lumbar puncture needle, under continued fluoroscopic control. Tilting of the table in an appropriate direction allows pooling of the contrast fluid at the needle's tip and in this way—given the exercise of patience by the operator—much, or even all of the medium may be withdrawn.

However, adverse reactions are few and little evidence exists that harm is likely to result from allowing 'Myodil' to remain in the theca. Some radiologists do not advise or attempt its removal. To do so completely is often difficult: it sometimes causes pain: it entails

inevitably an appreciable extension of the procedure: it may necessitate a second lumbar puncture. If the needle is left in place at the
first operation it must be continuously protected during the X-ray
examination, usually by means of a 'stop' which prevents the
fluoroscopic screen from approaching close to the skin surface. Even
so, it is possibly liable to displacement through movements of the
subject.

It is customary before the patient leaves the X-ray table to make
certain that none of the 'Myodil' is within the cranium and to
collect it in the lower part of the theca. It will become fixed there
in the nerve root sheaths and gradually will be absorbed at the rate
of about 1 ml in 12 months. A patient who has had myelography
performed will show evidence of it in plain radiographs of the
lumbar region taken even some years afterwards.

The patient should be removed from the department on a trolley
in the same manner as his arrival. If he is to lie supine, there should
be light support for the head and shoulders with a pillow in order to
retain the contrast medium in the spinal part of the subarachnoid
channel. On his return to the ward the after-care of the patient will
be similar to that following clinical lumbar puncture. He is likely to
suffer from a general malaise, with headache and nausea and
possibly a sharp rise in temperature. Usually these effects do not
persist longer than 48 hours.

AIR ENCEPHALOGRAPHY AND VENTRICULOGRAPHY

These examinations have been included for completeness' sake in
surveying radiological techniques applicable to the central nervous
system. However, for reasons later apparent, it is not intended to
give them detailed notice from those aspects of preparation which
we have hitherto considered.

In so far as both refer to a contrast examination of the ventricular
system of the brain, the terms *encephalography* and *ventriculography* are synonymous. Distinction is made between the methods
used to introduce the radiological contrast medium.

ENCEPHALOGRAPHY

In this procedure radiographic contrast is provided by air, introduced intrathecally following the withdrawal of an equal volume of

cerebro-spinal fluid. The injection is made usually by lumbar puncture; occasionally by cisternal puncture at the base of the skull. If the patient is maintained erect during this operation, the air naturally will rise in the subarachnoid space above the level of the cerebro-spinal fluid and thus will outline the ventricular system; these cavities are otherwise not apparent on a radiograph owing to the similar density to X rays of the cerebro-spinal fluid and the cerebral tissues.

Since the basis of the procedure is lumbar puncture the preparation of the patient and the trolley is closely comparable, if not identical with that required for myelography and described in the earlier pages of this chapter. A further account is hardly necessary to the student. In those instances when cisternal puncture is indicated, preparation of the patient must include shaving of the head.

VENTRICULOGRAPHY

By this method the contrast agent—usually air but in some instances a positive radio-opaque medium ('Myodil')—is introduced directly into the lateral ventricles of the cerebral hemispheres, following trephining of the skull. It is a surgical procedure which will be undertaken in an operating theatre and on reaching the X-ray department the patient will be immediately ready for radiography.

Dressings on the head should be left in position: good liaison with the theatre staff will ensure that these are small, so that anatomical landmarks are not needlessly obscured and thus accurate radiographic positioning made more difficult to obtain. The importance of having the room and its specialized equipment fully prepared in advance should not be overlooked, but other forms of preparation are not expected to be the responsibility of the X-ray staff.

Care of the Patient

Patients referred for cerebral investigations are seriously ill. These procedures in themselves are unpleasant for the subject. Encephalography always results in severe headache and frequently vomiting occurs. The patient, even if responsive on arrival in the department, during the course of the examination may become drowsy and unable to co-operate to any useful extent. In spite of these difficulties it is essential in the patient's interest to secure a full series of radiographs in erect, supine and prone postures, and to obtain accurate projection in each instance. It must be recognized that these cerebral examinations are extremely exacting from everyone's point of view. They require unremitting attention to detail, a high standard both of technical radiography and of patient-care.

In many cases the patient may be only partly conscious, or he may be mentally confused. However distrait he appears, this must never be a reason for altering our behaviour towards him. Standards of professional demeanour should be absolute: it is unforgivable if we vary our treatment of a patient because he is incapable of sensation or understanding.

Although to a large degree we may believe that the patient is 'not with us', it is often true that he perceives better than we realize. Whenever possible an attempt should be made to convey to him an explanation of the procedure, what is going to happen and what is required of him. In these circumstances it is even more—never less —important that we talk to the patient simply and calmly, that we reassure him throughout its stages of the good progress of the examination, and that we continuously encourage him to give us what co-operation he can.

In the presence of an apparently unconscious patient, it is important to remember that he may be able to hear. During general anaesthesia, and in other forms of unconsciousness, hearing is the last of the special senses to fade and the first to return. In these circumstances no discussion of the patient's condition should occur, nor should any remark be made which ordinarily we would not voice in the patient's company. He may indeed be present with us through his ears, though unable to indicate his awareness, and afterwards feel anxiety or hurt when some overheard observation is fully or partly recollected.

CHAPTER XIV

WORK WITH A MOBILE X-RAY SET

The student radiographer quickly discovers that not all the diagnostic radiography done in the hospital is undertaken in the X-ray department. The need for radiographic facilities at the patient's bedside and in the operating theatre involves the radiographer in what might be termed extra-mural activity. The availability of equipment which is portable and mobile gives the means to meet this demand.

Work with a mobile X-ray set needs adaptability in the radiographer. Conditions can never be ordered in the way that departmental practice is controlled, and the radiographer must be prepared to adjust technique to meet the particular situation which is found. The variations of this are wide in scope and unpredictable in detail.

The need for correct judgment of technical considerations against an unfamiliar background will therefore tend to occupy fully the radiographer's mind. As experience extends in using the equipment, and in doing radiography with the added stress of these special conditions, so the proportion of concern occasioned by technical difficulties will diminish. While it is great, however, it is likely that the amount of thought given to the patient as a person will be reduced. This is understandable, but every effort should be made to realize that there are aspects of patient-care to be considered in work with a mobile set.

It might seem that when the radiographer visits the ward or the theatre to take films of a patient unable to come to the X-ray department, this patient is already in the care of others and the radiographer has no responsibility in the matter. This is a misconception, as a little thought shows. Some features of the patient's care and treatment are certainly in the hands of others, as indeed they are bound to be for any patient at any time, but as a member of the medical team the radiographer *always* carries responsibility. It is just as easy for the heedless and uninformed to damage the patient

173

by some lack of attention to his care in the ward or the theatre as it is when the radiographer is quite alone with the patient, and carries for a while an extended responsibility.

It is not possible that every circumstance encountered in work with the mobile set could be foreseen here and counsel given on the necessary procedure, but some general outline can be indicated which may serve as a guide to the particular.

It is not intended that technical and radiographic factors should be fully discussed, for such is not the purpose of this book, but it may be useful to have the student's attention drawn to some special features of the equipment.

THE X-RAY SET

X-ray equipment to be used at the patient's bedside or in the operating theatre may be classified as portable or mobile. The terms are not interchangeable. A portable set usually means one that is fully portable, capable of being dismounted, packed into carrying cases, and transported easily enough in a car to the patient's own home (where it may have to be taken up steep and narrow stairs), or to some place at a distance from the hospital.

A mobile set is usually taken to mean an X-ray set that is movable in the sense that it is on wheels and can be taken from place to place within the hospital, but it cannot be dismounted into smaller components and carried about with the freedom of the truly portable equipment. Mobile sets are altogether larger and heavier than portable sets, which constitute the simplest type of X-ray equipment available. The simplicity implies certain limitations (for example low tube currents and lack of very short exposure times), but endows the set with its truly portable character.

Both the mobile and portable equipment will be operated from a wall plug in the way of other electrical apparatus with which we are domestically familiar. These wall plugs provide an electrical supply which in the U.K. is usually at an electrical 'pressure' of 200–250 volts, and they are arranged to give a certain maximum current. This may be 5, 13, 15 or 30 amps, there being some variation in the local supply arrangement.

Observation in our own homes makes us familiar with these features of electrical devices, and we know that while we may operate one or two small lamps from the same 5 amp wall plug, equipment such as large electric fires and hot-plates cannot be operated at all from this lower supply, and must be connected to a source of greater current, for example, a 15 amp wall plug. This is distinguished by the greater size of the outlet socket on the wall and the plug top which fits into it, the wider spacings of the 'pins' on the plug and the added thickness of the electric flex.

The same rule applies to the use of X-ray equipment. The electrical power which the set consumes is related to the X-ray output; similarly the amount of power consumed by fires and lamps is related to the intensity of heat and of light which they give. The departmental X-ray sets which give high X-ray output, have tube currents up to 500 mA or more, and tube voltages up to 100 kVp or beyond that into the 'high kilovoltage' range, demand a large amount of electric power, even although for very short instantaneous periods of time. Such sets draw high mains currents, much in excess of the domestic 13 or 15 A, and need to be operated at supply voltages greater than 250 V. They are usually connected to the mains supply at about 400 V, and are provided with cables capable of carrying the high currents that are necessary.

However, portable and mobile equipment must be operated from available wall sockets either against a domestic background, or in the wards and theatres of the hospital. While it is possible to arrange in hospital for the installation of high-power sockets at certain points where mobile X-ray equipment is likely to be used, this is obviously not the case in private homes where the existing arrangements have to be accepted. A small portable X-ray set should be suitable for operation on a 5 amp supply.

These limitations in the electrical supply are an important factor in setting the upper limit to the X-ray output which the set can be expected to give. If the set is to draw from the mains a current which does not exceed 5 amps, the limit on the tube factors is likely to be 10–15 mA for the tube current and in the region of 80 kVp for the tube voltage, and it will probably not be possible to use the maximum tube current and tube voltage both at the same time.

Mobile sets to be operated from a 13 A or a 15 A socket can be expected to give greater X-ray output. Tube currents of 50–60 mA and tube voltages of 85–90 kVp can be used over a range of exposure times. Mobile sets providing 100 mA and 100 kVp may also be used off 13 A or 15 A sockets, but for short 'momentary' exposure intervals only.

Since limited X-ray output involves the use of longer exposure times, there has been a tendency for radiographers to demand mobile sets with greater and greater output. Patients for bedside radiography are often very ill and find it extremely difficult to keep still in the radiographic positions imposed on them, so that short exposures are appreciated by radiographers as an aid to the improvement of image quality. There are at present available mobile X-ray sets which are really high powered and give an output comparable with that from departmental installations. It must be realized, however, that these sets cannot possibly be operated at their full output from ordinary power supplies available at wall sockets, and high-power sockets with special wiring must be arranged in order to use them at full capacity.

Trying to use the X-ray set at a greater output than can be supplied from the mains power available at the wall outlet may result in a blown fuse. This is an electrical safety device put into the circuit to prevent overload. It consists of a wire which is heated by excess current to the point when it fuses and breaks, thus opening the circuit. This can be an embarrassing source of delay, for the fuse has to be replaced before any further radiography can be done from that point of supply. In hospital an electrician can doubtless replace the fuse without much loss of time; in a private house the radiographer may have to search for the fuse box in a corner that would be dark even if the lights could be switched on.

In either case the delay can be seen as an aspect of failure in patient-care, since an ill patient, and perhaps an anaesthetized patient, a surgeon (whose responsibility for the patient will make him unhesitant to express dissatisfaction), and theatre staff may all have to wait until the equipment can be used. There is also the danger that a blown fuse will cut off the supply to other important electrical apparatus in an operating theatre.

The X-ray set must therefore be used within the limits of the power supply. It is good sense if possible to make a test exposure to ascertain that the fuse will carry the required load. This saves the embarrassment of blowing the fuse at the stage when the patient, the film, and the tube have been positioned relative to each other, and the radiographic exposure is being made. Where the tube current cannot be pre-set a test exposure will certainly be necessary. The tube voltage should be selected and the mA control turned down nearly to zero before the test exposure is begun, the control being then gradually turned up during the exposure to give the tube current required. To begin the test exposure with the mA control in an advanced position will often result in blowing a fuse, especially on a 5 amp supply.

In a private house the radiographer will be wise to find out first of all the location of the fuse box, and to carry such accessories as spare fuse wire for 5, 13 and 15 amp supplies, a screw driver, a pair of pliers and a torch. In some old electrical installations in this country sockets may be found which carry two-pin plugs instead of the more usual three-pin arrangement. The lack of the third pin means that the equipment will not be earthed, and use should be made of an 'earthing reel' in this circumstance. This consists of a length of cable, one end of which should be fastened by means of a metal clip (for example a 'bulldog' paper-clip) to part of the X-ray set, while the other end may be attached to a mains water pipe, or taken out of doors and sunk in the earth by means of a metal pin (for example a screw driver, the wire being attached to its shaft).

Radiographers gain most of their experience, and certainly their initial experience, with portable and mobile equipment in hospital. The work will be considered here in two sections; (i) in the ward, and (ii) in the operating theatre. In either case the first step towards success is fully to understand the request form which is sent to the X-ray department, so that the exact nature of the X-ray examination and the reason for it are both appreciated. Only then can the needed equipment be properly assembled. To do otherwise is to risk arriving at the scene of operations with films of the wrong size or wrong speed or insufficient in number, or perhaps without facilities for fast processing when these are required. All this gives rise to unnecessary delay, and wastes the time and energy of everyone involved—the radiographer's by no means in the least degree.

Working with a mobile set away from the department the radiographer must be careful to put cassettes which are ready for use, or have been used, in a place where they will not be fogged by radiographic exposures. Exposed and unexposed cassettes must be kept separate or differentiated from each other so that there is no risk of exposing each cassette more than once.

WORK WITH MOBILE EQUIPMENT IN THE WARD

Requests for radiography with a mobile set will reach the X-ray department from both medical and surgical wards. Medical cases are generally X-rayed in the ward because they are too ill to come to the department, and the examination most often requested is a plain film of the chest. Surgical cases will include as well as those who are too ill to come to the department a proportion of patients who are unable to leave their beds because they are secured to a frame which is applying traction to a fracture. Such patients, especially if they are young and agile and have had time to get used to the traction, often present a lively appearance and are able to co-operate with the radiographer very well within the limits of their defined area of movement.

Having arrived at the ward with the necessary equipment, the radiographer should first report to the nurse in charge and announce which patient is to be X-rayed, and the examination to be done. This is not only a courtesy to the person in charge but will enable the radiographer to find out in which part of the ward is the patient to be X-rayed, and also to receive any special information concerning him—for example, the extent to which he may be asked to co-operate by sitting up and moving about the bed. If the patient is very ill, the nurse may feel that the radiographer should have the assistance of one of the nurses who is familiar with the patient and his treatment. It is not difficult, therefore, to see the importance of telling those in charge when the examination is being made.

It is a kindness to the patient to go in to see him without the equipment, and give an explanation of what is to be undertaken. If he has never been X-rayed before with a mobile set, he can view only with apprehension the advance down the ward of a large piece of machinery, and find himself on a pinnacle of alarm when he realizes that *his* bedside is its destination. The radiographer propelling it may hope to ease matters by a smiling approach, but it is the equipment which occupies most of his vision and he may be almost unaware of its human director.

Obviously it requires a little more time and effort from the radiographer to go in to see the patient before fetching in the equipment, but it is certainly of benefit to the patient and is not entirely without value to the radiographer. These few minutes will enable the radiographer to assess the patient's capacity for co-operation and any special difficulties which are present—for example, traction frames. Perhaps at this stage the need for assistance from the ward staff may become obvious, and it can then be sought.

Clearly it is not possible to do the radiography without *some* disturbance to the patient, and the aim should be to make this as little as is compatible with an efficient examination. Few of us fully realize what busy lives some patients lead. The doctors' rounds, visits from the physiotherapist, the performance of various special examinations and tests such as the taking of blood and other specimens for laboratory investigation—all these may leave the patient with the impression that he is getting hardly any rest at all. The radiography we have to do is to us one incident in a busy day; we do not always perceive that to the patient it may be something of the same, and the radiographer but one more person to disturb his peace with requests and instructions.

The patient should be given privacy for the X-ray examination, and either screens or cubicle curtains should be pulled round the bed. After the radiographer has finished, the patient should be made as comfortable as possible in a bed restored to neatness. The equipment should be put away with the supply cable tidily coiled and the tube column and tube head locked in a position which prevents dangerous projection before it is taken from the ward.

Many special conditions will be met in using a mobile set, and indeed every excursion may seem to present a challenge to technical ability. However, there are certain features with regard to the patient which are likely to recur, and an indication of these may be given here as some guidance to the student.

The Patient Having Oxygen Therapy

The need for giving the patient additional oxygen in the air he breathes, and methods of administration are discussed somewhat more fully in Chapter xvi of this book. Here it can be said that patients having continuous oxygen therapy for a period will be encountered in the wards. The oxygen is supplied from a cylinder or through a piped supply to the patient's bedside, and it is administered to him in one of three ways; (i) by enclosing him in an oxygen tent, (ii) by means of a mask fitting over his mouth and nose, and (iii) by means of tubes inserted up his nasal passages.

N

There are two important points to remember when doing radiography on patients who are having oxygen. Firstly, the risk of fire and explosion. Oxygen while not itself flammable is a strong supporter of combustion, and any material which burns in air will burn very much more rapidly in air with increased oxygen content. The use of any electrical apparatus carries the risk of a spark when the equipment is functioning, so that it is important that while the X-ray set is operating the oxygen supply is switched off and discontinued.

The second point arises from this need to stop the supply of oxygen in order to use the X-ray set. The patient having oxygen therapy is likely to be very ill and dependent on the supply of oxygen to ameliorate his condition. It will therefore cause him distress if not actual harm to be without it for an appreciable time. If the radiography is to be done with the least disturbance to him, then all must be made ready with regard to the X-ray set and the patient before the oxygen supply is cut off, so that this is done for the shortest possible time.

If the patient is receiving oxygen through nasal catheters, the supply is turned off, the catheters being left in place; if by mask, the supply is cut off and the mask removed; if in a tent, the supply is cut off and the patient is taken out of the tent for the required period. It is not likely that this procedure will be left entirely to the radiographer, for it is the responsibility of the ward staff to see that the patient is receiving the oxygen correctly at the prescribed rate of flow. In the case of an oxygen tent which has been opened, it is usual for a short period afterwards to increase the rate of flow of the gas through it in order to raise the oxygen concentration.

If a member of the nursing staff is not required to give assistance with the patient throughout the X-ray examination, the radiographer's responsibility in regard to the oxygen supply may be summarized as being first to see that it is turned off before the X-ray set operates, and secondly to see that the ward staff are informed *immediately* the radiography is finished so that the oxygen supply can be restored.

The Patient in a Respirator

Patients with virus infections involving the central nervous system (for example, acute anterior poliomyelitis) may have paralysis of the respiratory muscles. They therefore require mechanical aids to maintain respiratory movement.

The so-called 'iron-lung' is one such apparatus. The patient is enclosed in a metal tank within which the pressure is altered. In one type of respirator the pressure is alternately below atmospheric pressure and at the same level as atmospheric pressure. During the period when the inside pressure is below that of the atmosphere surrounding the patient's uncovered head and face, air enters and expands the lungs; it is then expired by the recoiling action of the thoracic cage during the period when the air inside and outside the respirator is at the same pressure level.

Whatever type of respirator is encountered, it can be realized at once that the case is very similar to that of the patient having oxygen therapy—although there is no fire risk. The patient is very ill and is dependent on the respirator to maintain his breathing. He is likely therefore to feel desperately alarmed when removed from it, and it may be that he can be left without the respirator for only a very brief space of time. The radiography must be done efficiently and speedily with the assistance of ward staff who fully understand the patient's needs and the management of the respirator.

The Patient Having Intravenous Infusion of Fluid

In various cases as part of the patient's treatment it may be necessary to give him fluid by a method other than oral administration. This may be because the patient is unable to take anything by mouth owing to such causes as a mouth injury, surgery to the gastrointestinal tract, or a comatose state. It may be that the patient *can* take fluid by mouth, but it is required that a severe fluid loss (due to vomiting or diarrhoea or some other cause) should be quickly replaced in order to restore the correct fluid balance of the body. If the patient requires additional blood in order to make up loss by haemorrhage, transfusion of blood is similarly undertaken by an intravenous route.

A patient receiving such an infusion has an intravenous needle fixed into a vein usually in his arm. This needle is connected to a bottle which is hung upside down from a hooked stand above the patient. Not far below the bottle, the tubing which connects it to the needle is interrupted by insertion of a drop counter, in which the fluid can be seen dripping down to the needle. Above the drop counter, between it and the bottle, is a tubing clip which regulates the rate of flow.

In modern practice the equipment for giving a drip infusion is often disposable. This disposable equipment comes with its inner parts pre-sterilized by the manufacturer—that is, there is a sterile pathway for the flow of fluid through it. Some parts of the exterior of the equipment are sterile and are protected by sheaths which are removed before use.

The first part of the equipment (Fig. 25) consists of two transparent plastic chambers set one above the other. The upper is the filter chamber and it has in it, suspended from its top edge, a filtering sac through which the fluid which is to be infused must pass as it enters the chamber; the lower one is the drip chamber and contains a float ball. This float ball closes the exit from the chamber in the event of its having been allowed to become empty.

The upper chamber has projecting above it a piercing needle enclosed by a sheath. In use, the sheath is removed from the needle and the piercing needle is then forced through the closure of the bottle of fluid which is to be given to the patient. When the bottle is suspended with its closure downwards, the fluid fills the filter chamber by gravity and drips through a narrow tube communicating with the drip chamber: 15 drops will be approximately equivalent to 1 ml of fluid.

A length (about 1.5 metres) of plastic tubing leads from the bottom of the drip chamber. The lower end of this tubing is protected by a sheath which is removed so that the tubing can be attached to an intravenous needle for insertion into the vein that is to be used for the infusion. The plastic tubing carries a device which can be used to control the flow of fluid along it. In Fig. 25 the sheaths protecting the piercing needle and the lower end of the plastic tube have been removed.

The second part of the equipment (not shown in Fig. 25) is an air-inlet assembly to allow air into the suspended bottle so that the fluid running out is replaced by air. The air-inlet assembly is a short (about 40 cm) length of narrow plastic tubing with a short-bevelled needle at one end and a small wire hook attached to the other end, which is open; both ends are protected by sheaths which are removed before use. The needle on the air-inlet tube is forced through the bottle closure as far as it will go and when the bottle is suspended the air-inlet tube is hooked up in a suitable position by

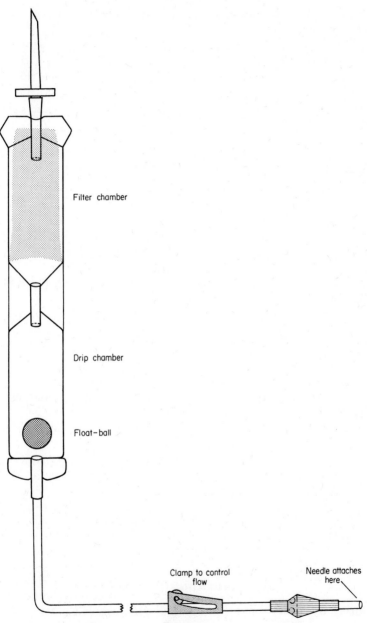

Filter chamber

Drip chamber

Float–ball

Clamp to control flow

Needle attaches here

FIG. 25
Disposable equipment for giving a drip infusion.

means of the little hook attached to it. Air can then enter the bottle through the plastic tubing.

The radiographer has no responsibility for altering or setting the rate of flow of an intravenous infusion, but while dealing with such a patient should observe certain points. It must be seen that the needle does not become dislodged from its site in the vein, and that in moving the patient the tubing is not kinked or compressed so that the rate of flow is obstructed.

The patient may have his arm bandaged to a splint so that he may move it without disturbance of the needle, but some care will nevertheless be necessary to see that the needle is not pulled or jerked out of place. While with the patient, the radiographer should observe the drop counter or drip chamber every so often to see that the fluid is continuing to flow properly, and should also occasionally look at the patient's arm. If the needle has dislodged itself from the vein and is still in the tissues, there will be a flow of fluid into the tissues of the arm and a swelling will develop around the needle site.

If the needle comes right out of the patient's arm, the tubing clip must be used to clamp off the flow of fluid, and pressure should be exerted for a few minutes at the injection site to prevent extravasation of blood into the tissues. All these occurrences—cessation of the flow of fluid, suspicion that the needle has been moved out of the vein, or total dislodgement of the needle from the arm—must be reported immediately to the ward staff.

In moving the X-ray equipment, the radiographer must notice the position of the suspended bottle and take care not to strike it with the X-ray tube head. The bottle and its wheeled stand can be moved about a little if care is taken to see that no strain is put on the tubing, but the bottle should not be lowered from its position above the patient. If the bottle is seen to be nearly empty the attention of the ward staff should be drawn to this fact.

The method of intravenous drip infusion may be used to give a radiographic contrast agent for urography. The technique supplements simple intravenous urography.

The Patient with a Tracheostomy

During the course of their work radiographers encounter patients who have had tracheostomies. A tracheostomy is a surgical procedure in which a rounded opening is made in the upper trachea just below the cricoid and thyroid cartilages which enclose the vocal cords. Through this hole in the trachea a tube (known as a tracheostomy tube) is passed, keeping the hole open and giving an airway and access to the patient's trachea, bypassing his nose, mouth and pharynx.

The procedure achieves the following:

(i) it overcomes (through bypassing) any obstruction in the air passages above the tracheostomy opening (i.e. in the mouth, the oro-pharynx and the larynx);

(ii) it allows secretions to be readily removed from the trachea and bronchi by suction (in a patient who cannot cough effectively);

(iii) it improves effective ventilation of the lungs;

(iv) it facilitates mechanically assisted respiration and it is positively indicated as a procedure to be carried out for any patient who is to have prolonged artificial ventilation of the lungs;

(v) it prevents (by separating the larynx and the pharynx) the inhalation of food, fluid and secretions by a patient who has paralysis of the muscles involved in swallowing.

Tracheostomy is performed on increasing numbers of patients as a planned procedure in the management of various disorders. It is used in treating (a) patients who have ventilatory failure; (b) patients who are comatose; (c) patients who have lost the nervous control of the act of swallowing; (d) patients who have undergone laryngectomy (surgical removal of the larynx) and in such cases the tracheostomy is permanent. When the tracheostomy is temporary, as the patient's condition improves the tube is removed and the hole in the trachea is allowed to close.

Examples of disorders in which tracheostomy may be used are: crush injuries to the chest when multiple fractures to the ribs and sternum are interfering with the adequate ventilation of the lungs and the patient is to be aided to breathe by means of a mechanical respirator; poliomyelitis involving paralysis of muscles in the pharynx and of the respiratory muscles, when mechanical ventilation will be used as in the previous example; fractures of the cervical spine with spinal cord injury paralysing nerve supply to the thorax (here also mechanical ventilation will be used); severe unstable fractures of the mandible which can cause obstruction of the respiratory tract in its upper parts.

It may be concluded from this list that radiographers using mobile equipment in intensive care units are likely to deal with patients who have had tracheostomy and they may also encounter in the X-ray department patients whose tracheostomies are permanent.

THE TRACHEOSTOMY TUBE

There are three main types of tracheostomy tube as follows.

(i) A plain metal tube. There are three components associated with this type of tube. First there is an outer tube (see Fig. 26) which has a flange at one end to which the neck piece is attached. The neck piece fits across the front of the patient's neck over the tracheostomy opening, the tube lying within the lumen of the trachea, and it carries tapes which are fastened round the patient's neck and keep the tube in place. Secondly there is an inner tube which fits into the outer one and can therefore easily be changed and cleaned. The third component is a device called an intro-ducer, basically a blunt-ended rod with the same curvature as the

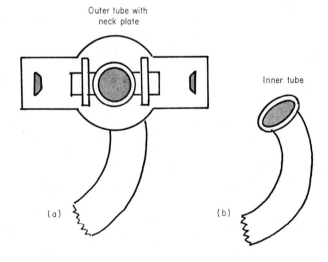

Outer tube with
neck plate

Inner tube

(a)   (b)

FIG. 26 (a). A sketch to show the outer tube of a plain metal tracheostomy tube. The proximal end is shown with its flange and neck-plate.

(b) The proximal end of an inner tracheostomy tube which fits into the outer metal tube.

tracheostomy tube. The surgeon undertaking the tracheostomy puts the introducer with the tracheostomy tube over it into the window he has made in the anterior tracheal wall. He removes the introducer when the outer tube is properly in place and then puts the inner tube into the outer one. The purpose of the blunt-ended introducer (which protrudes from the tracheostomy tube) is to prevent the tube from damaging tissues as it is directed into place.

(ii) A plain plastic tube. In the past plastic tubes have had no inner tube and (being softer than metal and hence less likely to damage tissue) no introducer. Today three-component plastic tubes are available. Inner tubes make cleaning easy as it can be done without disturbing the outer tube and an introducer makes insertion easier.

(iii) A plastic tube with an inflatable cuff towards its distal end (which lies in the lumen of the trachea). Such a tube is sketched in Fig. 27. The cuff can be inflated by means of a syringe attached to the tubing. When the cuff is inflated as much as is required, the air is prevented from escaping by clamping the tubing between the pilot balloon and the syringe or else by attaching a spigot to the end of the tubing (the end of the tubing is not shown in the figure). The purpose of the pilot balloon is to indicate whether the inflatable cuff (which the operator cannot see as it is inside the patient's trachea) is airtight. The inflatable cuff has two functions to perform. If air, oxygen or anaesthetic gases are being pumped into the tracheostomy, all should enter the lungs and none should escape upwards through the larynx. As Fig. 28 shows, the inflated cuff can prevent upwards escape as it maintains contact with the walls of the trachea. Secondly the cuff is a barrier to secretions from the upper part of the respiratory tract and prevents their entry to the lower trachea and bronchi.

Choice of the sort of tracheostomy tube to be used will depend upon why it is being used and what conditions are present in the patient. If the patient does not need a mechanical ventilator for his respiration and if he can swallow properly and can cough effectively and thus eject any inhaled secretions, then a plain metal or plastic tube (not cuffed) is used. If the patient needs artificial ventilation or is likely to inhale secretions from his mouth or oro-pharynx, lacking the ability to swallow or a cough reflex, then a cuffed tube is necessary so that a barrier may be placed between the upper and the lower parts of the respiratory tract.

The tracheostomy tube is held in place by tapes attached to its neck-piece. The tapes are tied at the side of the patient's neck, where they are less likely to cause discomfort and are more accessible than if they were tied at the back. The tie is by a single bow knot with short loops and long ends. Tapes obviously must not be tied so tight as to constrict the neck but when they are too loose they are dangerous. Loose tapes allow the tracheostomy tube to come out of the lumen of the trachea and yet keep its tip in contact with the tissues immediately in front; here the tube may do a great deal of damage, even to the extent of rupturing the innominate artery.

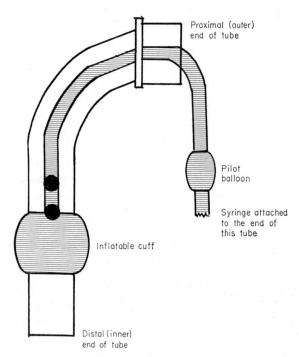

Fig. 27. A sketch of a cuffed tracheostomy tube.

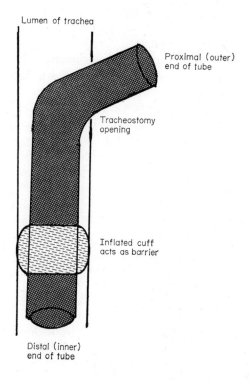

Lumen of trachea

Proximal (outer)
end of tube

Tracheostomy
opening

Inflated cuff
acts as barrier

Distal (inner)
end of tube

FIG. 28. A sketch to show how the inflated cuff of a cuffed tracheostomy tube fits against the walls of the trachea and acts as a barrier so that gases cannot escape upwards and secretions cannot travel down from above the tracheostomy.

CARE OF THE PATIENT

For a patient who has had a tracheostomy performed as part of the treatment of ventilatory failure, proper nursing care of the tracheostomy is extremely important. On it depends the successful treatment of the patient's grave condition. Where care of the tracheostomy is inadequate, complications such as infection and loss of patent airway often occur. We need hardly say that such complications can kill the patient. Clearly a radiographer does not need to know all the details of caring for a tracheostomy but it may be of help if we indicate important points in the routine care and show what observations a radiographer may usefully make.

Routine Nursing Care

The routine nursing care of a tracheostomy involves the following procedures.

(i) Caring for the wound.

(ii) Ensuring the securing of the tracheostomy tube in its place.

(iii) Ensuring the removal of secretions which may block the tube and cause respiratory obstruction.

(iv) Ensuring by the use of various devices that the air which the patient takes in is humidified. This is necessary because the tracheostomy bypasses the upper parts of the respiratory tract in which the air is warmed and humidified in normal breathing. Humidification has an important part to play in keeping secretions fluid; they are then less likely to crust and block the tracheostomy tube.

(v) Changing the tracheostomy tube to prevent the formation of an increasing layer of dried secretions which will narrow the lumen and lead to respiratory obstruction.

(vi) Care of the inflatable cuff of a cuffed tracheostomy tube. This cuff must be inflated to just the right amount. Too little and the cuff will fail to act as a barrier in the way it should; too much is dangerous because the cuff may compress blood vessels and damage tracheal tissue. When correctly inflated the cuff must apply some pressure to the tracheal mucosa and to minimize damage to the tissues the cuff is deflated every so often for a brief period (e.g. 2 minutes per hour).

Care by the Radiographer

A radiographer dealing with a patient who has a tracheostomy as part of the treatment of ventilatory failure should keep the following points in mind.

(i) The patient cannot speak. Unless the tracheostomy is permanent, this loss of normal phonation is only temporary and the patient regains his voice within a few days of the removal of the tube. (Patients who have a permanent tracheostomy after a laryngectomy can be taught to speak without a larynx by using the mouth, tongue, oesophagus and diaphragm; the speech of such patients may sound nearly normal but may be only a whisper.) The speechless conscious patient must communicate with the radiographer by signs and by writing and he will probably have pencil and paper at the bedside. The radiographer must be understanding and must unfailingly remember that the patient has *not* lost the use of his eyes and ears as well as of his vocal cords. He may feel that his lack of speech makes him an embarrassing nuisance to his attendants. Nothing must be said or done to increase his sense of frustration, the annoyance of his impediment and the feelings of anxiety and depression which his situation brings.

(ii) The outer end of the tracheostomy tube must not be inadvertently occluded. The tube clearly must be maintained as a patent airway for the patient. As soon as it ceases to be patent he suffers respiratory obstruction and if this is complete and maintained he dies. Partial occlusion is distressing as insufficient air gets through and respiration requires more effort. The patient is very conscious of his dependence on the tracheostomy tube as the means of taking in air and the radiographer should understand his apprehensive attitude towards it.

(iii) While with the patient, a radiographer should observe the tracheostomy tube, checking that it has not slipped out of position —as it may do if the securing tapes are too loose. If the tube does come out of position the help of nursing staff must be sought *at once* so that it may be restored to its proper place. The danger that, with the tube removed, the tissues will immediately come together and close the hole in the trachea is present in the first 24 to 48 hours postoperatively. During this period the tube must be replaced or tracheostomy dilators inserted very quickly. After 48 hours there is no danger that the hole will close but it remains important not to delay replacement of the tube because its absence may allow secretions to flow into the trachea eventually causing collapse of the lung.

(iv) The patient should be observed for signs of respiratory obstruction. Obstruction which is sudden and complete is very infrequent; it could be caused by flakes of dried secretions which have detached themselves from the wall of the tube and are lying across the lumen. Within seconds the patient is cyanosed. Help must be summoned *at once* so that the obstruction may be relieved.

Respiratory obstruction after tracheostomy is much more likely to occur slowly over days from slight beginning to a more advanced state. The causes of such respiratory obstruction may be that the tube is out of position, or being gradually blocked by secretions, or that a tube of too narrow a diameter has been inserted so that insufficient air is reaching the lungs. It is most important that anyone noticing signs of respiratory obstruction in a patient should report the matter to responsible ward staff so that the patient's condition may be investigated and the situation rectified. The signs to be observed are: pallor or cyanosis; an increased and later irregular pulse rate; greater effort in respiration, possibly with widening of the nostrils; reversed or 'see-saw' respiration in which the chest wall moves inwards (instead of outwards as is normal) on inspiration; restlessness; loss of consciousness or deepening of a comatose state.

(v) It is worth noting the state of the tapes which hold the tracheostomy tube in place. If they seem loose the matter should be reported to ward staff. If they become untied they must be re-tied at once and at no time should the tracheostomy tube be left entirely free. The common error is to tie them too loosely. In connection with tying the tapes, it is to be remembered that when the neck is flexed its diameter is less than when the neck is extended. So tapes which are tight when the neck is bent forward will be tighter still when the neck is extended with the head back; and tapes which are loose with the neck extended and the head bent back will be looser still with the neck flexed. It is usual to tie the tapes with the neck flexed to avoid the situation of their being too loose.

The Patient with a Drainage System

Systems for the drainage of various body cavities will be encountered during work in the wards, particularly in the surgical wards. The patient has a length of plastic or rubber tubing inserted into whichever cavity it is required to drain. In modern practice the container for any fluid which is being drained is usually a plastic bag hanging from the side of the patient's bed; the bag has a metal frame at its upper edge with hooks that hang on the side of the bed. The bag may be marked with a scale to show how much fluid is in it.

During operations on the gall bladder the surgeon often inserts a tube of T shape into the bile ducts, the long arm of the tube being taken out of the abdomen to drain bile into a container after the abdominal opening is closed.

The urinary bladder may be drained by means of a catheter inserted through the urethra, and this may be done if the patient is unable to pass urine naturally, or if it is wished to keep the bladder empty and unexpanded. The catheter may be of the self-retaining type or may be inserted supra-pubically, and the urine drains continuously away.

In approaching such patients, the principles of care should by now suggest themselves to the student from indications previously given. It is necessary to notice the presence of any external containers and to avoid striking them or compressing tubes with the X-ray equipment. In moving the patient tubing must be watched to see that is does not get kinked and that the drainage system does not become open in any way. Care must be taken to see that strain is not put on the tubing. This increases the risk of the tube coming out and of connections pulling apart, and in some cases may cause the patient pain.

The Patient on Traction

Patients on traction are often subjects for ward radiography. This form of extension is frequently used in the treatment of fractures, being employed to correct overriding of fracture fragments and bony displacements of various types. The required continuous pull is achieved either by a system of weights, or by fixing the part to a splint; the traction is applied sometimes through strapping to the patient's skin, and sometimes to the bone by means of a metal pin inserted distal to the fracture. Such pins will be encountered at the lower end of the femur, the upper end of the tibia, and through the os calcis. Traction may be applied to the cervical spine by means of weights and either pin fixation to the skull or the use of a leather harness applied to head and chin.

Patients on traction frequently have the end of the bed raised on blocks in order to put a slope on it, and there is an overhead beam with pulleys. Approaching such a patient, the radiographer should observe the presence both of the blocks underneath the bed and of the overhead framework. Failure to appreciate these features may result in the bed being pulled off the blocks by an unobservant attempt to move it, and in the X-ray tube head being crashed against the overhead structures as the mobile set is wheeled into position.

Since any weights applied are intended to give a continuous pull, they must not be lifted or allowed to rest on anything so that the cord holding them becomes slack.

Limbs being supported in splints for the application of traction will be seen to rest in broad flannel slings, arranged so that each sling has its proximal edge overlapped by the distal edge of the one above it; this prevents any pressure from the edges. The slings are often attached to the splint by 'bulldog' clips. These are likely to obscure certain radiographic projections, and they may with due care be replaced by safety pins for the period of the X-ray examination.

WORK WITH MOBILE EQUIPMENT IN THE OPERATING THEATRE

Earlier in the chapter reference was made to the psychological effect on the radiographer when radiography is undertaken in conditions other than the controlled ones of the X-ray department. This effect is likely to be intensified when radiography in the operating theatre is being done. This work is regarded as being of an emergency nature, and the time factor is important. The aim always in surgical procedures is to be as quick as is consistent with efficiency, for prolonging the length of time that the patient is undergoing surgery and is kept under anaesthesia increases the risk that he must run. The burden of responsibility for the patient's well-being which rests upon the surgeon makes him exacting in his requirements and the radiographer must be prepared to produce good X-ray films without delay.

It is likely that the patient will not appear to the radiographer as a person at all, for he will probably be anaesthetized before the radiographer encounters him, and he will appear therefore simply as a human body and a certain operation field. There will seem to be many other people in the theatre more directly responsible for his welfare—the surgeon, the anaesthetist, the nursing staff—and the radiographer's share in the proceedings will appear as almost wholly a technical one directed to the production of radiographs. This technical responsibility is of sufficient weight and the radiographer who successfully and calmly meets it in whatever crises and stresses may arise is indeed a worthy member of the team.

Nevertheless there *is* a patient there, the sole reason of the whole exercise, and if the radiographer is to be of the best possible help to him there must be an understanding of certain aspects of theatre work.

There are many technical features to be considered, but they are not within the scope of this book, and discussion will be limited to some general principles relative to operating theatre technique and the patient's safety.

On first going to the theatre, the radiographer must check that all the required equipment has been brought and is ready for use, and that the X-ray set is plugged into the right power supply and is working correctly. It is inexcusable to wait until the surgeon requests the taking of a film to discover a fault in the equipment.

Explosion Risk in the Operating Theatre

Although it may be something which does not impress itself immediately on the newcomer to the operating theatre, there is an explosion risk present due to the use for anaesthesia of gases which readily ignite or promote ignition. It has therefore been considered important to reduce the chance of a spark occurring, and in designing equipment for the theatre attention has been paid to this point.

Possible sources of ignition which suggest themselves are hot surfaces such as theatre spotlights and bulbs, and all electrical instruments which may be used in the theatre. A less noticeable but equally important source is due to the phenomenon known as static electricity.

Static electricity is present all the time. It is produced when insulated objects have friction applied to them, even if this friction is only that given by passing through the air. Very high potentials or electrical 'pressures' can be produced, and when two objects which have acquired electric charge in this way are brought close to each other, charge is transferred from one to the other. The object which is at the higher potential will transfer electric charge to the one at lower potential, and this creates a spark. The spark may be very small and not perceived by the eye, but even an infinitely small spark can cause an explosion in an atmosphere filled with flammable gases.

Various safety 'anti-static' devices and precautions are used, the aim being to keep everything in the theatre if possible at the same electrical potential or pressure, and to try to prevent the accumulation of static electricity. Many operating theatres are now designed with floors which will conduct electricity and allow it to leak slowly

o

away. Stretcher trolleys are usually given a length of chain which drags on the floor as they are pushed about the hospital, and provides a pathway for the dispersal of the electric charge which they might otherwise collect; some of them have 'anti-static' wheels. Certain synthetic fibres show readiness to acquire electric charge (many girls will have heard the 'crackle' of electricity as they pull a nylon petticoat over their heads in taking it off, and perhaps even seen a spark if the bedroom is dark). In some theatres the wearing of nylon underclothing is forbidden to the theatre staff on duty.

X-ray equipment operates at high voltages, and no matter what safety precautions exist in the theatre itself no one can guarantee that the X-ray apparatus is spark-proof. It is part of the radiographer's responsibility to understand, and to see that others understand, the risk involved in using X-ray equipment in conjunction with gases which readily ignite or promote ignition. Surgical procedures which require radiography should be undertaken with anaesthetic gases not flammable in character.

Surgical Asepsis in the Operating Theatre

Explanation has already been given of the risks of infection to patients during surgery (Chapter IV), and of the need to undertake surgical procedures in conditions of asepsis which exclude the presence of living organisms. When mobile X-ray equipment is brought to the operating theatre there is not only added risk of explosion, but threat to the sterility of conditions in the operating field.

The mobile equipment may not be reserved exclusively for use in the theatre but may move throughout the hospital, collecting fluff and dust from the wards as it goes. It is thus a potential carrier of bacteria, and it is furthermore a piece of equipment which it is impossible to sterilize completely.

It is the radiographer's responsibility to see that the X-ray set and accessories are clean and free from dust. Since the X-ray tube head in many instances will be placed directly over the operating field, particular attention should be paid to it. In some theatres it may be the practice to enclose the tube head in a linen or polythene cover, and this is one way of making quite sure that no particles fall from it into the field of operation.

As an aid to lessening the risk of explosion, reducing the threat to asepsis of bringing to the theatre a piece of equipment which travels throughout the hospital, and to improving the quality of X-ray films taken, some modern theatres are equipped with permanent X-ray installations which are high-powered sets. The X-ray tube may be mounted on a wall bracket or ceiling suspension so that it may be manipulated above the operating table or brought alongside it; or the equipment may be free-standing and mobile about the theatre suite. The high tension generator providing the power, and the controls for it, are situated in a separate room, a system of communication between this and the theatre being incorporated in the arrangements.

However, it is likely to be some time yet before this admirable system is so widely used as to make the appearance in the theatre of a mobile X-ray set something unusual.

With regard to personal clothing in the operating theatre, the radiographer must follow the rules applying to theatre staff. Almost certainly a clean gown, a face mask, and covering for the head will be issued, together with some form of special footwear (such as pumps, rubber boots, or cotton coverings to tie over the shoes). All these are designed to ensure that the radiographer does not bring into the theatre bacteria from other parts of the hospital.

The theatre may be considered as having two areas:

(i) the sterile area,
(ii) the non-sterile area.

The *sterile area* is primarily the operation field, and in it are included the patient and the operation wound, the surgeon and his immediate assistants (both medical and nursing staff), all the instruments and equipment which they will directly handle, and any trays, trolleys, or tables which hold equipment in readiness for them.

The rest of the theatre constitutes the *non-sterile area*. In it are the anaesthetist and his equipment from which the anaesthetic gases are supplied, the rest of the theatre staff, and diverse accessory equipment. The radiographer and the X-ray apparatus are in this group.

Those working in the theatre have a duty to see that no contamination of the *sterile* area occurs from the *non-sterile* area. The radiographer must be careful not to touch, either personally or with any of the X-ray apparatus and accessories, anything in the theatre which is sterile. This will need care in the manipulation of the mobile set and in positioning cassettes. Movement about the theatre should be restricted to avoid disturbance of the air; this might carry organisms from the floor and other non-sterile regions into a sterile field. Similarly to reduce the risk of droplet contamination, talk in the operating theatre should be kept within the limits of necessity.

When the surgeon views radiographs he will have to move from the sterile area in the immediate vicinity of the operating table out to the non-sterile area in order to get close to the X-ray illuminator. It will be seen that he is careful not to contaminate himself by touching his gown or his hands against anything not sterile; he will hold his hands folded together in front of him. The radiographer must be equally careful not to contaminate the surgeon as the X-ray films are being shown.

The sterile areas in the theatre are often distinguished by special coloration, all the towels, gowns, and drapes over the patient or trolleys being coloured green (in some cases blue) so that there is visual reminder of their sterility.

RADIATION SAFETY

Radiation risk to the patient during radiographic examinations is discussed more fully in another part of this book (Chapter XIX). We include here a few notes on the limiting of radiation dose to staff and others during examinations with mobile equipment. It cannot be too strongly emphasized that wherever X-ray equipment is being used by a radiographer the responsibility for radiation safety rests on that radiographer, unless a radiologist is present and is taking charge of the examination. The radiographer *must* see that the conditions of use are safe and that the patient and staff are not excessively or unnecessarily exposed to X rays; this may entail giving an authoritative opinion to senior people highly trained in their own specialty but not trained in the use of X rays.

There are three features of work with mobile equipment which are likely to increase the radiation risk to staff.

(i) The patients are often ill and may require support during the radiographic exposure.

(ii) The radiographer will usually be closer to the X-ray source and to the patient than in departmental practice, receiving thus a bigger dose from scattered radiation.

(iii) Difficulties in precisely positioning the patient and centring the X-ray beam often result in the use of a beam less strictly limited than is customary with departmental installations.

No one other than the patient under examination must be in the line of the direct beam. This point requires particular attention when the beam is directed horizontally and may include in its range patients in adjoining beds and staff in the ward or operating theatre. If necessary, beds must be moved away and staff should be warned to keep clear while the exposure is made.

The radiographer should wear a lead-rubber apron if close to the patient and the X-ray tube. Any supporting of the patient should be done by a nurse or other non-radiographic staff (not the same assistant too often), and a lead-rubber apron and if necessary gloves should be worn.

The X-ray beam should be limited with cones or diaphragms to cover the region under examination; the use of a light-delineator will greatly assist in this, giving visual indication of the area covered.

With recognition of the sources of risk and careful attention to these relatively simple precautions, the use of mobile equipment should have a level of protection equivalent to that available to the radiographer at work in the X-ray department.

CHAPTER XV

THE INFECTIOUS PATIENT

The student will by now appreciate the risks of cross infection in hospital and understand procedures designed to prevent any patient from acquiring in hospital an infection which he did not have when he was admitted. As well as the detailed techniques of surgical asepsis (which can form only a small part of the radiographer's daily duties), attention must be paid to general considerations of hygiene in the X-ray department; these are not less important than techniques for asepsis. Most patients for X-ray examination will not be involved during the course of it in surgical procedures; *all* patients will be dependent on departmental practice in hygiene to protect them against infection.

Routines of cleanliness both for staff and patients as indicated in Chapter II must be unremittingly undertaken. Disregard of detail in this leads to generally careless practice which increases everyone's risk—particularly that of the patient, who is more susceptible and more exposed. It may be assumed here that this general care is applied to all patients. Patients known to have a disease communicable to others require particular additional precautions.

Communicable diseases may be spread in various ways. If the question is asked: 'What is infectious about a patient?' the following have to be considered in the answer.

(i) Droplet discharge from patient's nose and mouth.
(ii) Faeces.
(iii) Urine.
(iv) Sputum.
(v) Discharge from wounds, sores, and body cavities.

As examples, the organisms of anterior poliomyelitis and cerebrospinal meningitis are contained in the nose and throat secretions of those who have the diseases, and may be conveyed by droplets when such a patient coughs, breathes, and talks. In other diseases, such as typhoid fever and dysentery, the infectious materials are the patient's excreta (urine and faeces) from which infection may be conveyed to bedpans, bed linen, and other things. The bacteria of pulmonary tuberculosis are contained in the sputum. Some bacteria can live in the dried state.

Communicable diseases can be spread by direct contact between the patient and other people; also through an intermediary, an

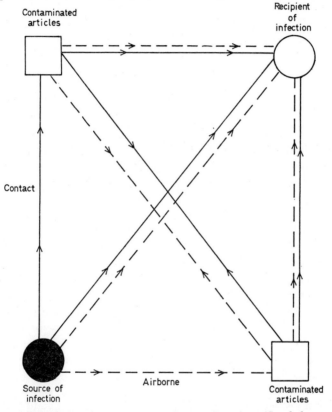

FIG. 29. Illustration of the spread of infection. *Copy from 'Staphylococcal Infection in Hospitals' by kind permission of the Controller of H.M. Stationery Office.*

article which has been in contact with the patient. All things in contact with the patient can be considered as infected because of contamination which may reach them directly, may be air-borne, may be conveyed by the patient's hands, and may reach them from other articles previously infected.

In caring for such patients, isolation technique is designed to stop the spread of the disease to other people by close control of the area within which contact occurs. The word contact in this sense embraces all three elements—the patient, other people, and things.

However, it is important that the patient should not be made to *feel* isolated by a sense that he is 'untouchable' or an impression that the staff are afraid to be in contact with him. It is possible to practise the correct techniques without such emphasis and such reluctance of approach as to cause the patient to see himself as an outcast.

THE INFECTIOUS PATIENT IN THE X-RAY DEPARTMENT

If possible the infectious patient should not be allowed to come to the X-ray department, but should be examined by means of a mobile X-ray set taken to the ward. If an infectious patient does come to the X-ray department, he must be there for the shortest time consistent with an efficient examination, and he must be kept away from other patients while he is in the department. If there is choice of the time when he attends, then this should be at a period when the department is not busy and there are few other patients present. This will make it easier to ensure the isolation of the infectious one, and the lack of pressure from other work will expedite the processing of films and their subsequent viewing. Thus the patient will not be kept long in the department. If there is little or no choice of the time when he attends, then he must be given priority over other patients, and must be X-rayed as soon as he arrives in the department. After the examination it will probably be necessary for him to wait a little time until the films are viewed, and he should be isolated from other patients during this period, which should be made as brief as possible.

When the patient comes to the X-ray room, it should be ready to receive him with the table covered with a clean sheet and the pillow in a clean pillow case. Sheets are to be used in preference to blankets, since blanket fluff carries bacteria very readily and disperses infection through the air. The use of disposable paper sheets and coverings recommends itself here. If the cassette is to be put in direct contact with the patient, or if he is to be positioned against a vertical Potter-Bucky stand or cassette holder, a clean pillow case, clean dressing towel, or disposable clinical sheet should be available to cover these. Any linen or disposable coverings used for this patient should be removed as soon as the examination is finished.

If the patient has to wait for films to be viewed before the examination is declared complete, it is really better that he should wait in the X-ray room, even although this may delay the use of the room for other patients. To remove the infectious patient to another waiting place, make the X-ray room and the radiographer ready for another patient, and then again revert to the infectious patient if further films prove necessary demands an elaborate procedure that is time-consuming and more prone to error than the simpler form. Once the X-ray room has been given over to the examination of the infectious patient, it is more truly careful of the others to keep them waiting a little longer until this examination is complete and the patient has left the department.

The radiographer should wear a mask and a clean gown covering all uniform, but leaving the arms bare to the elbows; the disposable type of mask will be very suitable. Once having touched the patient, his clothes, or anything which has been handled by him, the radiographer must be regarded as a 'contaminated' person. This contamination will be conveyed to anything else the radiographer touches, unless the hands are well washed for 2 or 3 minutes with soap and warm water; this effectively removes from the skin recent contamination. Disposable paper towels should be used for drying the hands.

It should be remembered that this transfer of contamination by the radiographer's hands must apply also in the case of any personal articles belonging to the radiographer which might be used —for example, a watch held in the hand, a pen, or a handkerchief, and some attention should be given to avoidance of these ways in which infection may be spread. Such articles should not be handled until after the hands have been washed.

A radiographer working unaided is clearly required to handle accessories and the controls of the X-ray set as well as the patient; this necessitates either frequent washing of the hands during the X-ray examination after every contact with the patient before anything else is touched, or a careful disinfecting afterwards of *everything* with which both the radiographer and the patient have been in contact. This must include cassettes manipulated by the radiographer, the controls of the X-ray set, the tube head and tube column. The cassettes must be thoroughly and carefully wiped with disinfectant before being taken into the dark room. A hygienic way of using the antiseptic or disinfectant is to apply it as an aerosol spray and wipe with a disposable tissue. The radiographer in a contaminated state should try to handle cassettes as little as possible, touching them only by the corners and edges.

It will be better if the radiographer can work with an assistant. The radiographer will help and position the patient, and the assistant will manipulate the equipment, set the controls, and make the exposure. This assistant will wear a mask but need not wear a gown, and must *not* touch the patient or anything with which the patient is in contact.

During the course of the examination, it may be necessary for the radiographer who has been in contact with the patient to leave the X-ray room in order to view films. If this is so, the radiographer must remove the gown, taking care not to allow its outer aspect to make contact with the inner aspect; the outer aspect is contaminated, the inner one is 'clean'. The hands must then be well washed and scrubbed with soap and warm water before the radiographer leaves the room. It should be noticed that if the taps cannot be turned off with an elbow and there is no assistant available, the radiographer must put a tissue or disposable towel over the taps before turning them on. The towel is then discarded; once the hands are washed they may be used for manipulation of the taps, as they are now clean. On returning to the X-ray room and the patient, the radiographer must again put on the gown, observing the same precautions as when it was taken off.

When the examination is complete and the patient has left the X-ray room, the radiographer disposes of any coverings which have been in contact with the patient. If they are to be laundered, it may be necessary to see that they are disinfected before being sent to the general laundry; a suitable procedure would be to place them in Izal (1–100 solution) for 12 hours.

The radiographer then washes the hands well, removes the gown, folding it so that the inner side is outwards, washes the hands again, and removes the face mask, taking care to handle only the tapes. Attention should be given to any part of the X-ray equipment which has been contaminated by contact with the patient and the radiographer. All such parts should be cleaned thoroughly with a suitable disinfectant (for example, Izal 1–300 solution). Finally the hands should be well washed once again before attending to the next patient.

THE INFECTIOUS PATIENT IN THE WARD

As has been explained, it is preferable that the patient with a communicable disease should be X-rayed in the ward by means of a mobile X-ray set.

Such a patient will be nursed with an isolation technique which is called isolation nursing because the patient is in a room by himself. Usually there will be a notice on the door drawing attention to the isolation nursing; a radiographer who is in any doubt about the situation must ask the ward staff. Very occasionally the patient may be in a corner of a general ward. This is called barrier nursing. It is unsatisfactory because it is not possible to limit the infection by keeping it within the barrier zone; air and dust, for example, can circulate from there through the whole ward.

All utensils used by the patient—bedpans, urinals, toilet articles and feeding utensils—will be reserved for his sole use. Disposable paper plates and cups and plastic cutlery which have only a single use are a great aid. Equipment for clinical examination—such as a stethoscope and a sphygmomanometer—is kept in the room and so is a supply of linen. Everything in the patient's room or within an arbitrary area round his bed if he is in a general ward is considered to be infected. If the patient is in a general ward, the area round his bed within which contamination occurs is usually defined by screens. Anyone who enters the patient's room or this circumscribed area and touches anything within it—including any furniture and the floor—is regarded as being contaminated.

Gowns and masks will be provided for those who attend the patient, and the practice is for these things to be put on when entering the room and removed when leaving it. It is usually the practice to keep two or three gowns hanging at the door inside the room, and anyone entering to attend the patient takes one of these. As the purpose of the gown is to prevent contamination of the clothes of the staff by which infection could be carried to other patients, it is clear that the outer and inner aspects of the gowns must not make contact with each other, as the inner is the 'clean' side. Often the outer side is clearly marked—for example by a broad band of bright colour round the hem. It may be difficult to ensure that the inside of each gown stays clean; they should hang on separate hooks as an aid to this. Masks will be worn by one person only and discarded, and for this purpose the disposable type of mask is extremely suitable. A supply is kept ready outside the door with a bin into which to discard them. In the room close to the entrance there will be facilities for washing the hands.

Before entering the patient's room, the radiographer puts on a mask and bares the arms to the elbows; and on going into the room puts on one of the gowns which are there. The hands should then be washed in soap and water and dried on a paper towel which is discarded.

If the radiographer has to work quite unaided, then it must be recognized again that the apparatus used will become contaminated. This includes the cassette, which the radiographer must handle after it has been in contact with the patient, the controls of the mobile set, the tube column and tube head, and the supply cable which is drawn over the floor.

As in the case of an infectious patient being examined in the X-ray department, it will be better if the radiographer works with an assistant, for in this way much of the equipment can be spared contamination. This assistant should wear a mask but need not wear a gown, and should be *very* careful to avoid any physical contact with the patient, the bed, any of the furniture in the room, and those parts of the X-ray set which have been contaminated by contact with the bed and the floor. The gowned radiographer positions the patient, and the assistant positions the X-ray tube head, sets the controls, and makes the exposure.

The cassette should be enclosed in a clean pillow case, dressing towel, or paper towel of adequate size. After use the assistant will remove it, the radiographer holding the cassette in its wrapping in such a way that the assistant can remove the cassette without touching the outer parts of whatever has enclosed it. The assistant can then take the cassette to the darkroom.

If more than one cassette is to be used for the examination, the assistant must bring them in one at a time from outside the patient's room. If the radiographer is working without assistance, all the necessary cassettes must be brought into the room at the start so that the gowned radiographer does not have to pass in and out of the room several times. They will have to be safe-guarded from radiation fog and must all be considered as contaminated, being thoroughly wiped with disinfectant before being taken to the dark-room. (The disinfecting process must not be carried out with an enthusiasm that leaves the cassettes wrecked by fluid! The use of an aerosol spray with care and of disposable tissues for wiping is recommended.)

When the examination is finished and the patient is made comfortable again, the radiographer should wash the hands well and then move the X-ray set away from the bed and disconnect it from the mains. The radiographer then takes off the gown, returns it to the hook from which it came, and washes the hands once more. The X-ray set and all contaminated parts are thoroughly cleaned with disinfectant; this includes the supply cable, which must now be coiled up in its place in readiness to take the set from the room when the radiographer leaves. The mask is then discarded, care being taken to touch only the tapes as the mask is removed.

CHAPTER XVI

SOME PRACTICAL NURSING PROCEDURES

TEMPERATURE, PULSE, RESPIRATION, BLOOD PRESSURE

The taking and recording of the patient's body temperature, his rate of respiration, and the rate, force, and rhythm of his pulse beat are basic procedures in medical care. Knowledge of the state of these features in any given patient at a given time provides the doctor with information concerning the condition of the patient, and can give a valuable indication of his general state.

For example, infection gives rise to an increased metabolic rate (this may be defined roughly as the rate at which the body consumes its nutritive fuel), and the increased metabolic rate gives rise to a raised temperature and a faster pulse. Haemorrhage results in a lowered temperature because of the heat loss through loss of fluid, and at the same time the pulse rate increases because the oxygen-carrying capacity of the blood is reduced by blood loss; a low temperature and a rapid pulse may be the first signs given to the doctor that haemorrhage has occurred.

Shallow and slow breathing is found in a state of shock. Laboured and difficult breathing may indicate heart failure. Noisy inspiration is a result of obstruction of the upper air passages.

These are only a few indications of the way in which observation of these features can tell the doctor what is happening in the patient's body, and it is not difficult to see the necessity for meticulously recording them as a part of general nursing care. In the X-ray department the observation of the patient's temperature, pulse, and respiration (sometimes seen abbreviated to T.P.R.) is not required as a routine procedure, and indeed may seldom be done by a radiographer. However, in the event of something untoward happening to the patient while he is in the department—for example, if he collapses or complains of feeling suddenly unwell—it may be necessary to make these observations, and the radiographer should know how they are done.

Temperature

The temperature is taken by means of a clinical thermometer, an instrument of which the general features must be familiar to most of us by the time we are old enough to work in hospital. It is made of narrow-bore glass tubing with a wall relatively thick in relation to the bore, and it is filled with mercury. It terminates in a bulb which is the 'business end' of the thermometer, and above this bulb there is a narrowing of the bore so that the mercury level does not fall after the thermometer is taken from the patient.

The normal body temperature remains almost constant in health, although individuals show variation between each other when they are compared. This range of variation is between $35.5°$ C $(96°$ F) and $37.2°$ C $(99°$ F), and the average normal temperature is taken as $36.8°$ C $(98.4°$ F).

The scale of the clinical thermometer is calibrated from $30°$ C $(86°$ F) to $43°$ C $(109.4°$ F). With regard to the upper and lower limits, temperatures above about $41°$ C $(105.8°$ F) and below about $35°$ C $(95°$ F) are harmful to the life of the body cells, and life cannot long be maintained if the body temperature is a few degrees beyond these upper and lower limits.

It is usual to find the average normal temperature of $36.8°$ C $(98.4°$ F) marked on the thermometer with a distinguishing point on the scale such as a red line or an arrow head. The thermometer may also be marked with the time it takes to register. It is the usual practice to leave it in place for at least 3 minutes for an accurate record.

Clinical thermometers in hospital are generally kept ready in a suitable disinfectant solution, such as chlorhexidine 0.5 per cent in water, and the thermometer should be wiped clean before use. It is the modern practice to supply in-patients with an individual thermometer for the period of stay in hospital, each thermometer being kept in its own container at the patient's bedside.

Before being used, the thermometer should be inspected to see that it is in good order and not damaged, and it should then be shaken down so that the mercury is at its lowest level before the thermometer is in contact with the patient. The thermometer is shaken by flicking the wrist to and fro with the thermometer held firmly in the fingers. Care should be taken to see that it is not inadvertently struck against anything during this process. The patient's temperature can be taken in the mouth, or by contact with skin surfaces in the axilla or groin.

Taking the Temperature in the Mouth

It is customary to use the mouth unless there is some reason why it should not be used. It would be contra-indicated if the patient were irresponsible because of his mental state or because he was a young child, if he were unconscious, had a mouth injury or inflammation, if his breathing were difficult or if breathing had to be done through the mouth because of injury to his nose. It should be ascertained that the patient has not recently had any hot or cold drinks.

The bulb end of the thermometer is inserted in the mouth, the patient being instructed to hold the thermometer under his tongue and to keep his lips but not his teeth closed. Needless to say, he must not attempt to talk while the temperature is being taken. The thermometer must be read as soon as it is removed, and the reading should be recorded before the mercury is shaken down again.

In ward practice it is usual to keep a record of the patient's temperature and other data on special charts which present the information in the form of graphs, but in the X-ray department the completion of this type of record is not likely to be necessary.

Taking the Temperature in the Axilla or Groin

Since the temperature is being taken in this case by contact between the thermometer and skin surfaces, it is important to see that the contact between the skin and the bulb of the thermometer is well made. This method is therefore not very suitable for extremely thin patients. The skin area should be dried first, and it should be ascertained that the patient has not recently washed the part. If the axilla is being used, the arm is maintained close to the side with forearm flexed across the chest, so that the thermometer is held in the axillary fold. The temperature registered will be $\frac{1}{2}°$ lower than that found in the mouth.

The groin is seldom used except in children, but the same considerations apply as in the use of the axilla.

The Pulse

The patient's pulse can be felt at various points in the body where a superficial artery passes over bone, for what is being felt is the expansion of the vessel when the heart chambers contract and pump blood through it. The rate of the pulse beat therefore varies with the rate of the heart, and it will be found normally to be slower in states which slow the heartbeat (for example during rest or sleep), and faster in conditions which increase the rate of the heartbeat (for example during and after vigorous physical exertion by the athletically untrained).

The usual place for taking the patient's pulse is his wrist, where the artery can be compressed against the palmar aspect of the radius close to the radial styloid process. For this, the person taking the pulse should use the middle and index fingers of one hand to feel the artery, and the patient should be at rest when it is done; if he is not already lying down he should sit, and the arm should be conveniently supported.

Before beginning to count the rate of the pulse beat, the radiographer should observe its regularity of rhythm and its volume (is it a forceful beat or a weak one?) as these features can be significant. It is also possible to gain an impression of the degree of tension in the artery.

As with the body temperature, the rate of the pulse beat when the patient is at rest and in health varies little for any one person, although individuals show variation between each other when they are compared. The average normal pulse rate is taken as 72 beats per minute, although rates much slower and much faster than this are considered to be within normal limits for particular individuals. The rate is faster in the newborn and in infants, and is slower in old age. Any condition which decreases the metabolic rate slows the pulse rate.

Unless the rhythm is irregular it is not necessary to count the pulse rate for a full minute; it can be taken for $\frac{1}{2}$ a minute and the figure obtained is then of course multiplied by 2 to give the rate per minute.

Respiration

The rate of the patient's breathing should be taken without his knowledge. Respiration and the chest movements can to some extent be voluntarily controlled, and once the patient becomes aware that the rate is being counted he may feel self-conscious about it, and it may be difficult to arrive at a true estimate of what the rate is. It is usual to count the respiration with the fingers still on the pulse,

P

and in this way the patient does not know that it is being done. If the patient's hand and arm are laid across his chest with the palm down and the pulse is counted, then the respirations can be noted by the rise and fall of the arm and chest together.

The normal respiration rate is increased by physical exercise and also by emotion. In the average adult at rest the chest rises and falls about 15–20 times per minute. As with the pulse, the rate is quicker in the newborn and in infants. In addition to the rate of respiration, its qualities of depth and regularity are important, and observation should be made of whether the breathing is noisy or quiet.

Blood Pressure

The term blood pressure refers to the force exerted by the blood upon the walls of the vessels through which it circulates. This force is related to (i) the force of the heartbeat, (ii) the degree of elasticity of the vessel walls, and (iii) the amount of blood which is circulating. Various conditions therefore influence the blood pressure.

For example, exercise, emotion, and change of posture from the supine to the erect position all have an effect upon it. As the body ages, hardening of the arterial walls reduces their elasticity so that they offer greater resistance to the blood in circulation; blood pressure therefore rises. A fall in pressure can result from excessive loss of fluid, for example after haemorrhage or severe diarrhoea. Patients in a state of shock also have lowered blood pressure. A maintained rise in blood pressure is called *hypertension*, and a maintained low pressure is called *hypotension*.

When the heart is actively pumping (that is during the systolic phase in the cycle of heart movements), the pressure will support a column of mercury 120 mm high. This figure—120 mm—is the average systolic pressure, and it is higher than the pressure during the diastolic phase when the heart is relaxed and its chambers are re-filling. The average diastolic pressure is about two-thirds of the systolic—that is 80 mm. An expression of the blood pressure usually gives both figures thus: 120/80.

The apparatus which is used to record the blood pressure is known as a sphygmomanometer (Plate XII facing page 214). This incorporates a mercury gauge on which the pressure in millimetres of mercury will be recorded. In using the apparatus, care must be taken to see that it is so placed in relation to the patient that he cannot see the scale of this gauge. There is also a rubber cuff connected to the gauge (the cuff is generally in a cotton cover), and this cuff is fixed evenly round the patient's arm and is inflated with a hand pump to which it is connected. The patient should be reassured as to the ease of the procedure. He must be lying down when the blood pressure is taken or the result is misleading.

The cuff is put on the patient's arm above the elbow with the centre over the brachial artery. The pulsations of this can be found above the elbow at the medial margin of the biceps by pressure directed posterolaterally. The cuff is then pumped up by means of the hand pump, and after a while the pressure on the artery is enough to obliterate the radial pulse. A small threaded screw on the hand pump is then released letting the air escape, and the pressure of the band on the brachial artery falls. This should be allowed to occur slowly while the radial pulse is felt for its just perceptible reappearance. The height of the mercury column then is the systolic pressure.

Estimation of the diastolic pressure is adequately done only by using a stethoscope to listen over the brachial artery. It is not a method likely to be of use to the unpractised, and almost certainly will not be required of the radiographer.

LAYING UP A STERILE TROLLEY

Detailed requirements in setting up trays or trolleys for sterile procedures will clearly depend on the nature of the treatment or examination for which the equipment is being prepared. Certain principles of technique, however, are basic and common to many procedures, and should be understood if conditions of asepsis are to be preserved.

It is a general rule that when a trolley is being laid up with both sterile and unsterile equipment, the top shelf is reserved as the sterile field, while the lower shelf holds unsterile accessories which may be needed—for example, bandages, lotions, and possibly containers for used instruments and dressings. A suitable container for used instruments is a jar filled with disinfectant solution. Containers for soiled swabs and dressings should properly be closed, and bins with lids operated by foot pedals have long been used, these bins standing upon the floor. An alternative modern disposal method makes use of paper bags into which the soiled dressings and used instruments are put. These bags are clipped to the sides of the trolley with 'bulldog' clips or plastic clothes-pegs, the one for used instruments on the left side, and the soiled dressings bag on the right. After use, the top of the dressings bag is closed with a twist, and it is put in the dirty-dressings bin for incineration. The instruments are either washed, boiled, and put away in the department, or are returned to a central sterile supply according to the practice of the hospital.

In the diagnostic X-ray department the changing of surgical dressings is not likely to be often undertaken, and the use of an open bowl or receiver placed upon the floor for a soiled dressing may just be allowable. It should be realized, however, that this practice leaves uncontrolled a possible source of infection by dispersal of infected particles in the air, and as soon as the procedure is finished soiled dressings and swabs should be at once disposed of without being directly handled.

The hands are always to be considered as non-sterile unless they are in sterile rubber gloves, and they therefore must not come in contact with any sterile material. Before preparing for or undertaking a sterile procedure, the hands must be properly washed with warm water and soap, and well dried upon a disposable paper towel; wet articles and wet areas favour the spread of bacteria.

People concerned in sterile procedures and in handling sterile equipment should wear masks, although it is not generally the custom to do this when the procedure being undertaken is a simple intravenous injection. The mask covers both mouth and nose and is made of layers of muslin, often with a sheet of cellophane inserted between the layers. The cellophane makes the front of the mask impervious to the moisture produced by respiration; a wet mask will be an inadequate barrier against droplet infection from the nose and mouth of the wearer. Disposable masks of paper are available, but these must not be worn for periods which are longer than an hour as they are penetrable by moisture eventually. In some hospitals, nurses no longer wear masks when doing a round of dressings because in these circumstances paper masks are worn too long to be of any help.

A trolley very commonly prepared in the X-ray department is for intravenous injection in the procedure of intravenous uro-

Plate XII   A sphygmomanometer
Showing mercury column, cuff (folded up), rubber bulb for inflating
cuff, and the release valve. *By courtesy of A. C. Cossor & Son
(Surgical) Ltd.*

graphy. The technique for setting up a sterile trolley will be described in terms of this as it is so commonly undertaken. It is hoped that the student will understand from this the applications of correct sterile technique to other procedures.

The description here is for a trolley; an alternative method is to lay on a sterile tray the contents given here of the upper shelf, and arrange the items of the lower shelf on an adjacent table.

The trolley should be washed or sprayed with a solution such as 'Hibitane' (chlorhexidine 0.5 per cent in 70 per cent spirit), dried with a paper towel and then laid. If the equipment is not of the prepacked and pre-sterilized variety and is to be prepared by the radiographer, it should be checked to make sure that it is in good order—that the needles provided are neither blunted nor bent, that the needles fit the syringe and that the piston of the syringe fits the barrel. The requirements on the trolley are the following.

Sterile (upper shelf)
A 20 ml syringe and a 30 ml syringe, each with eccentric nozzle.
Needles to fit these and suitable for intravenous injection—for example, No. 1 and No. 2.
A container for 3 or 4 gauze swabs and dressing towel.
A container in which to place syringes and needles.
A pair of dissecting forceps.
One cannula for filling the syringe.

Non-sterile (lower shelf)
The agent to be injected, usually in a sealed single-dose ampoule. This must stand in a container of warm water.
One file.
One sphygmomanometer or tourniquet.
A bottle or aerosol spray of some antiseptic for cleaning the skin—for example, 'Hibitane', surgical spirit, or cetrimide.
A receiver for used swabs (these can safely be put in an open receiver as they will not be grossly infected).
Sandbag for supporting the patient's arm.

In the absence of a central sterile supply service or the use of disposable pre-sterilized equipment, all the sterile requirements apart from the dressing towel and the gauze swabs will be sterilized in the department. The swabs and towel will be sterilized by auto-claving, and will probably be taken from a drum of sterile dressings.

The clean trolley should be brought close to the sterilizer or autoclave. There should be available a pair of *sterile* Cheatle forceps in a jar of disinfectant solution. The Cheatle forceps are used to remove the sterile articles from the autoclave or sterilizer. These forceps must be lifted straight from the container and must be kept uncontaminated by any contact with the sides of the jar, the trolley, and anything which is not sterile.

Sterile equipment laid on the upper shelf of the trolley should not be put too close to its edges. The procedure is as follows.

Using the sterile forceps.

(i) Remove from the sterilizer or autoclave the container for needles and syringes, and place it on the trolley top, taking care to allow no contamination of the *inner* surfaces of the container.

(ii) Remove from the sterilizer or autoclave the dissecting forceps, the syringes, the needles, and the cannula for filling the syringe. Lay them one by one in an orderly manner in the instrument container.

(iii) Remove from the sterilizer or autoclave the lid of the instrument container and, holding it carefully with the inner side down and allowing no contamination of the inner side, set in place on the container.

(iv) Remove from the sterilizer or autoclave the container for swabs and dressing towel and set it similarly on the trolley.

(v) Take the dressing towel and gauze swabs from the drum of sterile dressings and put them in the container.

(vi) Remove the lid of this container from the sterilizer or autoclave and set it in place.

(vii) Put the Cheatle forceps back in their jar of disinfectant.

If pre-sterilized supplies are available, the equipment needed for a simple sterile procedure is delivered to the department already sterile and enclosed in suitable packs

Dressings and gallipots of metal foil may be in a paper bag, and syringes and forceps within separate cylindrical metal containers. Needles may be of the disposable type.

This service makes the procedure much less time-consuming as it is necessary only to open the packs with proper maintenance of sterility and lay out the contents. A syringe may be slid from its container into the doctor's hand when he is ready to use it, and the needle in its turn taken directly on to the syringe by inserting the nozzle of the syringe into the open end of the needle container.

Fig. 30 on pages 223–6 shows the use of sterile packs for a dressing and indicates how such packs should be handled. It is very important in opening any sterile pack to avoid contamination of the contents as they are taken from it. Although the pack should be designed to minimize the risk of contamination, careful withdrawal of the contents is necessary; they should not be freely shaken out of an enclosing bag.

ASSISTING AT AN INTRAVENOUS INJECTION

There are many applications of the intravenous injection in administering drugs, and it is the method chosen when rapid absorption of the drug is required, and when it is necessary to give a large amount. In the diagnostic X-ray department intravenous injections are used for introducing radiographic contrast agents, and it is at this type of intravenous injection that the radiographer will be required to assist most often.

Intravenous injection is a procedure undertaken by a doctor, and the usual site for injection is one of the superficial veins at the elbow, the median cephalic or the median basilic vein. As an alternative, veins in the leg may be used if those at the elbow prove unsuitable, and the short saphenous vein just above the ankle would be a probable choice.

All intravenous injections must be given in conditions of strict asepsis, and careful maintenance of these in preparing the tray and assisting at the injection is one of the radiographer's duties. The radiographer must be aware of sharing a weight of responsibility with the doctor in seeing that this injection is given to the patient correctly—the right drug to the right patient in the right way.

It is *most important* that the agent to be injected should be checked at every stage of the procedure—when the trolley is prepared and again when the agent is taken into the syringe. The radiographer must check it and must see that the doctor also checks it *before* he gives the injection. From time to time disasters occur in hospital because a patient has been injected with the wrong substance; failure to check constantly and efficiently allows these things to occur.

The trolley will be prepared as described in the previous section in accordance with the requirements of the examination that is

being undertaken, and the radiographer will give a reassuring explanation to the patient of what is to be done.

When the doctor comes to give the injection, the cuff of the sphygmomanometer (or the tourniquet) should be put round the patient's
arm sufficiently far above the elbow to leave the bend of the elbow
well clear as the injection site. The band is inflated (or the tourniquet tightened) enough to distend the veins, and it will assist in this
if the patient can help by opening and closing his fist several times.

If the agent to be injected is contained in a single dose ampoule,
this will be opened by the radiographer when the doctor is ready.
The ampoule neck is marked with a file. The ampoule should be
wiped with a swab moistened with spirit or other antiseptic, and
broken at the filed neck, being held for this purpose in a piece of
sterile gauze. The radiographer then holds the ampoule while the
doctor draws the contents into the syringe.

The radiographer should check the name on the label and see
that the doctor also checks it. As has been indicated, the importance
of this can hardly be over-emphasized.

The radiographer will give such assistance as may be necessary
by lifting the lids of sterile containers (or opening sterile packs) and
pouring or spraying the skin cleansing agent. The lids of sterile containers should be lifted by hand, care being taken to see that the
contents are not contaminated; as they have been standing for a little
while the lids may be considered to have lost their sterility, and
should not now be manipulated with the sterile Cheatle forceps.
If the skin cleansing agent is being poured, it is important to see
that nothing sterile is touched with the unsterile bottle, and that
the interior of the cap of the bottle is not contaminated during the
process of handling it. When the bottle is tilted to the horizontal
for pouring, it should be done so that the label is uppermost (that is
against the palm of the hand), so that drips do not subsequently
deface it.

Cleansing of the patient's skin at the injection site may be
done by the doctor just before he gives the injection. The radiographer will steady the patient's arm, which should rest on a small
sandbag or firm pad, and will observe and reassure the patient.
When the needle is in the vein, the doctor will check that it is so by
drawing blood back into the syringe before he proceeds with the injection. At this point, when the blood is seen in the syringe, the
radiographer deflates the sphygmomanometer cuff or releases the

tourniquet, making quite sure that the patient's arm is not moved in the process.

After use, the needle and syringe (unless they are disposable) are cleaned immediately, first in cold water and then in warm soapy water. The water should be several times drawn up into the syringe through the needle and expelled in order to make sure that it is clean and not blocked. They must then be very well rinsed in clean water.

A SIMPLE STERILE DRESSING

Surgical dressings of operation wounds and burns (the latter are considered to be particularly liable to infection) are undertaken in the wards in controlled conditions of asepsis. It is most unlikely that a radiographer in the diagnostic X-ray department will be called upon to deal with a major dressing. If a patient comes to the department with a dressing in place which contains radio-opaque elements such as 'Elastoplast' or jaconet, it should not be summarily removed. Advice should be sought from the ward or department from which the patient has been referred concerning the removal of such a dressing and its possible replacement.

If the patient comes to the department with a surgical dressing in place which during the course of the examination becomes dislodged, or becomes wet with blood or other discharge from the wound, fresh sterile dressings should be applied to cover the previous one, and the ward or department referring the patient should be told of the occurrence.

Undertaking a simple sterile dressing *may* come within the province of a radiographer, and it should be understood that the important principle to be observed in doing it is the maintenance of asepsis by correct sterile technique. A trolley must be prepared, reference being made to the methods and precautions described in preparing a trolley for intravenous injections. The requirements for the trolley are the following.

Sterile (upper shelf)
A covered container holding sterile dressings—3 or 4 cotton wool balls; 3 or 4 gauze swabs, approximately 3 inches by 3 inches.
A covered container holding 3 or 4 pairs of sterile dissecting forceps and a pair of scissors.

A pair of sterile Cheatle forceps in a jar of disinfectant solution.
A sterile gallipot turned upside down in a sterile bowl.

Non-sterile (lower shelf)
A jar holding disinfectant solution for discarded instruments.
A bin, bowl, or receiver for discarded dressings.
A container (bowl or tray) holding accessories such as masks,
    bandages, pins, adhesive strapping, and a pair of scissors.
A skin cleansing agent such as 'Hibitane' 0.05 per cent in aqueous
    solution.

The container for discarded dressings and the jar for used instruments may be replaced by two paper bags attached with clips to
the trolley, one for instruments on the left side and the soiled dressings bag on the right side.

The technique employed is described as a 'no touch technique',
and this means that the hands do not touch any part of the wound
or the area round the wound, or any material which will be
applied directly to the wound. The dressing must be managed with
sterile forceps. If this cannot be done sterile rubber gloves must be
worn; it is here assumed that the straightforward type of dressing
most likely to be encountered in the diagnostic X-ray department
can be managed with forceps alone.

Before the dressing is begun the patient should be placed in such a
position that the area to be dressed is horizontal. When this is so,
dressings can be laid in place without risk of their falling off, and
it will not be necessary to hold them in place with forceps while outer
dressings are applied.

The hands of the person undertaking the procedure should be
preserved from contact with grossly contaminated material such as
soiled dressings. The outer dressings may be removed by hand, but
the inner ones should be lifted away with forceps. The procedure
is therefore as follows.

(i) Wash the hands and dry them on a clean paper towel.
Disposable paper towels are excellent for this purpose.

(ii) Put on a mask. The mask may be of the disposable type as
the procedure will not take long.

(iii) Carefully remove the bandages and main outer layers of
the dressing which is in place and discard them into the receptacle
provided.

(iv) Wash the hands again in warm soapy water and dry them on a clean paper towel.

(v) With the Cheatle forceps, set the gallipot upright in its sterile bowl. Put the Cheatle forceps back in the jar.

(vi) Fill the gallipot with skin cleansing agent, taking care not to touch the unsterile bottle against the sterile gallipot.

(vii) Using the right hand (if right-handed), remove the lid of the sterile instrument container (keeping it with the inner side downwards). With Cheatle forceps in the left hand, take up a pair of dissecting forceps by grasping them at mid-length. Replace the container lid, and with the right hand thus freed take hold of the dissecting forceps, being careful not to touch with the fingers the tips of the Cheatle forceps. Restore the Cheatle forceps to their jar.

(viii) Use the dissecting forceps to remove the last layers of the dressing which is in place, and discard the dressing and then the forceps into their appropriate receptacles.

(ix) Using the method previously described, take a fresh pair of dissecting forceps and use them to lift a swab from the container of dressings, managing the lids of the containers as before.

(x) Using the dissecting forceps to hold the swab, soak the swab in the skin cleansing agent in the gallipot, and clean the skin and the wound. Each swab should be used for one stroke only and not scrubbed back and forth along the wound. For a linear wound stroke in one direction only along (not across) the wound, working from the clean to the dirty end if there is a noticeable difference between the two ends. If the lesion is circular rather than linear, make a stroke round its outside edge and then with a fresh swab make a similar stroke round the inside. (It is arguable which to do first; some people say that the inside should be done first.) Discard the swab into the appropriate receptacle.

(xi) Use the forceps to apply fresh sterile gauze and then outer dressings to the wound. If at any time it is necessary to replace forceps on the trolley after they have been handled, or to take out of the container and lay on the trolley a spare pair of forceps, so that two may be ready for use, it is important always to place them on the trolley with their points inwards. The handles will lie towards the edge of the trolley so that the points are within (and the handles are outside) an arbitrary line defining the sterile field.

The dressing is finished by applying bandages or strapping to hold it in position.

The trolley is cleared away, the soiled dressings being discarded into a bin and the instruments washed in warm soapy water, rinsed and boiled. Any dressings not used should *not* be returned to the drum from which they were orginally taken, but may be kept and used for filling the drum again when it is due to be re-autoclaved.

If the hospital makes use of a central sterile supply system, the procedure of preparing for a small sterile dressing becomes very much simpler. A prepared pack containing all that is necessary for a small dressing will be issued by the central sterile department. Typical contents are the following.

Four pairs of dissecting forceps.
Four cotton wool balls.
Three gauze squares (about 3 inches by 3 inches).
Two aluminium foil gallipots.
One large clinical sheet.

The top of the trolley is left entirely clear. The lower shelf holds:
(i) the sterile pack;
(ii) brown paper bags and pegs;
(iii) accessories such as masks, bandages, pins, adhesive strapping, and a pair of scissors;
(iv) a skin cleansing agent;
(v) a 7-inch pair of dissecting forceps (sterile) in a separate container.

It will be possible to open the pack without touching any part other than the outside, and the inner wrapping can be spread out to form a sterile field on top of the trolley (see Fig. 30).

There will usually be two layers of wrapping, the outer one perhaps being a paper bag. This outer layer can be removed after the hands have been washed and a mask put on at the start of the dressing technique. When the inner wrapping is spread out to cover the trolley top, the dressings and gallipot are lying directly on it.

As shown in Fig. 30, the large dissecting forceps are dropped from the container into the hand (the points not being touched). They are then used to arrange the contents of the pack.

The dressing is undertaken with a 'no touch technique' as described. As no Cheatle forceps are used, it will be necessary to lift the dissecting forceps by hand from the trolley top. Care should be

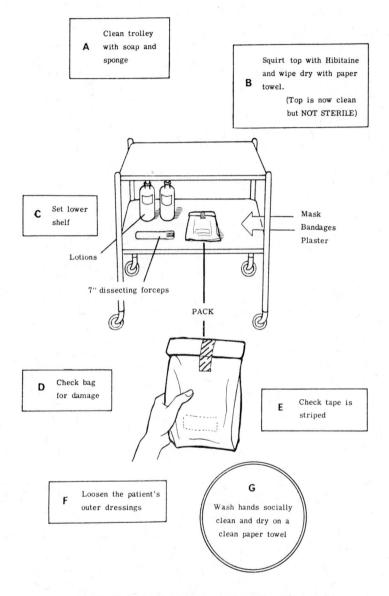

A Clean trolley with soap and sponge

B Squirt top with Hibitaine and wipe dry with paper towel.

(Top is now clean but NOT STERILE)

C Set lower shelf

Mask
Bandages
Plaster

Lotions

7" dissecting forceps

PACK

D Check bag for damage

E Check tape is striped

F Loosen the patient's outer dressings

G Wash hands socially clean and dry on a clean paper towel

FIG. 30. Basic dressing technique using sterile packs. *(Prepared in conjunction with Guy's Hospital and reproduced by kind permission of Guy's Hospital and the Bowater-Scott Corporation Ltd.)*

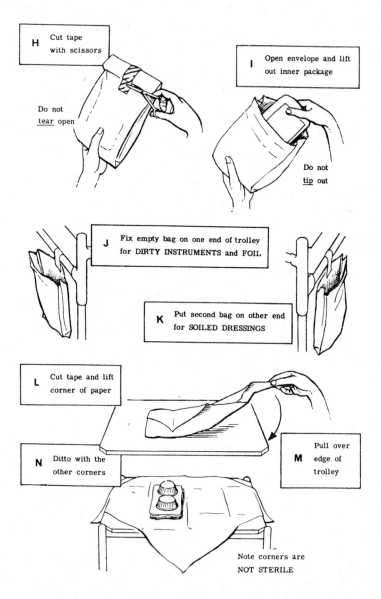

H   Cut tape with scissors

Do not tear open

I.   Open envelope and lift out inner package

Do not tip out

J   Fix empty bag on one end of trolley for DIRTY INSTRUMENTS and FOIL

K   Put second bag on other end for SOILED DRESSINGS

L   Cut tape and lift corner of paper

N   Ditto with the other corners

M   Pull over edge of trolley

Note corners are NOT STERILE

FIG. 30—*contd.*

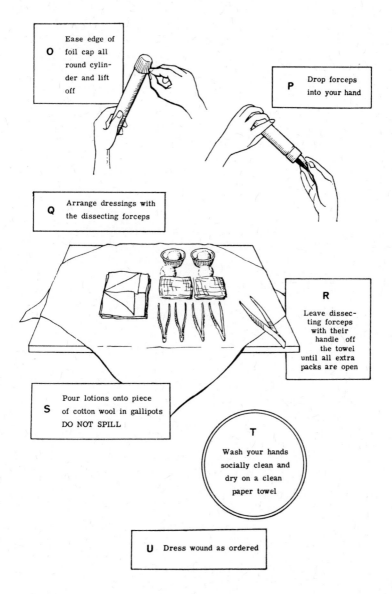

O Ease edge of foil cap all round cylinder and lift off

P Drop forceps into your hand

Q Arrange dressings with the dissecting forceps

R Leave dissecting forceps with their handle off the towel until all extra packs are open

S Pour lotions onto piece of cotton wool in gallipots DO NOT SPILL

T Wash your hands socially clean and dry on a clean paper towel

U Dress wound as ordered

FIG. 30—*contd.*

CLEARING UP

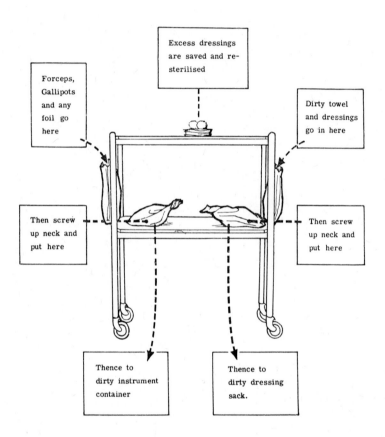

FIG. 30—*contd.*

taken to touch only the handles and not the points of any of the forceps.

When the dressing is finished, the gallipots, paper wrappings, etc., are discarded into the soiled-dressings bag on the side of the trolley, and the forceps are put into the soiled-forceps container for eventual return to the central sterile supply department.

A modern technique for ward dressings has been introduced in some hospitals in the United Kingdom. Complete dressing packs, sealed and sterilized by the manufacturer, are used. This is called a pre-set tray system and each pack contains equipment for a dressing (including wound-cleansing lotion in a plastic sachet) and a fresh pack is used for each patient. The contents are packed in a plastic tray with moulded gallipots as a part of it, and the tray acts as a sterile field while the dressing is being done. Everything, from the tray itself to the plastic and metal forceps, is disposable.

The pack is sealed within an air-tight and water-tight polythene covering and is sterilized by radiation before it leaves the manufacturer. These commercial packs are supplied under strict controls and provide a standardized sterile dressing which should be of great help in reducing cross-infection in all hospitals, from the largest to the smallest, where they are used. If the pre-set tray system becomes widespread general practice, central sterile supply departments in hospitals could be smaller and could devote themselves to the more specialized service of providing sterile supplies for operating theatres.

OXYGEN THERAPY AND RESUSCITATION

All the living cells of the body demand oxygen, and normally enough can be supplied by the act of respiration in ordinary atmospheric air. In certain circumstances, however, there will be reduced oxygen in the blood—a condition known as anoxaemia. It will show itself in the patient's face by blueness of his nose and the tips of the ears and about the mouth, and in his nails the blue coloration will also be detected. This blue tinge is known as cyanosis.

This state of affairs can arise when respiratory capacity is diminished by obstruction to the air passages, by diseases of the lung, by chest injuries and chest surgery. It can also arise in shock and in cardiac failure because the blood circulation and the oxygenation of the blood by passage through the pulmonary system are not adequate. It may be seen in the type of circulatory collapse which

Q

sometimes follows the intravenous injection of radiographic contrast agents. Loss of blood can also give rise to anoxaemia because there is insufficient volume of circulating blood to provide enough oxygen for the tissues. So there are many conditions in which the patient can benefit by the administration of oxygen, and there are various ways in which it can be arranged for him to breathe an additional amount in the air which he inhales.

The Oxygen Supply

Oxygen is supplied commercially compressed into cylinders. Cylinders of medical gases are standardized as to size and colour, being provided in a certain range of sizes and in a colour individual to the gas contained in the cylinder. Oxygen cylinders are black with white shoulders and upper part where the outlet valve is situated. The name or the symbol O_2 (and sometimes both) may be seen painted upon the outside of the cylinder. It is obviously important at all times to be able to distinguish a cylinder readily and quickly, so that the risk of the patient being given the wrong gas in a moment of crisis is reduced.

In hospitals oxygen is often piped directly to the wards and certain departments from a central supply in the basement. Oxygen is then available at the patient's bedside by means of this pipeline. It is, however, less likely that the X-ray department will be included entirely in this arrangement where it exists for the wards; sometimes one or two rooms in a department may be equipped with piped gases which would include oxygen. The department must therefore maintain as part of its emergency equipment complete apparatus for delivering oxygen to the patient. This apparatus must be regularly and frequently checked to see that it is in good order, for when it is needed there must be no loss of time in getting it into operation.

Oxygen is not itself flammable, but increased concentration of it in air increases the rate at which materials will burn. There is therefore considerable risk of fire and explosion associated with the use of oxygen, and possible sources of ignition must be controlled in regard to a patient having oxygen therapy.

When a patient in the ward is having continuous oxygen therapy for a period, no naked lights are allowed in the immediate vicinity, and if electrical apparatus (such as mobile X-ray equipment) is to be used, the supply of oxygen must be turned off while the equipment is functioning. Oil or grease must not be used on the fittings of oxygen cylinders.

There is a device which has been demonstrated to increase the margin of safety in using oxygen cylinders. It is said to eliminate fire and explosion risk, and it consists of a plug which has a low-temperature melting point. This fuses and seals off the oxygen cylinder at a given temperature.

The Oxygen Cylinder and Regulating Valve

For use, the oxygen cylinder has attached to it a regulating valve. This fitment has a threaded end which goes into the upper end of the oxygen cylinder, and is locked in place by means of a nut which may be of the wing type. This nut is tightened by a special spanner which is also used to turn the main tap on the cylinder which releases the oxygen flow.

The regulating valve incorporates a pressure gauge which shows the amount of oxygen present in the cylinder, and a regulator which can be adjusted to control the flow of oxygen. A flowmeter which shows the amount of oxygen being used is another feature of the cylinder fitting, and such a meter may be either a dial or a dry bobbin type; in the latter case a bobbin moves up and down inside a glass tube which is calibrated with scale markings, the height of the bobbin against the markings indicating the flow. Both the dial and the bobbin type of flowmeter record the flow in litres per minute. The usual rate at which oxygen is given is 4–6 litres per minute.

The regulating valve fitment, with its pressure gauge and flowmeter, is attached to the oxygen cylinder (as has been explained) by means of the threaded end which inserts into the valve opening at the head of the cylinder. Before this is done, the main tap of the cylinder should be opened a little and some of the oxygen allowed to escape. This will dislodge any small impediments which may have collected around the valve opening. With the valve closed again, the threaded end of the regulator fitting is inserted and tightened in place by means of the nut for the purpose. (At this stage the regulator controlling the flow of oxygen through the flowmeter should be in the 'off' position.) The main tap on the side of the regulator is then turned on. The pressure gauge recording the contents of the cylinder will register 'Full' when the cylinder is a new one.

The cylinder is now ready to supply oxygen to the patient when the regulator valve is opened to produce the required rate of flow as registered on the flowmeter.

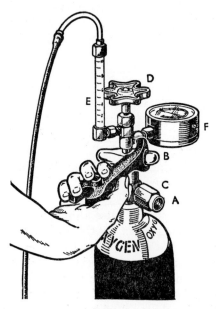

FIG. 31. An oxygen cylinder fitted with a fine adjustment valve. The illustration shows: A, main tap for turning on flow of oxygen; B, wing nut for attaching regulator, etc., to the cylinder (this nut may be loosened with a special spanner); C, lock nut; D, fine adjustment valve; E, flowmeter; F, pressure gauge. *By courtesy of Baillière, Tindall & Cox Ltd.*

The cylinder with its regulator fitment and meters constitute the apparatus necessary to *deliver* oxygen. In order to administer it to the patient certain further equipment is needed. The nature of this will depend on the method of administration.

Methods of Administering Oxygen

The three main ways of administering oxygen are:

(i) by means of an oxygen mask,

(ii) by means of nasal catheters (that is, tubes inserted into the nasal passages),

(iii) by enclosing the patient in an oxygen tent.

Any of the three may be employed for continuous oxygen therapy when the patient is in the ward, but for emergency use in the X-ray department only the first method can be applied, the other two being unsuitable to this application.

Oxygen Masks

(i) *The Boothby, Lovelace, Bulbulian (B.L.B.) Mask*

An oxygen mask may be either nasal (covering only the patient's nose), or oronasal (covering the patient's nose and mouth). The nasal type can be used only if the patient has no obstruction to the nose, and can co-operate to the extent of breathing through his nose and not his mouth. For emergency use the oronasal type of mask is a better choice. The mask can be attached to the patient's face by means of rubber straps.

In the B.L.B. apparatus, a rubber mask (usually of a type which fits over the patient's nose and mouth) is connected to a thin rubber bag. The oxygen passes from a cylinder into an inlet pipe to the bag, connection being made with tubing of rubber or polythene thick enough not to kink easily. A single tube leads from the upper part of the bag and, at the patient's chin, this tube divides to form two tubes which pass one on each side to enter the sides of the nose piece of the mask.

When the patient breathes out the expired air is mixed with incoming oxygen in the bag, and the patient subsequently inhales a mixture of air and oxygen from the bag. This process both warms and moistens the oxygen. Dry oxygen is very irritating to the respiratory tract, and unless the mask can act as humidifier in this way it will be necessary to moisten the gas by bubbling it through water.

Fig. 32.

'B.L.B.' apparatus. *By courtesy of Baillière, Tindall & Cox Ltd.*

After use the parts of the B.L.B. mask should be sterilized by boiling or by immersion in disinfectant solution.

(ii) *Polythene Mask*

This is a disposable mask of light transparent plastic on a wire frame. It fits over the patient's nose and mouth, and is held in place with narrow cords over his ears. The mask consists of a double plastic bag, oxygen passing from the cylinder (again by means of rubber or polythene connecting tubing) into the space between the inner and outer layers of the bag. The inner layer has two holes which allow the oxygen to enter the inside of the bag and reach the patient. Some moist expired air goes into the space between the layers and humidifies the incoming oxygen, so this type of mask also acts as a humidifier.

Oxygen Administration by Nasal Catheter

In this method two fine rubber tubes are passed into the patient's nasal passages, one up each nostril. The two tubes from the nostrils are connected by a Y-shaped junction to a single tube which receives oxygen from the cylinder bubbled through a bottle of water.

Fig. 33. Disposable polythene mask. *By courtesy of Ballière, Tindall & Cox Ltd.*

The Oxygen Tent

There are several types of oxygen tent in use which may show variety in detail but are similar in basic construction. The tent is of light transparent plastic material fixed to a frame, the whole assembly being mounted on wheels so that it can be wheeled into position over the patient's bed. The canopy of the tent is capacious enough to allow its free edges to be tucked in at front, sides, and back, so that the patient is totally enclosed. Oxygen is fed into the upper part of the tent.

The tent has certain features of design to prevent the air inside becoming too hot and damp, cooling of the air usually being done by passing it through an ice box. Some tents incorporate forced circulation of the oxygen and improvement of ventilation by means of a motor.

Maintenance of Emergency Oxygen Equipment

The oxygen cylinder on a wheeled stand so that it can be readily transported, the regulator valve and meters fitted to it, and a mask for administering oxygen are important parts of emergency equipment in the X-ray department. They should be maintained assembled and ready for use. Large departments will certainly have more than one set of such equipment.

Each oxygen cylinder should be daily checked to see that it is full; if it is nearly empty it must be replaced by a full one, and not left until it is nearly exhausted. When the cylinder is being changed, the main escape valve should be turned off before the regulator fitting is removed.

The oxygen key or spanner which opens the main escape valve on the cylinder should be kept attached to it with a tape so that it is to hand for instant use. The mask should be inspected regularly to see that it is in good order, and without holes or defects which would allow escape of oxygen intended for the patient. If the mask is of the B.L.B. type, the rubber bag should be examined to make sure that it has developed no splits along the seams.

GIVING A PATIENT A BEDPAN

The use of a bedpan is probably one of the procedures most dreaded and disliked by any patient who contemplates a period in hospital in the course of which he may be immobilized in bed. This is a very understandable view. In the first place, he will be embarrassed about asking for the bedpan when he needs it. According to his age, he may feel that a young nurse (junior nurses who deal with bedpans tend to be young!) is too nearly the age of his grandchildren, or of his children, or of his own friends for him easily to be able to mention such basic functions to her. A woman patient may escape the embarrassment but may share a reluctance to make a demand on busy nurses and a worry as to whether the nurse will bring the bedpan in time to prevent the delay making itself disastrously evident in the bed.

In the second place, once the patient is on the bedpan he finds it difficult to use, and this of course applies to women patients too. A patient supine in bed, or a patient sitting up in bed on a bedpan which is balanced on a yielding mattress, is in a position very different from those assumed naturally for the performance of the functions with which the use of the bedpan is associated. It is difficult to use the abdominal muscles effectively. There may be a feeling of insecurity and a fear of falling which tend to impair concentration on the physical functions. So for various reasons the bedpan is a disliked object.

In modern hospital practice the bedpan is used only when it *must* be. Patients who can walk to the lavatory are encouraged to do so, and certainly need little encouragement in most cases. Those who are able just to get out of bed can use commode chairs which are brought to the bedside. A commode chair is a chair which can take a bedpan in the place of its seat and a patient using it finds it much more like using an ordinary lavatory. Even those on complete bed-rest are often today allowed to get out of bed and use a commode chair because the effort and worry of this are much less than those associated with the use of the bedpan in bed. However, it is clear that bedpans must be used sometimes, and it is useful if radiographers in the X-ray department know how to deal with them.

The first step is to ensure privacy for the patient; a sense of lack of privacy is one of the trials to a patient in his life in the hospital ward. He should use the bedpan in a room where he can be private and not, for example, in a waiting bay or corridor surrounded by other patients. The bedpan should be brought to him with a cover over it. In modern hospital practice this cover is disposable, being paper, and its once-only use is a great aid to hygiene.

The bedpan should be clean and dry and neither too hot nor too cold. A cold pan is uncomfortable but is not so dangerous as a pan which is too hot. Carrying a bedpan, the radiographer should hold it firmly with both hands, keeping it away from all contact with the unprotected uniform coat; this is important for reasons of hygiene. Unlike nurses, radiographers do not usually have to issue a number of bedpans at a time and are therefore spared the temptation to load themselves up with a pile which is desperately clutched to their white-coated chests and abdomens in order to prevent the pans falling.

If the patient cannot help himself two radiographers assist him. They place themselves one on each side of him; the radiographer at the patient's left side puts her right arm under the patient's body at

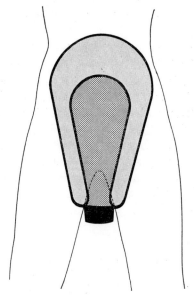

FIG. 34.
Placing a bedpan under a patient.

just below waist level, and the one on the patient's right side puts her left arm in a similar position. One radiographer then puts a free hand under the upper part of his thighs and together they raise the patient's body. The radiographer with one hand still free uses it to push the bedpan from the side to a position under the patient's buttocks. The sketch (Fig. 34) indicates the placing of the bedpan for a supine patient; if the 'front end' is not visible at the patient's crutch the bedpan is too far up his body to be useful.

If the patient is a very heavy weight it may take two radiographers and four hands to lift him, while a third radiographer puts the bedpan in place. If the patient can lift himself ably, it is of course easy for one radiographer to manage the procedure unaided.

Should the patient be able to sit up on the bedpan, care should be given to him to see that he does not fall off, particularly if he is liable to feel faint or dizzy or is not agile. Toilet paper should be available to be used.

When the bedpan has been used it should be removed by manoeuvres similar to those which placed it. The patient should be made comfortable and should be given the means—a bowl of warm water, soap and a paper towel—with which to wash and dry his hands.

The patient may have used the bedpan simply to evacuate an enema given to him in the X-ray department as preparation for or as part of a diagnostic procedure. In this case, once the results have been noted the bedpan, unless it is disposable, may be emptied down the lavatory and then washed and sterilized in readiness for further use. Disposable bedpans and urinals require special machinery for their disposal. The patient may be on a regime which involves saving his excreta through 24 hours for various tests or measuring his urine output. The radiographer should ascertain from the ward what must be done in regard to urine and faeces that may be passed while the patient is in the X-ray department.

GIVING AN ENEMA

Fluid may be injected into the large bowel via the rectum for various purposes, and it may be given either to be retained or to be returned. The purposes for which enemata are given are as follows:

(i) to cleanse the bowel and empty it of faeces,

(ii) to introduce drugs,

(iii) to introduce fluid if the patient is unable to take the normal amount by mouth and supplementary fluid is required,

(iv) to introduce a radiographic contrast agent for diagnostic purposes.

The radiographer's practical experience of enemata in the diagnostic X-ray department will be limited to the first and last of these purposes. Since specific aspects of the diagnostic enema are discussed in another place (Chapter vi), and certain general details of its administration are the same as those in the giving of a cleansing enema, in this section the practical aspects of giving an enema will be considered in relation to a cleansing enema and a rectal wash-out.

A Cleansing Enema

The fluid used may be either water or normal saline solution, or a soap and water mixture, and the quantity given will vary from several millilitres for a young child up to 1–2 litres for an adult. Ordinary tap water is used.

The soap and water enema is a long tried and traditional preparation; in hospital green 'soft soap' is often used, and should be dissolved in the proportion of an almond-sized piece (30 g) to 0.5 litre of water. It should be well dissolved in a small quantity of the water, the balance of the water then being added, and the solution strained before use.

Since the rectum and the bowel are not sterile body cavities, equipment used for the giving of an enema does not need to be sterile but it should be clean, and catheters and receivers should have been boiled after previous use. The trolley prepared is therefore not a sterile trolley; it is set up with the immediate requirements for giving the enema laid out on the upper shelf, and various accessories put in readiness on the lower shelf.

Trolley (upper shelf)

A large funnel or enema can. If a small quantity is to be given the funnel will be convenient, but for the larger amounts an enema can is the better choice.

A piece of rubber tubing 45–60 cm long connected to the funnel or enema can.

A glass connection to connect the rubber tubing to a rectal tube or stout rubber catheter. A Jacques oesophageal tube, size 8–12, may be used. The value of the glass connection is that as well as acting as a connection it allows visual assessment of whether the fluid is running properly.

A spring clip.

The first four items should be assembled together, and put in a bowl or receiver on the trolley top.

A jug containing the enema fluid.

A lotion thermometer to test the temperature of the solution.

It should be given at a temperature of 38° C (100° F); if it is too hot or too cold the fluid may be returned at once.

A suitable lubricant such as vaseline.

A gallipot containing squares of lint or clean rag with which to apply the lubricant.

Trolley (lower shelf)

A bedpan and cover. It is the usual practice to cover a bedpan when it is brought to the patient and removed, but the use of a cloth cover is often unhygienic, and the best cover is a disposable paper towel which is used once only.

A mackintosh or plastic square for putting under the patient's buttocks and a square of cellulose for covering it.

A receiver.

A bowl containing toilet paper and wool swabs.

Occasionally a Higginson's syringe may be used for giving an enema, and this replaces the enema can or funnel. The fluid to be injected is put into a bowl, and withdrawn from it by means of the Higginson's syringe.

The Higginson's syringe has certain disadvantages in use, so that it should not be chosen as preferred equipment for the giving of an enema. The disadvantages are (i) that considerable pressure can be achieved with this syringe, the operator having no close control over or knowledge of the pressure at which the enema is being given; and (ii) that the rigid bone nozzle of the syringe may perforate the rectal wall. This latter possibility may be prevented by attaching the usual rubber catheter to the nozzle of the syringe. The lack of control of pressure remains as an important reason for not using this method.

If the patient is not already in bed, he will have to lie down on a bed or examination couch in order to receive the enema. The patient must be given an explanation of the procedure before it is begun, this explanation being expressed in reassuring terms. The trolley is taken to the right-hand side of the bed or couch, and the patient is told to lie down on his left side with his knees and thighs flexed. He is so positioned that his buttocks are brought to the edge of the bed. Bedclothes should be turned down to mid-thigh level. The bed is protected by means of the waterproof square covered with cellulose.

With the enema can, tubing, and catheter connected together, the tip of the catheter should be well lubricated with vaseline applied by means of a tissue. Some of the fluid to be injected is poured into the can and allowed to run through the catheter into a receiver to dispel air in the tubing; there should be some fluid still in the can at the end of this procedure, or air will enter the system again at the top. The catheter is clipped with the spring clip, and it is then ready for insertion in the rectum.

In doing this, the radiographer must have no hesitation in making sure that it is possible to *see* what is being done. There must be a good light, and one hand should be used firmly to part the buttocks at the natal cleft so that the anal orifice is fully revealed. Only in this way can the catheter be inserted with the ease and sureness that make it least disagreeable for the patient. Inspection will show whether the patient has any haemorrhoids, a condition which will require very gentle insertion of the catheter, as the area is extremely sensitive; in the case of a female patient it will also allow the radiographer to be sure that the catheter is being inserted in the right orifice. It is easier than might be supposed for someone lacking experience and the wisdom to *look*, to put a catheter into the vaginal opening instead of the rectum.

It relaxes the anal sphincter and makes insertion easier if the patient is asked to bear down during the process. Without using force, the catheter is gently passed forwards and upwards until 7–10 cm of it have been inserted. It will be seen to be gripped by the anal sphincter. After a brief pause in which the enema can may be filled up, the tubing clip is released and the fluid is run in.

The enema should be given at low pressure, the pressure and speed of administration being controlled by the height of the enema can above the patient's body. This should be about 30 cm at the start, and should not exceed 45 cm. If the can is too high and the enema is given too quickly, the fluid will not flow right round to the caecum, the patient may not be able to take the full amount, and the fluid will be returned quickly. So time should be allowed for the enema to be given slowly and evenly, a pause being made if the patient complains of pain or the desire to evacuate. He should be encouraged to take the full amount. For evacuation of the colon up to 1 litre is required.

When the enema has been given, the catheter is removed from the rectum, disconnected from the tubing (which should be clipped off if the remaining contents of the can are not to escape), and placed in a receiver. When the patient's needs have been given attention, the catheter is flushed with cold water, and both it and the receiver are washed with warm soapy water to remove all grease, rinsed and then boiled for 5 minutes.

If the patient is able and mobile and the lavatory is closely adjacent, he may be sent to the lavatory to evacuate the enema. However, the radiographer should remain at hand to see that all goes well, and that the patient does not become ill or faint while he is in the lavatory; it is wise to advise him to leave the door unlocked, the radiographer giving an assurance to see that no one goes in while he is there. In a modern building a lavatory intended for patients' use may be fitted with a bolt which can be released from outside the door by means of a screwdriver or the rim of a coin.

If the patient is not well able to go to the lavatory, or if it is particularly important to observe the result of the enema, then he must be given a bedpan. The result should be observed as to amount, colour, character, and presence of blood.

By way of summary, the steps of the procedure are listed below.

(i) Collect the equipment;
(ii) explain to the patient and prepare him;
(iii) lubricate the end of the catheter;
(iv) run the enema fluid through the tubing and clip off;
(v) insert the catheter in the patient's rectum;
(vi) allow the enema fluid to pass into the rectum;
(vii) when the enema has been given, remove the tube;
(viii) give the patient a bedpan;
(ix) note the result;
(x) clear away the equipment.

A Rectal Wash-out

This is a means of cleansing and emptying the bowel, and it is undertaken as preparation for various procedures—for example, sigmoidoscopy, surgery to the rectum or colon, and the giving of a diagnostic enema in radiological investigation.

The fluid used is plain water or normal saline, and the quantity required will be up to 3.5 litres. It is given at a temperature of 38° C (100° F) and should therefore be prepared at a few degrees higher than this. The equipment needed is almost the same as that required for the giving of an enema except for the following: a large funnel is used instead of an enema can; the tubing connected to the funnel should be of a larger lumen to allow for the return of faeces; the bedpan is replaced by a large pail which is stood upon a square of waterproof material on the floor. It may be wise for the operator to wear a waterproof apron. The jug used for the wash-out fluid should be a large one in view of the quantity to be given. A small amount of disinfectant fluid should be put in the bottom of the pail.

With observance of the same technique as in the giving of an enema, the fluid is run in slowly, the funnel being kept filled from the jug. When 0.25–0.5 litre has been given it is siphoned back by inverting the funnel over the pail. More is then given, and the process is repeated until the returning fluid is clear.

THE CATHETERIZED PATIENT

Catheters are hollow tubes designed to be passed into cavities and passages of the body. The present section refers to the catheterization of the urinary bladder.

This may be undertaken for a variety of reasons—for example in cases of urinary retention when the patient cannot micturate naturally, a catheter is passed to relieve distension of the bladder. Catheterization is also done to obtain an uncontaminated specimen of urine so that it may be bacteriologically examined, and to empty the bladder prior to special procedures such as cystoscopy or surgery to the pelvic organs. After pelvic surgery, a self-retaining catheter may be inserted in order to keep the bladder wall collapsed, or to prevent contamination of an operation area. This catheter may be connected to tubing which drains urine into a bottle or plastic bag. There may also be an arrangement for tidal drainage of the bladder. In this process, a suitable lotion is dripped from a container into the bladder via a catheter, the fluid emptying by siphonage into a container.

In the X-ray department it may be necessary to catheterize a patient, and this will usually be done by a doctor or nurse. It is very important for the student to realize that the bladder, unlike the rectum, is a sterile body cavity, and that infection of the urinary tract can occur extremely easily when instruments and catheters are passed into it.

Catheterization is therefore always undertaken most carefully with regard to the sterilization of the catheters, and their subsequent manipulation into the tract, so that no contamination occurs.

Infection can occur from the catheter, the operator's hands, and the patient's skin. Some patients may require frequent catheterization (for example, paraplegic patients), and it is often the practice to give such patients chemotherapy in the form of drugs to combat any urinary infection which might arise.

It can be seen that preparing a trolley for catheterization of a patient involves the preparation of some sterile equipment. The technique of preparing a sterile trolley has already been described in an earlier section of this chapter, and need not be given again in detail. The methods for preserving sterility of the equipment which were stated in preparing for an intravenous injection should be meticulously applied to *any* procedures requiring sterile technique. They are therefore applicable in preparing a trolley for catheterization of the urinary bladder.

Various types of catheter are in use and any particular type of catheter will be available in different sizes. In modern practice catheters are usually made of plastic and are pre-sterilized by the manufacturer, each catheter in its own paper pack. Some may be of the self-retaining type. Ureteric catheters are straight fine catheters which are used for exploring the ureters, draining the pelvis of the kidney, and introducing a radiographic contrast agent in retrograde pyelography.

The requirements of a trolley prepared for catheterization are set out below. The provision of more than one sterile catheter allows for one to be accidentally contaminated, in which case it will be discarded and another used in its place.

Sterile (upper shelf)

Two or three sterile catheters.

Two pairs of sterile dissecting forceps (these may be used to hold the catheter for its introduction into the urethra).

A sterile bowl holding 8–10 sterile swabs and 3 sterile dressing towels.

A sterile bowl containing lotion for swabbing (for example, 'Hibitane' 1 in 10,000 in aqueous solution).

A large sterile receiver in which to receive the urine.

A graduated container in which to measure the urine.

For a male patient a lubricant such as sterile liquid paraffin. This may be issued in a small container holding enough for one use only; from this it will be poured into a sterile gallipot.

A gown and mask.

Non-sterile (lower shelf)

A light.

A mackintosh sheet and dressing towel to put under the patient's buttocks.

A container for used swabs.

A jar for used instruments.

These last two items may be replaced by paper bags attached with clips to the sides of the trolley, the one for used instruments on the left side and the bag for soiled swabs on the right.

If it is required to send a sterile specimen of urine for bacteriological examination, a screw-top sterile specimen jar should be included in the contents of the lower shelf.

It should be recognized that if the patient comes to the X-ray department with a catheter in place, then all parts of the catheter which are in the urethra and bladder or allow entry to the bladder (that is, all the *inside* of the catheter and some parts of the outside as well) are a sterile system. If the catheter is connected by rubber tubing to a container for drainage, then the inside of the tubing and of any container are included in the sterile system.

In handling and moving a catheterized patient, the radiographer must be careful at all times to see that the sterile system does not become open. If the catheter is closed with a spigot and the patient asks for the catheter to be released, then the spigot must be set down with care in a sterile container so that only its outer terminal is contaminated by the hands, or else it must be replaced with a fresh sterile one. The urine drained out of the catheter must be kept in a suitable container until the nurse in charge of the patient's ward can be notified of the amount and character of the urine passed.

If the catheter is connected to a tube and drainage container and it becomes disconnected while the patient is in the X-ray department, the catheter should be clamped, and the tubing and container returned intact to the ward with the patient, a report being given of what has occurred. If the catheter should come partly out, it should not be pushed back as this would mean insertion into the sterile area of a part of the catheter made unsterile by its extrusion. For the same reason no attempt should be made to replace a catheter which has come out completely. The ward should be notified of either of these occurrences.

R

Something has already been said of the patient who comes to the X-ray department with ureteric catheters inserted prior to retrograde pyelography. (Chapter VII.) If catheters have been placed in both ureters, they are generally strapped each to the inner aspect of the appropriate thigh with their ends placed in test-tubes. The right and left sides must not be confused, and the catheters should be handled carefully when they are withdrawn from the test-tubes for the pyelographic injection.

THE USE OF A SUCKER

In some patients it is necessary to remove the secretions of the trachea and the bronchial tree by a mechanical method that applies suction; this draws the secretions upwards through a catheter as a vacuum cleaner draws up its tube the dust from a carpet. This method is called mechanical aspiration of the secretions and the suction apparatus that does it is called briefly a sucker. It is usually electrically operated from a wall socket. Equipment is available which is independent of a mains supply, being operated by a foot pedal, and is thus suitable for taking to the scene of an accident.

A patient who cannot effectively cough up his own secretions requires the use of the sucker. There may be various reasons why the patient is unable to clear the secretions from his airways:

(i) he may be unconscious;

(ii) he may be debilitated;

(iii) he may have a depressed cough reflex as an effect of certain drugs;

(iv) he may have disabilities such as fractured ribs or muscle paralysis which limit coughing power;

(v) the secretions may be copious, viscous and so tenacious that they are difficult to cough up completely and the patient cannot clear the bronchial tree unaided.

If the secretions are left without attempt to remove them they run down into the bronchi. Here they block some region of the air tract and the normal passage of air is halted in that part of the lung which is distal to the block; air neither enters the lungs on inspiration nor leaves it on expiration. If this process occurs on a large scale the patient drowns in his own secretions and death is certain. It is to prevent this that suction is used. It may also be used in emergency resuscitation of a patient to make sure that he has a clear airway.

Catheters for attachment to the suction apparatus are of a soft plastic, are pre-sterilized by the manufacturer and are disposable, a new one being used for each session of suction. They are available with different diameters. One end of the catheter—the proximal end—is attached to the suction apparatus which is to draw up the secretions through the catheter and deposit them in a bottle or jar (usually filled with antiseptic solution) on the apparatus. The other end of the catheter (the distal end) is inserted into the patient's trachea.

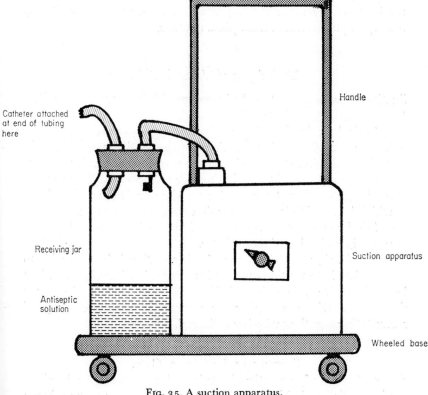

FIG. 35. A suction apparatus.

The way in may be through the patient's nose or mouth; if through the mouth it may be down an airway which has been inserted or through an endotracheal tube which has been placed in the trachea via the mouth *(endotracheal* means *inside the trachea)*. Or entry may be through a tracheostomy tube in an opening made in the upper trachea (see page 185 in Chapter xiv).

Fig. 35 is a sketch of one type of suction apparatus. Mounted on the wheeled base is the electrically driven machine which provides the vacuum pressure for suction. Controls on the metal cover make it possible to switch the machine on and off and to vary the vacuum pressure. Also mounted on the base is a glass jar into which the sucker discharges any matter which it brings up. A piece of tubing can be connected to the aperture on the cover of the jar and to the free end of this tubing (not shown in the illustration) the catheter in use is joined. The machine has a tall handle over it so that it may readily be pushed about from place to place.

Techniques of Using Suction

Suction may do a great deal of damage if it is incorrectly applied. Its dangers are threefold:

(i) the introduction of (or the increasing of an existing) infection by the use of techniques which are not sterile, particularly in patients who have had tracheostomy performed recently;

(ii) the collapse of part of a lung or of the whole lung because suction is continued for too long a time or because a catheter which is too wide is used through a tracheostomy tube;

(iii) damage to the mucous membranes of the tracheal wall by rough introduction of the catheter.

In considering the techniques of using suction it is reasonable to differentiate between those proper for a nurse looking after a patient in an intensive care unit and the techniques used in the X-ray department where a sucker may serve in the emergency of resuscitating a patient who has collapsed.

Suction in Intensive Care

A nurse looking after a patient in an intensive care unit may be given the instruction to 'suck him out' every so often—say every 2 hours —after a tracheostomy has been performed. The need for suction because a patient cannot effectively cough up his own secretions is one of the indications for performing this operation to make a hole in the trachea and place a tube in it (see page 184 in Chapter XIV). The nurse thus has an easy route for the catheter attached to the suction apparatus. She uses a sterile technique because it is important to protect the tracheostomy against infection, washes her hands before she touches the catheter and puts a sterile disposable glove on the hand which she is to use for handling the catheter, keeping the other hand for the 'dirty work' of controlling the suction machine.

The importance of the size of the catheter inserted down a tracheostomy tube is as follows. Once the suction has achieved its purpose of withdrawing sputum (this can be done in a few seconds), continued suction only draws air from the region of the lung where the catheter tip lies. Provided that this air can be easily replaced at once, all will be well (unless suction goes on for a long time), but if the air is not easily replaced, collapse of the lung follows as a serious consequence. Now if the catheter is smaller in diameter than the tracheostomy tube in the trachea (it should be not more than half the internal diameter of the tube) air rushes in from outside around the catheter in the tracheostomy tube to replace what is being sucked out and no harm is done. But if the catheter is nearly as wide as the tube, no air can easily get in and the rate of withdrawal can exceed the rate of replacement and trouble follows.

So the nurse selects a catheter of sufficient diameter to pass thick mucus but narrow enough to be less than half the diameter of the tracheostomy tube. The distal end is dipped into sterile normal saline solution (the purpose of this is to wet the catheter as a way of lubricating it) and after the solution has been allowed to drain off it, the catheter tip is put into the tracheostomy tube. The catheter is then gently pushed down as far as it will go. The outer end of the catheter is attached to the sucker via a length of sterile plastic tubing and suction can be applied from the apparatus. To lessen the risk of collapsing the lung it is the practice to apply suction only as the catheter is being gradually withdrawn and for no longer than about 3 to 5 seconds.

SUCTION IN THE X-RAY DEPARTMENT

In the X-ray department a sucker can be a useful piece of equipment in an emergency of resuscitating a patient who has collapsed (see pages 250–259 in Chapter XVII). If the patient has stopped breathing and expired air resuscitation is to be used, it will be a waste of time to apply it and to continue it if the patient has not a clear airway. The suction apparatus can be used to clear an airway, the catheter being inserted into the patient's mouth and the tip passed round the mouth, pharynx, larynx and upper trachea to draw out matter which may be obstructing these parts of the respiratory tract. It will take only a few seconds to do.

CHAPTER XVII

FIRST AID IN THE X-RAY DEPARTMENT

First aid is the immediate treatment given to a patient by those who are present when an emergency condition arises. While working in the X-ray department, radiographers may be required to help patients in various states that need immediate treatment or immediate assistance. It is clear that certain first aid procedures (for example treatment of victims rescued from drowning or found with coal gas poisoning) are *not* likely to be used in the X-ray department. There are, however, several conditions which will be quite commonly encountered (for example epileptic fits, faintness, nausea and vomiting), and knowledge of what to do for the patient in these circumstances is certainly necessary to a radiographer. Since accidents may happen in spite of every precaution, simple principles of first aid for certain types of accident should also be known.

It should be taken as a general rule by student radiographers that immediate seniors should be informed and fetched to the scene if something untoward happens to a patient who may be alone with the student, even if the incident appears to be transient in its effect. This does *not* mean that the patient should be abandoned while others are fetched. The student should stay with the patient to give such immediate aid as may be required, if necessary calling out to attract the attention of others. The student should *not* transmit to the patient a sense of anxiety, but should certainly report to seniors anything about a patient which gives cause for anxiety, though it may seem trivial.

Even if no medical assistance has been required at the time, it will be usual for the radiographer to report further what has happened—in some cases to the radiologist, in others to the ward staff or to the medical officer who referred the patient for X-ray examination. In the event of an accident in the department a full report must be made in writing at the time.

249

RADIOLOGICAL EMERGENCIES

The term *radiological emergency* has come to be associated in particular with a dangerous condition arising in a patient as the result of the use of a radiological contrast agent. (See also Chapter VII.) However, an emergency may be precipitated not necessarily by this but by some other cause, for example the administration of a local anaesthetic, pre-existent cardiovascular disease, or even an accident such as electric shock.

Depending on the cause, details of the treatment naturally will vary but the several treatments of serious emergencies overlap to a large extent. The professional responsibility of the radiographer does not extend to decisions about medical treatment. This section will be concerned only with those measures of immediate aid with which every radiographer should be conversant. It is upon the rapidity with which appropriate action can be taken by the person nearest at hand that the patient's life may depend; the nearest person is quite likely to be the radiographer making the X-ray examination or even a senior student who is assisting at it.

In any medical emergency of this kind, as has been said, the radiographer or student must at once call or send for medical assistance. X-ray rooms should be provided with an alarm system so that the radiographer may easily obtain help without having to leave the patient. The two most urgent situations are cardiac arrest (cessation of the heartbeat) and respiratory arrest (failure to breathe) and these are discussed below.

Cardiac and Respiratory Arrest

A patient whose brain is deprived of oxygenated blood for longer than 3–4 minutes is likely to suffer irreversible cerebral damage. It is consequently of supreme importance that the diagnosis of cardiac arrest be made quickly and treatment be begun quickly. Cardiac arrest cannot be treated on its own, since it will be accompanied by respiratory failure; restored cerebral circulation is of no use to the patient if the blood is inadequately oxygenated.

In a patient who appears to have collapsed the signs of cardiac arrest are:

(1) absence of a palpable arterial pulse;
(2) dilatation of the pupils (a late sign, not seen within 1 minute);

(3) pallor or cyanosis;

(4) failure to bleed (a scratch or incision about 2.5 cm long may be made on an accessible portion of the skin);

(5) convulsions (these occur sometimes as a secondary manifestation of diminished cardiac output).

The above observations should be made within 20–30 seconds of the onset of disaster. In the list, (2), (3) and (5) can occur from other causes. Absence of the arterial pulse is of decisive significance and the radiographer must not hesitate to look for it while awaiting the arrival of medical aid. In a later section of this chapter the pressure points for a number of arteries are given. In the present emergency the pulse may be palpated at any convenient point related to a large artery in the body. However, the carotid artery is perhaps the one of choice since it can be felt in either side of the neck relatively easily by the inexperienced. The two first fingers of one hand should be used to palpate the artery at the anterior border of the sternomastoid muscle, level with the upper edge of the thyroid cartilage (colloquially the 'Adam's apple').

If cardiac arrest is thought to have occurred, or even is suspected, the single-handed operator has to face the problem of whether to tackle first the cardiac or respiratory failure. If two people are present, then the conditions can be treated simultaneously by the methods listed below under the headings CARDIAC STIMULATION and PULMONARY VENTILATION. The worker who is alone is justified in assuming that, unless the respiratory failure has preceded the cardiac arrest, there will be a small amount of oxygenated air present in the lungs and should therefore concentrate on cardiac stimulation in the first instance; however, efforts at pulmonary ventilation should not be long delayed. If the respiratory failure has occurred first then obviously it will be treated first. In the case of a cardiac arrest occurring in the X-ray department as a result of the administration of a contrast agent, the presence of primary respiratory failure is not likely.

CARDIAC STIMULATION

(1) Lay the patient supine with the head low.

(2) Thump the lower part of the sternum sharply with the ulnar border of the hand. This is known as *praecordial percussion*. It may result in one or two irregular heartbeats which will be followed by a normal cardiac rhythm. If it is effective the pulse will

be immediately detectable and if necessary the percussion can be continued at the rate of 60 strokes per minute.

(3) Raise the legs and if possible the upper limbs as well. Another useful manœuvre is forcible flexion of the hips and knees to bring the thighs sharply against the lower trunk; it may produce a rush of blood into the right atrium which is sufficient to initiate a cardiac impulse.

If there is no response to this and to two or three praecordial thumps, proceed to:

(4) External cardiac massage.

EXTERNAL CARDIAC MASSAGE

External cardiac massage is perfomed by means of rhythmic manual compression of the sternum. For it to be successful the patient must be supine upon a *hard* surface. The floor or the X-ray table is suitable but if the patient is on a mattress he should be moved to the floor, or a board or similar structure, for example a large cassette, should be placed at the back of the thorax. The operator should make certain that the patient has a clear airway; the head should be tilted back.

To perform external cardiac massage the operator should position himself on the patient's right and should place the heel of the right hand over the lower sternum; the other hand is superimposed on its fellow in the manner shown in Fig. 36. Pressure is applied vertically downwards 80 times per minute. The operator should be in a position to make use of his body weight for each thrust—that is, his arms should be stiffened and the sternum should move 3–4 cm towards the vertebral column at every compression. The flaccid condition of the chest wall makes effective movement of the sternum relatively easy to attain. Between compressions the hands should be lifted slightly to permit the chest to expand. Excessive pressure should be avoided. If the operator is a male adult it is probable that external cardiac massage can be efficiently performed with the use of the right hand only, unless the patient is large and the chest unusually rigid. In children up to 10 years of age the force of the heel of one hand is always sufficient; in neo-natal infants probably no more than pressure from the fingers alone is required. Since in a young child the heart is relatively higher in the chest, the pressure should be applied over the mid-sternum. Circulation may be deemed adequate if the pupils are contracted.

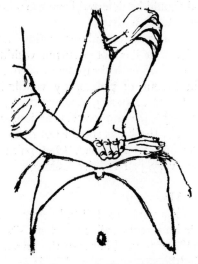

Fig. 36. Illustration of the technique of performing external cardiac massage. The upper drawing shows the way in which the hands should be positioned. The lower drawing indicates the correct site for applying the compression. *By courtesy of The British Journal of Radiology.*

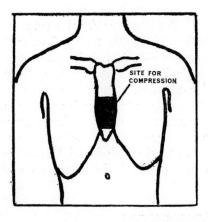

In the performance of external cardiac massage it is important to remember that the pressure should be applied *only* to the sternum: otherwise rib fractures, haemothorax and liver lacerations have been known to occur. The occurrence of extensive rib fractures necessarily diminishes the efficacy of the performance which depends partly on a general increase in the intrathoracic pressure. However, no one in hospital should be deterred from the manoeuvre by lack of much previous experience with it.

If cardiac massage is successful respiration may sometimes return spontaneously. If it has not occurred within 30 seconds and the operator is still alone with the patient, cardiac massage should be interrupted in favour of pulmonary ventilation and the two procedures then alternate. After 15 cardiac thrusts, give 2 pulmonary ventilations. If two people are present and able to perform the manœuvres in unison, the lungs should not be inflated at the same time that the sternum is depressed. One pulmonary ventilation should be made to every 5 sternal depressions.

Direct Cardiac Massage

Should external cardiac massage fail to be successful a physician on arrival may decide on direct cardiac massage. The thorax is opened and the heart itself compressed between the fingers of a hand introduced through the thoracotomy wound. It is *not* a procedure upon which any but a qualified medical officer should embark and is redoubtable enough even then, unless he is experienced in thoracotomy.

Pulmonary Ventilation

Despite its impressive syllables the term *pulmonary ventilation* refers to the simple processes by which it is sought to re-oxygenate the lungs of a patient who is in respiratory failure. These are:
(1) artificial respiration;
(2) the supplementary administration of oxygen.
A number of means of performing artificial respiration are known and have been used to good effect. However, at present the method most widely advocated is the one which is known properly as *expired air resuscitation* and popularly in magazines and newspapers as 'the kiss of life'.

Expired Air Resuscitation

The essence of this procedure is that the operator employs his own exhaled breath to inflate the lungs of the patient. He does this by placing his mouth either directly upon the patient's mouth, or to an airway in the patient's mouth, or sometimes to the patient's nose, the mouth being kept closed; in the case of a small child the mouth and nose can be entered simultaneously. Some anaesthetists suggest

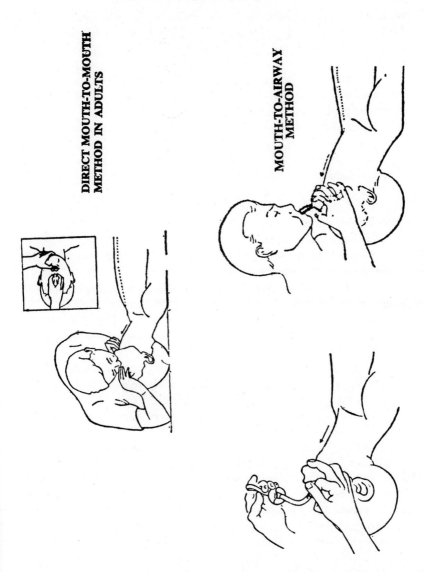

DIRECT MOUTH-TO-MOUTH
METHOD IN ADULTS

MOUTH-TO-AIRWAY
METHOD

Fig. 37. Illustration to show the technique of performing expired air resuscitation. The upper drawing shows the direct mouth-to-mouth method in adults. The lower drawing shows the mouth-to-airway method. *By courtesy of The British Journal of Radiology.*

that mouth-to-nose inflation is the easier of the two methods; this presupposes a clear nose and a mouth which does not sag open.

For the sake of simplicity the procedure will be described below as direct mouth-to-mouth respiration. Its steps are as follows.

(1) Make sure by swabbing the patient's mouth that no foreign material is present which may prevent him from breathing, particularly if he has been vomiting.

(2) Maintain a clear airway by pulling the patient's jaw upwards, using your left thumb placed between his teeth in the manner shown in the upper drawing in Fig. 37. Keep the head tilted back.

(3) Catch the patient's nostrils firmly between the flexed index and middle fingers of your right hand to prevent any escape of air by this route.

(4) Take a deep breath.

(5) Open your mouth wide and place it tightly over both the patient's mouth and your own thumb.

(6) Exhale—forcibly if the patient is an adult, in a gentle puff if he is a small child.

(7) The patient's chest should be seen to rise. If it does not do so, suspect the presence of an obstruction and check this possibility again.

(8) Remove your mouth to allow the patient to exhale (which he will do at first passively owing to the elastic recoil of his lungs), and yourself to take a fresh breath. Repeat from (4), continuing at the rate of one inflation every 5 seconds, until the patient is breathing naturally.

This method of artificial respiration needs little practice and little knowledge for successful use. It can be employed rapidly on the onset of respiratory emergency, since it does not require the patient to be moved, as do some other methods, into a special position which might necessitate his being taken off the X-ray table. It can be applied instantly by a radiographer alone with the patient. It can do no possible harm if it is begun by someone who believes, but is not absolutely certain, that the patient is lifeless.

The operator should take deep breaths, equivalent to about twice his normal tidal volume. The oxygen content of expired air is naturally lower than atmospheric air, being about 14–18 per cent as against 21 per cent. Deep inhalations provide exhalations which are of use to the patient and can maintain the oxygen tension in his

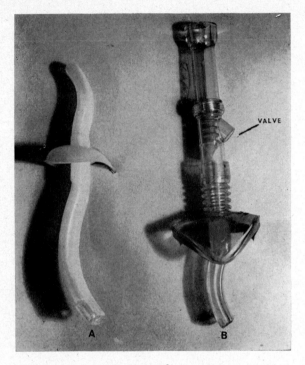

Plate XIII   Resuscitation airways. The airway on the left is of a simple type, the short end being suitable for a child and the longer end for an adult. The airway on the right is the Brook airway. (By courtesy of the *British Journal of Radiology*.)

arterial blood nearly at its normal level. The carbon dioxide present in the exhaled breath has a useful function in stimulating the respiratory centre of the brain.

Should the operator who has to continue the procedure for long become dizzy or feel himself grow faint he is suffering from the effects of over-ventilation and has probably been breathing too fast; he should decrease his rate in this event. Like most methods of artificial respiration, expired air resuscitation is tiring but should not otherwise cause physical disturbance. It is often said that the main objection to it is an aesthetic revulsion from mouth-to-mouth contact with a stranger. However, nice considerations of hygiene can hardly be of much weight when the patient is in such an extreme condition.

The procedure can be made to seem more hygienic and acceptable if an airway is available and can be inserted; this may be impossible if the jaw is tightly closed. The airway can be of a simple type; or the Brook Airway is one especially designed for expired air resuscitation. It incorporates a mouth guard which provides a seal against the escape of air directed at the lungs, an airway valve which allows the exhaled air of the patient to escape through an exhaust port, and a blow tube which fits into the airway valve and gives a mouthpiece for the person blowing so that his own mouth is not in direct contact with the patient's. The presence of the valve in this airway increases the resistance offered and the operator must blow a little harder.

Two types of airway are illustrated in Plate xiii. The simpler one is suitable for either an adult or a child; the other is the Brook Airway.

Administration of Oxygen

Oxygen administered by a face mask is helpful treatment in all instances of radiological emergency. The general procedure is described in a special section of the previous chapter and will not be detailed here. When expired air resuscitation is performed through an airway, oxygen may sometimes be used supplementarily. Fed gently through a narrow tube into a corner of the operator's mouth it will enrich his breath in the patient's favour. Obviously it would come as a second stage of treatment since, confronted with respiratory arrest, no one should lose time in any way before beginning resuscitation.

Equipment for Emergencies

In order to be prepared for the treatment of these emergencies X-ray rooms where contrast examinations are performed should carry certain equipment. This includes as essentials:

(1) an alarm system;

(2) an oxygen cylinder with a reducing valve and suitable mask or respirator (Chapter xvi);

(3) a Brook or other resuscitation airway;

(4) a mouth gag;

(5) a laryngoscope;

(6) a sterile pack containing the instruments listed at the end of this section;

(7) a supply of drugs in appropriate ampoules which may be used in resuscitation (Chapter iii).

To this minimum list of equipment may be added at the discretion of the radiologist in charge such other items as:

(1) suction apparatus (see page 244 in Chapter xvi);

(2) a tracheostomy set;

(3) a transfusion set;

(4) a sphygmomanometer and a stethoscope.

Furthermore, it is advisable to have certain other equipment available within easy reach for use when the first stage of emergency has been weathered. This need not be maintained in the X-ray room or even in the X-ray department: for example it might be kept in an annexe to the operating theatre or in the casualty department. The important things are that it should be readily accessible and that every member of the X-ray staff should know where to find it.

This accessory equipment should include an E.C.G. machine and an instrument known as a defibrillator. The first of these is an apparatus for visualizing and recording the heart's beat in the form of electrical impulses and tracings (electrocardiographs). The defibrillator also is an electrical instrument. Fibrillation is an abnormal twitching rhythm of the heart: isolated segments of its muscle contract, out of concert with each other. This condition may be corrected by the influence of an electrical shock. The machine is used to administer a single shock or a series of rapid electric shocks to the cardiac muscle which result in a momentary absence of systole. The heart is restarted under the control of a pacemaker which initiates a normal co-ordinated rhythm of contraction.

THE STERILE PACK

The emergency sterile pack should contain the following items.

Two 10 ml syringes with eccentric nozzles.

One 5 ml syringe of similar type.

Needles to fit the above and suitable for intravenous and hypodermic injection; for example Nos. 1, 2, 12 and 18.

These syringes and needles are usually of the disposable type and are already packed and sterilized.

Two fine exploring needles.

A cannula to fit the syringes for the purpose of withdrawing the contents of an ampoule.

A pair of Mayo scissors.

A large scalpel.

A pair of dissecting forceps.

One or two pairs of Spencer Wells artery forceps.

A few gauze swabs.

If it is not opened this pack will remain sterile for some while but should be regularly sent for autoclaving at intervals of a few weeks. The opportunity should be taken at this time to check the contents for good working order: for instance, a glass syringe may be found to have cracked during the last process of sterilization and at this juncture can readily be replaced. The scalpel blade should be renewed after alternate steam sterilizations as such blades quickly become rusty.

If the X-ray department is served by a system of central sterile supply, most of this equipment is likely to be available in a pre-packed or disposable form.

SHOCK

This state is an easily recognized condition in patients after injury. It is particularly liable to occur when there has been loss of blood or plasma. The blood loss may not be apparent as visible haemorrhage. For example, a fracture of the femur may result in a loss of 20–30 per cent of the total blood volume into the soft tissues of the thigh. Extensive burns give rise to severe loss of plasma.

While shock is more likely to follow a severe injury, patients

S

show variation due to differences in age, general physical constitution, and temperament, and the degree of shock which will follow any given injury is not predictable, though its likelihood can be foreseen. The physical injury may seem relatively trivial, for the condition of shock may be produced by mental forces acting on physical processes, and can follow from fright and alarm as well as other emotionally disturbing experiences. It is, however, generally agreed that the most important cause of shock is loss of whole blood or plasma from the circulation. Shock can be immediate or delayed, and can vary in degree from slight shock to a condition which is fatal.

The general picture presented by the patient is due to the fact that his body is without a full volume of circulating blood. His state is one of general depression of bodily functions in which the blood vessels are more flaccid than they should normally be and the heart beat has lost force. As has been said, there is usually reduction in the amount of blood available to circulate owing to fluid loss.

The patient has lowered blood pressure. His pulse is rapid as the heartbeat increases its rate in an effort to make more blood circulate and provide the patient with more oxygen. At the same time the force of the pulse feels weak. The patient is pale and cold, and he may be sweating and restless. His breathing may be shallow and slow, or it may be sighing in character.

The general treatment is to keep the patient lying down at rest so far as is possible, and to give him some degree of warmth without overheating. His head should be kept low and turned on one side unless there is injury to the head, chest, and abdomen; in these cases the head and shoulders should be slightly raised.

If the patient has vomited or seems breathless he should be placed so that he is nearly prone—half-way between lying on his side and lying face downwards (see Plate vi)—provided that he has no injuries which make it necessary that he should not be turned into this position. An atmosphere of reassurance and confidence will comfort him as he is mentally in an anxious state of distress.

The radiographer will see many patients in a condition of shock while carrying out X-ray examinations on those who have been injured. These general procedures of treatment indicate how such patients should be handled. The patient should not be put erect, or be uncovered more, or for a longer period, than is necessary for the purposes of the X-ray examination.

HAEMORRHAGE

Haemorrhage may be bleeding from a visible site, known as external haemorrhage, or it may be bleeding which takes place internally. In this case it may be revealed by escape of blood from a natural body orifice.

External Haemorrhage

Haemorrhage may be (i) arterial, (ii) venous, and (iii) capillary. When the bleeding takes place from an external wound the type of haemorrhage can be recognized by the colour of the blood and the way in which it escapes.

Arterial haemorrhage produces bright red blood issuing in spurts which may be of considerable force if a large artery has been damaged. *Venous haemorrhage* causes a steady flow of darker blood. If a large vein is damaged there is a rapid flow of blood, but this type of bleeding is easier to control than that which comes from arteries, when there is much greater pressure behind it. *Capillary haemorrhage* produces a general oozing which is not difficult to control.

Nature stops the bleeding first of all by contraction of severed vessel walls, secondly by clotting of the blood, and thirdly by lowering of the pressure of the blood within the vessel walls.

A patient who has lost a lot of blood shows paleness of skin and lips. As the reduced amount of blood is unable to carry sufficient oxygen, the body attempts to compensate for this by an increase in the rate at which it is pumped round by the heart; although more rapid, the pulse feels weak in force. The patient may breathe with deep and long inspirations because of his need for more oxygen. There is decrease in the body temperature because of the fluid loss, and his skin is cold and clammy. He is restless, anxious, thirsty, and feels faint.

The first aid treatment for haemorrhage is directed towards its arrest. If the haemorrhage is external, the first action should be to apply pressure to the wound, if possible with a clean, firm pad. It may, however, be more important to apply the pressure as quickly as possible (for example if the bleeding is arterial and profuse), and in that case the radiographer's thumbs should be pressed on the wound. Firm pressure should be maintained.

In order to aid lowering of the blood pressure, the patient should be put lying flat. His head should be lowered if possible, unless the bleeding is from head or neck. If the site of haemorrhage is a limb, the limb should be elevated unless there is suspicion of a fracture. Medical assistance should be sought, and the patient should be reassured. It is generally recommended that the patient should be kept warm, but overheating is to be avoided.

It may be presumed that in the X-ray department medical assistance will be available before much time has passed, and it is unlikely that the radiographer will have to maintain for long unaided first aid measures for haemorrhage. The direct pressure on the wound and the general procedures described are probably all that will be required.

If it is not possible to apply direct pressure successfully, indirect pressure may be tried at a point between the wound and the heart. The artery is compressed where it is superficial and lies over a bone against which it can be firmly pressed. Such pressure should not be maintained for longer than 15 minutes.

For example, the pressure point for the brachial artery is against the inner side of the humerus about half-way between the medial epicondyle and the axilla, the pressure being directed posterolaterally. The inner seam of a coat sleeve is in a position which approximately indicates the course of this artery.

The radial artery is compressible against the distal edge of the radius at the anterior aspect of the wrist joint.

Indirect pressure for the femoral artery is against the bony pelvis at a point where the vessel enters the thigh midway between the symphysis pubis and the anterior superior iliac spine—that is the centre of the groin.

In cases where pressure on the wound and over the main artery at a pressure point have both failed to arrest the haemorrhage, the application of a tourniquet has been described. There are certain risks attached to this procedure.

The tourniquet must be tight to be effective, and it will then cut off the entire blood supply to the limb (obviously a tourniquet cannot be applied to parts of the body other than the limbs). This deprivation of blood can produce a paralysis of the limb if it continues too long, and gangrene could be a later result. A tourniquet should be cautiously released after 15 minutes' application. In accidents occurring in the X-ray department it is unlikely that a tourniquet will be necessary, and probably the radiographer would be wiser not to consider applying one unless medical help is very much longer in coming than might be expected, and the bleeding proves impossible to control by other methods. If a tourniquet *is* applied, the time of application should be marked upon the patient (an ordinary ball-point pen can be used for skin marking); or some responsible person should be told of the time of application when the patient leaves the radiographer's care.

Revealed Internal Haemorrhage

Emergencies may arise in the X-ray department when patients have haemorrhage as a result of disease processes in the body. The patient may, for example, vomit blood from the alimentary tract, or cough blood from the lungs. The vomiting of blood is called haematemesis; the coughing of blood is called haemoptysis. Vomited blood is dark in colour, and blood from the lungs is bright red and frothy, readily distinguished from blood which is vomited.

Clearly there can be no question of applying pressure in either of these conditions, since there is no external wound. The first aid measures are the general ones previously described to be undertaken while medical advice is obtained.

The patient should be reassured and kept at rest as comfortably as possible in a place of privacy, even if the privacy can be only that provided by a screen placed round him. If he is continuing to vomit or cough, he should be assisted in this. The radiographer should provide a bowl and hold it for him, and wipe his mouth every so often with a clean tissue. He will find it easier if he can be supported sitting up, but if this is impossible (he may be too ill to attempt it), then he will have to be positioned and supported lying down with his head turned to one side. The best type of bowl to use is a kidney shaped receiver, as the concavity of the curve fits under the patient's chin and makes a more efficient arrangement. If the patient can take it, water may be given by mouth; in the case of haematemesis it will be beneficial if the water is ice cold. All vomited material should be saved for medical inspection.

Bleeding from the Nose (Epistaxis)

The patient should be supported sitting up with his head held forward, and he should be told to breathe through his mouth. Direct pressure is easily applied by compressing both nostrils firmly between finger and thumb, or by compressing the affected nostril with an index finger against the nasal septum. This is likely to be the most effectual way to arrest the haemorrhage in a young subject, when the bleeding is often from a point inside the nostril on the septum of the nose. If the bleeding is persistent and severe, medical advice should be sought.

In an elderly person the bleeding may be from within the bony part of the nose, and thus the point of haemorrhage cannot be compressed. The patient should lie flat with his face turned downwards, and he should be given a bowl into which the blood and saliva may flow. He should be told to breathe through his mouth and not to swallow; a cork placed between his teeth to hold his mouth open will aid him in carrying out both these instructions. He should be discouraged from hawking and spitting in an effort to clear his throat of any blood which has flowed into it, since this activity tends to prevent natural blockage of the nose by clotting which will occur to arrest the haemorrhage. If the bleeding is persistent and severe, medical advice must be sought.

First aid measures described for epistaxis usually include applications of cold, either as a cold compress or with an ice cube held to the bridge of the nose. These procedures can certainly do no harm, but they are in fact likely to be of little effect in arresting the haemorrhage.

BURNS AND SCALDS

These two are grouped together for both are injuries produced by heat, the burn by dry heat and the scald by moist heat. First aid treatment is the same for both conditions. The important features to appreciate with regard to this type of injury are (i) that it can be serious even though superficial in character if a large enough skin area is involved; (ii) the degree of pain and shock which will accompany an extensive burn, for such burns even if superficial result in loss of plasma; (iii) the danger of infection and sepsis, to which burns are particularly liable.

The best action to take *first* is to immerse the burnt area as soon as possible in cold water. This lowers the temperature of involved tissues and reduces damage. The affected part should be kept in the water until the heat and pain have decreased. The burnt area should then be covered as soon as possible with a dry dressing, preferably a sterile one; if not sterile, the dressing material must be clean. It should be material with a smooth surface so that there is no fluffiness or roughness of texture to stick to the burned part. If the area is large, sterile or clean dressing towels may be used. Clothing which covers the injury is best left as it is, and should not be cut and pulled away if it is burned on to the skin. In the case of a scald, if the clothing is soaked with boiling water it should obviously be removed.

The extent of the treatment required depends on the severity of the injury. If the burn is superficial and not extensive, the sterile dressing will be all that is needed. A more severe and extensive injury requires medical attention. A badly burned patient will be in great pain and a state of shock, and should be kept quiet and reassured while waiting for medical aid, which should be obtained as soon as possible.

LOSS OF CONSCIOUSNESS

Various causes produce loss of consciousness in a patient. The loss of consciousness may be partial, when it is called *stupor*; or it may be complete, when it is called *coma*. It should be possible to differentiate the probable causes of the state by observation of the onset and the condition of the patient.

The radiographer faced with this emergency should remember to notice such details as whether the onset was sudden or gradual, whether the patient's skin is dry or moist, hot or cold, whether his face is pale, red, or cyanosed, whether his body and limbs are rigid or slack or in spasmodic muscular contraction, and whether there is incontinence of urine or faeces. A clear report of details such as these will be of value to a doctor who may be called upon to diagnose the cause of the loss of consciousness.

Fainting Attack

The simplest cause of loss of consciousness is a fainting attack; this is due to a temporarily impaired supply of blood to the brain. The condition may arise through emotional causes such as fear or receipt of bad news, or through physical stresses such as being in a stuffy room, or in want of food, or in a fatigued state.

The patient looks pale and is sweating visibly on the forehead and about the mouth. He may complain of feeling dizzy, nauseated, or faint, for the loss of consciousness is not sudden. At this stage it may be prevented if the patient lies flat, on the floor if necessary.

If this assistance is to succeed in preventing loss of consciousness, it must be given at once as soon as it is recognized that the patient is feeling faint. It is useless to try to remove him to another place for he will probably faint before he gets there.

Sometimes it will not be realized that the patient is feeling faint, and the first intimation that something is wrong will be his loss of consciousness. This could easily occur, for instance, in the screening room where concentration upon the fluorescent screen and screening technique makes it difficult to maintain steady observation of the patient. If he has lost consciousness, he should be allowed to lie flat where he is (unless it is a position of danger). Tight clothing should be loosened. A plentiful supply of fresh air will help.

Usually patients recover from a simple fainting attack quite quickly. Afterwards the patient should rest for a while, and may be given hot tea or coffee or a drink of water. If he is slow to recover, medical advice should be sought.

Epileptic Fits

The epileptic fit is a common cause of loss of consciousness. It is readily distinguished from the simple fainting attack because it is entirely different in character, a convulsive stage preceding the stage of coma. During the convulsive period there are involuntary spasmodic contractions of muscles. The patient may be a known epileptic with a history of previous similar attacks.

There are certain stages of an epileptic seizure. The first of these may be known only to the patient. Its exact nature is peculiar to the patient and it is described as an 'aura'—it takes the form of a sensory disturbance of some type (for example a feeling of dizziness, a visual phenomenon such as flashes of light before the eyes, or a general sensation of unease). This warning may be of help to the patient, for if he is used to having epileptic attacks he will recognize it, and may be able to lie down before the seizure begins.

The warning is followed rapidly by the next stage of the fit. The patient usually cries out and then becomes unconscious. In this stage, which lasts for about half a minute, he is rigid and cyanosed, respiration having ceased, and the eyes are turned upwards.

The stage following is the convulsive one in which violent spasmodic movements of the limbs and body occur. Foam appears at the patient's mouth, and there may be incontinence of urine or faeces. This stage lasts for about a minute, and is succeeded by a stage of coma and often sleep.

The first aid treatment of any convulsive type of fit is directed to preventing injury to the patient if and when he becomes unconscious and during the convulsive stage. The patient with an epileptic seizure will probably have fallen to the ground by the time it is realized that he is having a fit, unless of course he was already lying down. If he has not fallen into a position of danger, he need not be moved, and tight clothing should be loosened.

When the convulsive stage is reached, the movements of the limbs should not be restrained unless they are likely to result in the patient hurting himself. If he is lying on an X-ray table, the spasms may cause him to fall off, and care must be exercised to prevent this happening. He is very likely to bite his tongue. To prevent this a gag should be put into his mouth between the teeth. In the absence of a Hewitt's peg (a wedge-shaped peg of wood for this purpose), whatever is to hand must be taken. For example, scissors with a handkerchief wrapped round the blades might be used if they are of the round-tipped type. A pencil is hardly strong enough and may break in the patient's mouth. A towel or several thicknesses of gauze, lint, or the disposable type of clinical sheet can be made to serve. Unprotected fingers can get bitten, and the radiographer should be careful to avoid the possibility when putting in the gag. No attempt should be made to prise open the patient's mouth and any gag should be inserted only when opportunity occurs.

When the fit is over, the patient should be allowed to rest. The occurrence of the fit should be reported and the patient (even if he is a known epileptic) should not be allowed to go home unaccompanied.

As well as the major epilepsy which has been described, there is a condition known as minor epilepsy in which the patient has loss of consciousness without the convulsive movements, the unconscious stage being very brief. The name *grand mal* is sometimes given to major epilepsy, and *petit mal* to the minor variant.

Other Causes of Loss of Consciousness

Two causes of sudden loss of consciousness in patients who previously may have appeared relatively well are (i) in diabetic patients, the insulin coma which was discussed in Chapter vi; and (ii) cerebral haemorrhage. This condition is commonly known as a stroke, and it is due to rupture of a blood vessel in the brain. The patient is often a man above middle age. He is completely unconscious, breathing stertorously, and may be flushed in the face. His cheeks may be seen to puff in and out as he breathes; this is due to laxity of the face muscles, for all muscles are in a flaccid state.

False teeth and spectacles should be removed and a clear airway maintained by turning the head to one side and pulling the lower jaw forward, as described on page 256. Medical assistance must be sought.

ASPHYXIA

In this condition the patient is unable to obtain air when he breathes. This may be because (i) there is some obstruction to his airway, as is the case after inhalation of a foreign body; (ii) there is some impairment of the physiological sequences of respiration, as is the case in paralysis of the respiratory muscles and inactivity of the respiratory centre of the brain which can result from certain infections and certain drugs; (iii) he is breathing a medium which gives him no air, as is the case in asphyxia by poisonous gases.

The first step in aiding a patient in this condition is to remove the cause of the asphyxia if this can be done, and to send for medical assistance. It should be made certain that the airway is clear, and it may be of help to give oxygen by mask. If the patient stops breathing some form of artificial respiration must be started immediately. The method of expired air resuscitation ('mouth to mouth breathing') is described in the first section of this chapter

FRACTURES

In medical terminology the word fracture means a broken bone. There are many types of fracture which can occur, some of them differentiated by special names, usually the name of someone who first described the fracture in relation to certain bones and certain displacements of the broken parts. Examples are Colles' fracture, involving the distal ends of radius and ulna, and Pott's fracture involving the distal ends of the tibia and fibula. The radiographer will often see such terms on request forms for X-ray examination of injured patients.

However, there are two *general* classifications of fractures which are important. Either the fracture is a *simple* one in which there is no communication between the fracture site and the open air; or it is a *compound* fracture in which there *is* communication between the fracture site and the open air through a skin wound.

Other considerations being equal, a compound fracture is the more serious injury, being liable to infection. No simple fracture should be allowed to become a compound one through careless handling. Any open wound should be covered as soon as possible with a sterile dressing; if this is not available a clean dry dressing must be applied.

The signs of a fracture include pain and tenderness at the site of the injury, loss of function, swelling, bruising, obvious deformity of the part. A doctor during examination may discover the un-natural movement between parts of a bone which gives further indication that a fracture has occurred. Some degree of shock may be present.

If an accident occurs in the X-ray department and there is sus-picion or certainty that the victim has a fracture, he must be referred for examination, and treatment by a doctor. In the meanwhile the immediate care given him must ensure that there is no aggravation of his injury, that no simple fracture is made compound, and that no movement takes place at the fracture site. Such movement can increase the degree of bony displacement which may already have occurred, and can cause the broken ends of bone to damage blood vessels, muscles, and nerves, and may result in bone piercing the skin and producing a compound fracture. In the event of there being doubt as to whether the patient has a fracture, he should be treated as if the injury were a fracture until it is proved otherwise.

These governing principles mean that the injured part must be adequately supported and immobilized when handling and moving the patient, and use must be made of splints and slings where neces-sary. If the patient has to be lifted, enough people must form the lifting team so that he may be moved easily, smoothly, and without risk. According to the nature of his injury, the degree of shock, and his general condition, it may be wise to keep him lying down. He should be reassured, made as comfortable as possible, and kept at rest and warm but not overheated, until medical attention is secured.

ELECTRIC SHOCK

An electric shock is the result of an electric current passing through the body. Electricity at high voltage is dangerous, but it is not the high voltage itself which causes the shock, but the current through the body which is produced by the high voltage in certain circumstances. These circumstances may exist when there is failure in protective systems incorporated in electrical apparatus.

Such apparatus is usually made safe to handle by two features.

(i) It is insulated. This means in general that the electrical conductors comprising the circuit are enclosed in non-conducting material, for example the sheathing on electric flex for lamps and fires and on the supply cables of X-ray sets.

(ii) Some part of the circuit is earthed. This may be done by connecting it to a metal plate buried in the ground or to a pipe (such as a water main) which goes into the ground. The earth can absorb a vast amount of electric charge, and connection of the apparatus to earth is a measure for the safety of those using it.

There is a tendency for electricity to escape to earth, and where there is failure in the provided safety devices, the path of least resistance may be through the body of someone handling the equipment. So an electric current passes through this person, and the degree of electric shock received depends on the strength of the current. If the body offers a high resistance to the passage of electricity, then the current will be low and the shock will be slight. If the body offers a low resistance to the passage of electricity, then the current will be high and the shock severe. Assuming the resistance of the body to be constant, a higher voltage produces a higher current.

In fact the electrical resistance of the human body is not constant and can vary considerably. Factors which alter it include the degree of wetness; this is why electrical equipment can be so dangerous in a bathroom, and why electric light switches in X-ray darkrooms either are controlled remotely by cords from the ceiling or are of a special design which enables them to be operated safely with wet hands. Features which increase the resistance of the body to electric current are the wearing of rubber gloves and rubber-soled shoes, and standing on dry floors and on insulating surfaces such as cork and rubber mats.

An electric current acts upon the muscles of the body and causes them to contract. In this way the victim of the shock may be unable to breathe because the respiratory muscles are affected, and his heart may stop beating because the heart muscle is involved. It is this muscular spasm which makes the victim unable to release his hold of a 'live' electric conductor if he is actually grasping it at the time. If he is simply touching it, the result of the spasm is the more fortunate one of withdrawal from the source of the shock. When the voltage is high, the effect of induced electricity may be to throw the victim away from the equipment; so that he may suffer fractures as a result of this or arising from the violence of a muscular contraction. If current flows through the body for a long enough time, irreversible damage to the body cells will occur.

The first thing to do immediately for the victim of an electric shock if he is still in contact with the circuit is to switch off the supply at the mains switch, so that the apparatus is no longer 'live'. In the X-ray department it will generally be possible to do this.

If for some reason it is not possible to cut off the supply and the patient has to be pulled away from the apparatus while it is still 'live', unless the rescuer is insulated from the current there will quickly be *two* victims of electric shock. The rescuer should therefore stand upon some insulating material—a cork or rubber mat or a thick blanket. This is particularly important if the floor is wet. A dry wooden floor and a dry floor with a rubber surface both provide reasonable insulation for mains voltage. A dry floor made of polyvinyl tiles provides insulation for voltages below 1000 volts, and therefore gives protection at mains voltage level.

The patient should be pulled away by the clothing and the rescuer's hands should be protected by insulating material, for example rubber or cloth. All articles used for the purpose of insulation must be *dry*. In the X-ray department lead-rubber aprons and gloves may be readily available, and may suggest themselves as suitable material for insulation. Lead-rubber will be adequate for voltages up to 400 volts, but is not reliable protection in the case of high voltage sources. It would be reasonable to use it if the electrical apparatus concerned were operating on the 230 volt mains supply. It should be realized that in the case of a.c. supplies the stated mains voltage is not the highest value reached during the a.c. cycle. The voltage increases to a peak value which is equal to the stated value multiplied by the factor 1.41. In the design of equipment, insulation requirements are based on peak values of voltage.

   Once the patient has been rescued from the source of the current, the treatment required will depend upon the injury sustained. The conditions which may be present are:

   (i) cardiac arrest,
   (ii) respiratory arrest,
   (iii) burns,
   (iv) fractures,
   (v) shock.

The rule in all first aid procedures is to treat the most serious condition first, and (i) and (ii) clearly require *immediate* assistance; (iii), (iv) and (v) are of less urgency.

   Arrest of the heartbeat has already been discussed in the first section of this chapter and the features of emergency treatment described. The radiographer can apply the appropriate immediate measures which have been mentioned. Artificial respiration must begin at once if breathing has ceased, and must be maintained while awaiting medical aid. The patient may require treatment for burns, fractures and shock.

   It is wise to regard electric shock seriously even if the results do not seem to be very severe, and to refer the patient for medical attention.

CHAPTER XVIII

MEDICO-LEGAL ASPECTS OF THE RADIOGRAPHER'S WORK

Reference to the medico-legal aspects of a radiographer's work may induce a sense of panic in the newcomer who feels uncertain of the implications of this alarming phrase. In fact it is necessary to understand in this only certain broad aspects of the radiographer's responsibility towards patients. It is, however, important that these aspects are fully understood, and they may be considered simply under three headings. These are:

(i) breach of professional confidence;
(ii) negligence;
(iii) procedure in the event of an accident.

BREACH OF PROFESSIONAL CONFIDENCE

Most people realize that doctors and others (in common with clergymen and lawyers) in their work are given knowledge concerning the personal history of those who consult them, and that they must regard such knowledge as strictly confidential. This bond of secrecy applies not only to medical details but to anything which the doctor may discover about his patient in consultation and treatment.

When a clinician refers a patient to the X-ray department for diagnostic examination, although the patient may never see the radiologist, he is in fact being referred for a radiological opinion. This opinion is related to appearances on radiographs, and is a statement from the radiologist as to the conditions which the radiographs in his belief show to be present; these conditions may be normal or pathological.

In order that he may form his opinion the radiologist must be admitted to the clinician's confidence, and therefore must be told facts about the patient relevant to his diagnosis and treatment which the clinician has discovered. Similarly the radiologist admits the clinician to *his* confidence, and tells him his opinion based on the appearances in the radiographs which have been taken. There is thus an exchange of confidential information, and these matters are properly within the triangle formed by the radiologist, the clinician, and the patient.

Radiographers are technical assistants to the radiologist, and in order that they may perform their duties they too are admitted into this area of confidence. Even the newest student in the X-ray department should realize that the work, through X-ray reports and case notes, gives access to information about the patient which must always be regarded as confidential. In the United Kingdom radiographers are State Registered, and one of the statutory functions of the Board which registers radiographers concerns itself with standards of professional conduct. It has been specifically stated by the committee concerned with these matters that one of the acts of infamous conduct by a radiographer would be knowingly to 'disclose to any patient, or to any other unauthorized person, the result of any investigations or any other information of a personal or confidential nature gained in the course of practice' of the radiographer's profession.

Strictly there are only two people with whom radiographers may freely discuss a patient and the details of his condition and case history; these two people are the referring clinician and the radiologist to whom the patient has been referred. In practice of course some discussion of patients must fairly and necessarily take place between various other members of the hospital staff; for example between junior radiographers and their seniors, and between radiographers and other nursing staff in whose charge the patients rest. These are legitimate extensions of the triangle of confidence previously mentioned.

No detail concerning a patient should ever be discussed with another patient or discussed outside the hospital. This applies (as has been said) not only to information on his medical history, but also to anything which may be discovered about a patient in the course of duty. The most junior student radiographer should recognize this obligation.

It is natural enough that if we are enjoying our work and are interested in it, we shall wish from time to time to tell our families some story of the day's events. If this is to be done it must be carefully done, in such a way that the patient cannot be identified. If you mention names you may find that the charlady of the patient's next-door neighbour has overheard you on a bus. This may sound far-fetched, but such things do happen.

It may be tempting to appear knowledgeable about a well-known patient—a footballer with a head injury, an actor with a nervous breakdown, a millionaire with a gastric ulcer—but we must see to it that we do not say more than might already have appeared in the daily press.

Not only must we not discuss the patient's medical and personal background with others, we must avoid discussion of his own condition with the patient himself. It is no part of our duty to tell the patient what is wrong with him, outline treatment, describe what has been done or may be done, speculate about recovery. It is rather a function of our responsibility *not* to tell him.

Patients of course ask radiographers questions about X-ray films which have been taken and seek information on what has been revealed. It is quite wrong to escape in the answer that 'they are all right'. In fact a direct answer should be evaded, and the question can easily be turned aside by some reply such as 'The doctor will see the films and he will be able to tell you', or 'I'm afraid we can't say until the doctor has seen the films all together'. Such answers should be made in as reassuring a manner as possible.

Even a simple piece of information can have an unpredictable effect upon the patient. It may seem easy to tell a patient that he has a broken toe, but this can fling him into a flurry of uncertainty as to whether he is likely to be unable to work and for how long, and if he has an active imagination or is a ballet dancer he can see his whole career jeopardized. He may even be just desperately anxious to take a certain girl to a dance that night. In fairness to both the radiographer and the patient, it is preferable that he should be told about his broken toe by the doctor who can provide answers to the questions that must surely follow.

NEGLIGENCE

Negligence in this context is simply a failure in care, a failure that arises by doing something (or failing to do something) that no reasonable person would do (or fail to do). In certain cases negligence becomes actionable in civil law. Negligence is actionable when there is a duty to take care, cast by law on someone or some people, and

T

there is a failure in that duty resulting in injury to another person or to others. In all our activities we have a duty to take care to avoid acts or omissions reasonably foreseeable as likely to injure others; this duty is based upon probabilities, not upon bare possibilities. This means, for example, that if you dig a hole in the middle of the pathway leading to the door of your house, and you do not put a fence round it or a strong cover over it, you are negligent. The injury to your friend who comes to call on you and crashes to the bottom of the pit is a foreseeable one—not foreseeable by your friend but foreseeable by any reasonable person who knew that the hole was there.

The degree of care required from us in law differs in different situations. The factors influencing this degree of care include (i) the risk involved, (ii) the known characteristics of persons exposed to risk, and (iii) the necessity. Those who do things intrinsically dangerous must exercise a higher degree of care, and certain groups of people will demand more care than others. The standard of care required in law is not the highest possible to which one can conceivably be expected to conform, nor is it the lowest standard of which one is actually capable. It is between these two extremes— the standard of 'the reasonable man'.

Radiographers must recognize that in their work they are certainly placed in the category of those who of necessity submit others to procedures which are intrinsically dangerous. Furthermore, the people who suffer these procedures have known characteristics which demand a higher degree of care. Children, old people, sick people of any age coming to the X-ray department as frightened strangers (for so they must be regarded) certainly need special care. The test to be applied is the foreseeability of injury to others, and any reasonable man would see that hospital patients need a special degree of care—even in as simple a matter as getting on or off an X-ray table—if foreseeable injury is to be prevented.

We must therefore give attention to detail in all aspects of our care for patients; not only in the technical procedures and use of our equipment, but in matters such as helping the patient in and out of the X-ray room and as he goes about the department. A radiographer who leaves even the most able patient alone to get down from the X-ray table after the simplest examination is as guilty of negligence as the one who fails to check the contrast agent injected for an intravenous urogram; the first situation has just as much possibility of foreseeable injury as the second. We are failing in our legal duties (quite apart from our humane responsibilities) if we do not keep this always in mind.

In using X-ray equipment radiographers have the duty of checking the controls of a unit before a diagnostic exposure is made or a treatment is given. In a judgement made in a specific case, the law placed this responsibility firmly on the shoulders of the radiographer, and it was said that all controls must be checked, including those customarily kept on one setting and not usually varied. Although in this particular case reference was made to the controls, the term should be interpreted as referring to *all* aspects of the equipment. This includes simple mechanical features such as the security and working order of such attachments as steps, hand-grips, shoulder-pieces, cones, and diaphragms. Protestations from a patient as to his lack of security on the X-ray table should never be ignored, and attention should be paid even to such non-technical considerations as the risk from a highly polished floor in the X-ray room.

Another aspect of negligence is failure to read properly requests for X-ray examinations. We all know the importance of this but in practice it may require an effort of conscientiousness from a busy radiographer seeing with dismay some illegible handwriting; but the effort must be made. If, for example, there is a request to 'X-ray the pelvis please' and we fail to elucidate the last erratic line which says 'Stone in the lower end of the ureter', we can take a useless radiograph and submit the patient to a dose of radiation which is not necessary. This is failure in care where there is a duty of care— in one word, negligence.

Negligence occurs, too, when a radiographer uses X-ray equipment without complete precautions to reduce to its necessary minimum the radiation dose received by the patient. There is certainly a duty of care in the use of radiation which our special knowledge fits us to meet and we must not fail to meet it.

Responsibility for Negligence

We are each of us personally responsible for any negligence of which we are guilty. In law an employer may also be vicariously responsible for the negligent acts or omissions of those he employs (called in this context his servants) when these acts occur within the scope of their work. This vicarious responsibility does not make the servants of the employer immune.

Radiographers in the National Health Service in the United Kingdom are considered in law as the servants of the hospital employing them. This means that if a radiographer is negligent, and a patient suffers injury as a result, in most cases the responsibility will be assumed by the employing hospital authority. If legal proceedings follow and damages are awarded to the injured patient, the hospital authority is liable for payment of these damages. There is, however, nothing in law to prevent the hospital authority from seeking to recover the damages from its servants. Such cases have occurred, a judgement being given in a specific case (not involving a radiographer) for an employing authority to secure a contribution of 100 per cent of the damages from its servant. It is possible too for the name of a radiographer to be joined with a hospital authority in a legal action, the radiographer being liable with the employing authority for damages claimed. This has occurred in a particular case.

These facts may sound alarming, but it is possible for radiographers to insure themselves against this type of risk; membership of certain professional bodies carries such insurance. The risk may not be very great, but radiographers considering the medico-legal aspects of their work should fully appreciate that it exists.

PROCEDURE IN THE EVENT OF AN ACCIDENT

It is obvious that even in the best X-ray department staffed by the least negligent radiographers accidents can and will happen, both to patients and to personnel. The procedures in such cases are in three sections.

(i) Care for the victim.
(ii) Reporting the accident.
(iii) Recording the accident.

Care for the victim is advisedly placed first, and is to be given immediately however slight the injury may seem to be. Detailed procedures in first aid and treatment clearly will be determined by what has happened, and need not be discussed here. Even if the accident seems trivial and the injury slight, it is wise to seek medical advice as part of the care of the victim.

Reporting the accident should be done as soon as is appropriate. For the student or the junior radiographer, this means giving a report of the accident to the superintendent or senior radiographer in charge. It will be reported also to the chief radiologist of the department. If the accident involves a ward patient, then the senior ward staff must be told what has happened, and if it involves a member of the staff of another department then the appropriate departmental chief must also be notified.

Recording the accident is of considerable importance. Hospitals have a form for this purpose, and this form should be completed as soon after the incident as is allowed by the more immediate concerns of first aid, treatment, and reporting to seniors. It must be done soon while the details of what has occurred are clear in the minds of those who are involved, and it must be done with complete honesty and frankness if it is to be of any value at all. The form has spaces for recording what happened, who was involved, what the results of the accident were, and what actions were taken in dealing with the incident.

The usefulness of this written account is twofold. Firstly, if any legal action arises out of the matter there will be available a permanent record of what the situation was at the time and what measures were taken. Secondly a clear account of the circumstances of the accident may serve to show how it has occurred. This may focus attention on some feature of the department—its equipment, its organization, its conditions, its practices, its staff situation—which made the accident more likely to occur and should be improved for safety. Through this it may be possible to stop the event repeating itself at a later date.

When an accident happens, particularly if it is a very alarming and serious accident, it is not always easy to report correctly afterwards exactly what has occurred. As trained people, radiographers must try to meet these situations as coolly as they can, and to retain unimpaired their faculties of judgement and observation.

THE IMPORTANCE OF RECORDS

From this particular case of recording an accident, it may be useful to proceed further to consider the importance of all records kept in hospital and in the X-ray department. The diagnostic radiograph is itself a record, a record of certain conditions existing within the body of a particular patient at the time the examination was made. The radiographic record (if it is to have value) must be completely identified as to the patient, the date, and the circumstances—for example its place in an intravenous urogram series or other sequence. It must also be capable of being found if needed. The record systems and arrangements for film-marking and filing used in X-ray departments are directed towards these ends.

Patients' records in hospital are intended partly for the transmission of information. This is done more clearly and with more saving in time and effort if the transmission is by written and not simply by spoken words. Another purpose of these records is the provision of a permanent account so that for diagnosis and treatment comparisons may be made between the patient's condition at different times. These permanent written records are independent of such factors as change in staff and in hospitals—the patient may be seeing another doctor in another place at a different time—and the fallibility of human memory.

Beyond the individual patient there is a much wider field of use for many types of hospital record and hospital statistics. Without them it would be impossible for medical science to advance, for financial assessments to be made, for services to be planned and developed to meet demands which are predictable by studying the records of previous activity.

In the X-ray department efficient (or even merely adequate) administration requires the keeping of records other than simple documentation of patients. For example, maintenance and renewal of equipment, supplies of films, chemicals, and drugs, movements of staff, holiday dates, personnel monitoring as part of radiation protection, collections of radiographs showing various abnormal and normal conditions—all these aspects of departmental work require detailed record systems of their own which are independent of changes in time and in staff.

While the keeping of records may often seem trivial, tedious, and consuming of time and energy upon which many claims are made, it must be appreciated that attention given to the task is by no means wasted. Records are of value and significance not only in particular instances, but generally in the provision of a competent service to patients, and this as has been seen is primarily the purpose of a hospital's existence and useful function.

CHAPTER XIX

THE PATIENT AND THE
RADIATION HAZARD

Even before their acceptance as candidates for training most student radiographers are aware that the radiations with which they will work have the capacity to harm and that excessive exposure to them will damage human tissue. Indeed this aspect of the work is one not only familiar to those occupationally in contact with ionizing radiations, but also widely known to the public at large. In many instances patients are sufficiently aware of the harmful potential of X radiation to become anxious and alarmed if what appears a large number of radiographs have to be taken.

THE NATURE OF THE RISK

In diagnostic X-ray examinations we are not concerned with doses of radiation within the 'excessive' category. To mention, as one instance, a radiation effect of which the public generally is cognizant, we are unlikely to produce sterility in a patient as a result of any diagnostic radiological procedure. However, in recent years the attention of research workers has been directed towards hazards which may be produced by low levels of irradiation and which subjects undergoing diagnostic radiography may well incur.

These risks are dual in nature. The first is *genetic*, that is, it refers to the possibility of undesirable effects upon a future generation, and it arises because of the ability of X rays—and other ionizing radiations—to bring about certain changes, known as *mutations*, in reproductive cells. Such slight alteration in the reproductive cells of each of a large number of subjects could lead to the existence of inherited defects in their descendants, not immediately apparent in their children but becoming manifest in the individuals of a far later generation.

In any population there is a certain mutation rate which is said to occur naturally. It is thought at present that perceptible genetic

damage would occur if there were irradiation of the whole popu-
lace sufficient to raise the natural mutation rate to twice its present
level.

Everyone receives naturally a small dose of radiation from his
environment, due to cosmic rays, radioactive materials in the
earth's crust and traces of radioactivity within the body which are
present as the result of small amounts of radioactive substances in
water, food and the atmosphere. This is an inevitable background
dose to which we are all subject. In addition to it many people
receive radiation from man-made sources. Reports show that in
those countries where extensive medical services are available the
largest man-made contribution to the genetic hazard comes from
medical radiology.

Even so, this contribution at present is relatively small: in the
United Kingdom it is not more than 20 per cent of that from natural
sources of radiation. Such a low figure reflects the care with which
diagnostic X-ray examinations in general are performed, and we
should recognize that to maintain it at this level, or less, requires
the unremitting attention of every radiographer, no matter how
trivial may seem the particular procedure at the moment concerned.
Results which are neither tangible nor likely to become evident
within a lifetime are prone to lack significance for us. It is important
that we each are actively aware of the reality of this obligation towards our patients, and that we take every step to ensure that the
radiation dose received in the course of *any* diagnostic X-ray examination is never higher than it need be.

The second type of hazard to which research workers have given
recent attention is that termed *somatic*. This refers to delayed
effects which may be seen in an irradiated subject after some varying
period of time, perhaps many years, following exposure. At the
present time it is not well understood whether these delayed effects
are ever caused by low levels of exposure and clearly it is difficult
to obtain clear-cut evidence on such a point. In the absence of proof
it is necessary—because we cannot safely do otherwise—to assume
that low levels of irradiation *can* produce somatic damage.

It is obvious that any measures taken to minimize the genetic
hazard from medical radiology, in general will minimize also the
somatic risk. In what follows consideration is given mainly to the
possibility of damage of the genetic kind.

It is unlikely that the patient himself thinks of this hazard in the performance of a diagnostic X-ray examination. When told that a further radiograph is necessary his fear no doubt is of possible sterilization or some vaguer immediate ill, and on this point we can freely assure him of his safety.

It must be recognized, however, that our awareness of the genetic risk and our concern to avoid unnecessary irradiation of those of child-bearing age should not sanction the acceptance of an incomplete examination. When clinical considerations have established that an X-ray examination is necessary, then whatever views are required for diagnosis must be included. For example, a survey of the lumbar vertebrae confined to the lateral projection is quite useless; and equally misleading may be the urographic series from which has been omitted the plain 'scout' film. To carry out a radiographic examination only partially on the ground of the radiation hazard is to protect the patient from one risk but to expose him to another—the possibility of incorrect diagnosis and treatment.

In accepting the principle that unnecessary exposure is to be avoided, our line of conduct should be to reduce as much as possible the dose incurred in the taking of necessary radiographs.

Radiography of the Pregnant

X-ray examination of a woman who is known or thought to be pregnant creates a particular problem in radiation protection because the radiation risk has special aspects. It is known that the maturing human embryo is potentially sensitive to ionizing radiations. The possibility exists of foetal malformations being produced as the result of a radiation dose delivered to the mother for the purpose of a diagnostic radiological examination. This is damage in the *somatic* category. It may be presumed that the *genetic* risk to a foetus is not greater than for other irradiated subjects.

It is thought that there is a period which is critical during embryonic development. It may be that there are a number of critical periods in the maturing of an embryo, embryonic organ or tissue, but knowledge of these matters is not yet complete. We do not know exactly when this critical period is: all we can say at present is that a foetus is at greater risk from irradiation early in intra-uterine life than when it is almost or fully mature. Ionizing radiations are known to alter chromosomes. As these control foetal development there may be a direct connection between such irradiation and chromosomal abnormalities resulting in a malformed child.

There are some grounds for believing that irradiation of the foetus in utero carries another risk. It has been suggested that leukaemia and other malignant diseases occur a little more often in children whose mothers have been subjected to diagnostic radiological examinations during the pregnancy.

For these reasons, X-ray investigations of pregnant women should be carefully controlled along the following lines.

(i) Unless the condition is one requiring immediate attention such patients should not have X-ray examinations of the abdomen, lumbar spine or pelvic regions, particularly procedures involving serial films or fluoroscopy: for example, tomography, intravenous urography, myelography and barium studies.

(ii) When a pregnant woman is referred to the X-ray department for obstetric reasons, repeat films should be avoided if possible and there is thus a special charge on the radiographer to obtain satisfactory radiographs in the first instance.

(iii) When the examination is not directly of the uterus or pelvis, for example during radiography of the lung fields or teeth, the radiographer has an unavoidable moral responsibility to protect the foetus as far as possible from both direct and secondary radiation by providing a suitable lead apron for the patient.

THE TEN-DAY RULE

In the human subject it is obviously difficult to obtain evidence—and impossible to conduct experiments—which would indicate numerically the size of the risk to a foetus irradiated during intra-uterine life. If there is a risk at all—and we cannot positively state that none exists—then it is necessarily greater for a newly formed embryo than for a mature foetus at a late state in the pregnancy. Radiography carries the highest potential for harm during the first six weeks of foetal life; that is, during a period when the patient concerned is unlikely to be aware that she is pregnant.

Because of this, in some X-ray departments a 'ten-day rule' is applied in relation to non-urgent examinations which entail irradiation of the lower abdomen and pelvis. This rule treats every woman between the ages of 13 and 45 as though she is pregnant until she is proved otherwise. Such patients are X-rayed only during the interval of not more than ten days following menstruation. Later than this, ovulation should normally have occurred and the woman potentially may carry a fertilized ovum. Even if the ovum which is present has not yet been fertilized at the time of the X-ray examination, the possibility cannot be disregarded that fertilization of a previously irradiated ovum is associated with the same kind of risk as when the sequence of events is the other way round.

Patients coming to the X-ray department understandably would not take kindly to questions from a receptionist or even a radiographer relating to sexual intercourse and consequently the only practicable policy is to assume the possibility of pregnancy, even in the unmarried.

There is no doubt that the use of the ten-day rule is ethically correct and that if we apply it in the X-ray department we no more than honourably discharge our responsibilities to our fellow human beings for the proper usage of the radiation with which we work. However, the rule has practical difficulties which mean that its implementation is by no means universal.

Abeyance of the rule can be defended on the ground that the hazard which it avoids is statistically too small to justify the expense and inconvenience of applying such a regulation. For example, it has been estimated that of 63,000 patients annually passing through a busy general X-ray department about 2,500 are women of child-bearing age and only about 1 per cent of these are in weeks 2–6 of a pregnancy.

Implementation of the ten-day rule has certain implications of difficulty which are indicated below.

(i) Patients who may have travelled some distance to attend hospital are required to make additional journeys in order to be X-rayed.

(ii) Consultant medical staff or staff in the X-ray department must give time to questioning each patient concerned about her menstrual history.

(iii) In some instances—owing to irregularity of menstruation or to many women's uncertainty over actual dates—the available ten days may be reduced to an effective five days.

(iv) The booking of extra appointments may intolerably increase the load on over-strained clerical staff in an already busy department.

SIGNIFICANT EXAMINATIONS

Genetic damage results from irradiation of the reproductive cells and consequently as a rule the most important (though not the only) dose to consider in diagnostic radiography is that received by the gonads of the subject. Any examinations which involve inclusion within the primary beam of the testes in the male and the ovaries in the female are clearly the worst offenders.

Also to be considered is the dose to the gonads from scattered radiation, when the site of examination in fact may be remote from the reproductive organs: for example, during radiography of the chest or teeth. The significance of the patient's position in X-raying the extremities should not be overlooked. For instance, the gonads of a male patient, seated on the X-ray table for radiography of his foot, may be irradiated, owing to the direction towards him of the tilted X-ray tube.

Much time has been given to the assessment of the mean gonad dose incurred during a wide variety of diagnostic X-ray examinations made under different conditions. From these published results certain conclusions can be drawn, for example:

(i) that when the pelvis is directly irradiated, the gonad dose received by females is greater than that received by males;

(ii) that when the dose received by the reproductive organs is due to scattered radiation (as distinct from inclusion of the gonads within the primary beam) then the quantity received by males is greater than that received by females.

Consequently it follows that the radiation risk from any particular X-ray examination is not the same for all patients, but may be greater or less depending upon the sex and size of the subject. For example, during radiography of the lumbar spine, renal tract, gall bladder or abdomen, the female reproductive organs are likely to lie within the primary beam. In examinations of the hip, the male organs most probably will be directly irradiated. Again, the greater gonad dose which may be received in their course makes X-ray examinations of the extremities more significant for males than for females.

PROTECTIVE MEASURES

The assessment of the dose received by the patient during diagnostic X-ray procedures, and methods by which it may effectively be reduced are complicated matters to which physicists have recently given serious attention and which no doubt are not properly within the scope of this book. It is, however, easily recognized that to implement such recommendations as may emerge from this work is the hour to hour responsibility of the radiographer—whether the most senior member of the department or its newest comer; it is a responsibility which is always with us and of which we should remain constantly aware.

In addition we have a responsibility to others than the patient. We should make use of the protective measures available for ourselves, our colleagues and anyone else who may be immediately concerned with a patient undergoing a diagnostic X-ray examination.

A full consideration of these problems must include a number of aspects which may not be within the immediate control of the radiographer who conducts the examination. These include the output characteristics of a particular X-ray set, the filtration of the primary beam, and the possibility of some leakage of radiation occurring from the tube housing. (This is referred to as 'leakage radiation'.) There are nevertheless a few simple measures the observation of which, whenever possible, reduces materially the gonad dose received by the patient.

(i) The use of the fastest screen-film combination or the fastest non-screen film which is consistent with the production of adequate radiographic detail.

(ii) The use of gonad shields or similar lead protection, when such shielding does not obscure areas of diagnostic importance on the radiograph.

(iii) Proper limitation of the area covered by the X-ray beam.

To these may be added:

(iv) the use of image intensification whenever possible during fluoroscopic procedures.

We shall consider (ii) and (iii) in the following pages, together with protective garments designed to reduce the dose received, not by the patient but by other people involved in his care. These are discussed first.

Aprons and Gloves

Student radiographers should not be long in X-ray departments before lead rubber aprons become familiar items to them. The purpose of these aprons is to protect from radiation and they should be worn whenever there is the possibility of unavoidable exposure either to the primary beam or to secondary radiation. Their use is obligatory in the following situations:

(i) whenever departmental, nursing, medical or other staff must stand close to a patient while an X-ray exposure or fluoroscopic examination is made;

(ii) whenever a relative, friend or any other member of the public, such as an ambulance officer or police officer, is required to support a patient during an X-ray examination. When possible, gloves as well as an apron should be worn if the hands must be exposed to radiation in either of the above circumstances.

Radiographers should condition themselves not only to putting on their own aprons but to handing an apron to anyone else in the vicinity in the X-ray room, or at the bedside in the ward, or in the casualty room, who may be without one. While members of the X-ray department's staff usually will request or obtain a lead rubber apron if the occasion requires one, others may not so readily make themselves heard. Outsiders do not fully recognize the risk and hospital staff—especially perhaps junior nursing members—may be reluctant to appear frightened or to give the impression that they are 'making a fuss' unnecessarily. We—who do understand the potential radiation hazard—have a moral duty to see that others are reasonably protected as well as ourselves. Even in the operating theatre, surgical and nursing staff who must remain continuously near a patient should be asked beforehand if they wish to wear a light apron.

However, although we know that individuals past child-bearing age need hardly be protected from the possibility of genetic damage, it is usually tactless to parade this knowledge in any of the above circumstances. On one occasion good relations between a certain X-ray department and a ward sister were fractured by a radiographer who came to the ward with a mobile X-ray unit, put an apron on herself but assured the sister that she would not need one as it was only people young enough to have children who mattered. It is wiser on the whole not to discriminate in the issue of aprons.

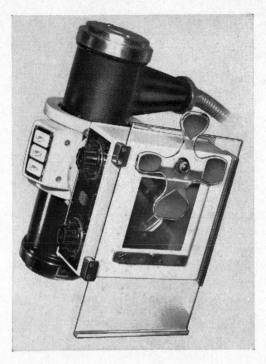

Plate XIVA   The Leicester Gonad Protector.
Four differently shaped lead masks (2 male, 2 female) are incorporated
in a rotatable Perspex disc. The radiation shielding corresponds to the
shadow the lead mask casts when the light beam is in operation. *By
courtesy of Watson and Sons (Electro-Medical) Ltd.*

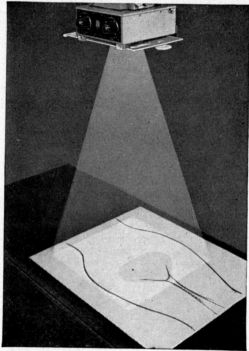

Plate XIVʙ   The Leicester Gonad Protector.

In this illustration the shape of the shadow cast by one of the masks can be seen. *By courtesy of Watson and Sons (Electro-Medical) Ltd.*

Lead rubber aprons come in a variety of styles and both they and the gloves should have certain minimum lead equivalents depending upon the kilovoltages generating the X rays to which they will be exposed. In many countries certain recommendations are published relating to protection from ionizing radiations and these include among other matters a statement of appropriate lead equivalents for aprons and gloves.

In the United Kingdom the relevant publication is *The Code of Practice for the Protection of Persons against Ionizing Radiations Arising from Medical and Dental Use*; student radiographers should study this. It states that both aprons and gloves must have a minimum lead equivalent of 0.25 mm for X rays generated at voltages up to 150 kV.

Manufacturers supply aprons in many styles and sizes, of lead equivalents ranging from 0.15 mm to 0.5 mm and of weights varying from $2\frac{1}{2}$ lb (1.1 kilograms) to 21 lb (9.5 kilograms). The substance used also varies in different examples. It may be lead-loaded rubber covered with cloth, or a suitable base impregnated with lead salts and faced with nylon and plastic materials. Plastics—as they are impervious to fluids—have the advantage of being easy to keep clean. Flexibility of material and general tailoring of the apron are important factors to the comfort of the wearer since none is light in weight as we usually understand the term and sometimes these aprons are worn for one or two hours continuously.

Aprons intended for the protection of the patient are briefly discussed on page 291.

Care of Aprons and Gloves

Protective aprons and gloves should be regularly inspected for signs of wear as deterioration in the protection provided may result. They should be kept clean, barium stains being those most likely to afflict both items.

Lead aprons are susceptible to damage by creases and folds. They should not be left hanging partially over the edge of a chair-seat or other article of furniture or lying doubled on a shelf. The coatee or two-sided type of apron can be put on a coat hanger but the ordinary variety of hanger is not strong enough for the load: a special hanger can easily be obtained from one apron manufacturer at least. An alternative method of storage is to drape the aprons over a wall-mounted rail, in the way that towels are kept in a bathroom. The rail should be several inches in diameter to avoid acute curvatures in the suspended aprons.

The Use of Gonad Shields

Where it is practicable direct shielding of the gonads with a lead sheet is clearly an efficient means of reducing radiation dosage. (Lead-rubber should not be used without a previous check to ensure that it will attenuate the primary beam to a sufficiently low level.) In most abdominal X-ray examinations, if the subject is a male, the scrotum may be shielded without likelihood of obscuring features of diagnostic significance. However, if the patient is a woman there are relatively few examinations involving irradiation of the pelvis and abdomen in which shielding of the ovaries would not be detrimental to the radiograph. In these circumstances it is necessary to rely on other methods of protection.

In the case of a child, gonad shielding may be inadvisable in practice, though theoretically possible. For example, in X-ray examinations made to detect the presence of congenital dislocations of the hip, the area of diagnostic importance is adjacent radiographically to both the testis and the ovary but sufficiently removed from them to permit their shielding—provided such protection can be accurately placed.

This will be recognized as a simple statement which covers sundry difficulties, the major one being that even if correctly placed in the first instance the appropriate lead shield is scarcely likely to remain at its post, when the subject is an active child expressing uninhibited disapproval of the entire procedure. The attempt to use such protection may well entail—through repeat radiographs—a higher dose to the patient than would have been the case had a gonad shield not been used in the first instance.

In some cases it would be desirable to protect the gonads for subsequent examinations, though not for the initial survey. This is true, for example, of accident cases involving the possibility of fractures of the pelvis. Clinical indications may suggest a particular site of bone involvement, but it is unwise to take radiographs only of a strictly localized area. In this type of case the exploratory examination should be made reasonably extensive. Later radiographs of a proven lesion are a different matter and here only the immediate area should be included, unless there are definite indications to the contrary.

There are in common use a number of devices which will protect the gonads from radiation. These most usually take the form of a lead strip, sometimes mounted on a T-shaped or triangular perspex base, which is placed on the patient in an appropriate position over the thighs or lower abdomen. A variant of this is essentially a mask placed at the X-ray beam's exit port from the tube-head; this must operate in conjunction with a light-beam collimator or diaphragm which visually delineates on the subject the area covered by the protector.

Apron Protection for the Patient

On page 288 was described the wearing of aprons manufactured from flexible lead-impregnated materials, as a means to reduce the dose received by departmental and other personnel associated with the care of patients during X-ray examinations. In some circumstances a similar apron may be advisable for the patient. The following are appropriate:

(i) an apron which can be worn by a patient seated in a chair for the purposes of dental radiography and provides cover for the front of the body from the level of the neck to that of the knees;

(ii) a waist apron which can be secured round the patient or suspended from adjacent supports in order to cover the lower back and abdomen during chest radiography. This is particularly recommended when the subject is pregnant but ideally should be used for any individual of child-bearing age.

Limitation of the Irradiated Area

This deserves particular attention simply because it can so readily be overlooked and its significance is not always appreciated. The radiographer exposing the film series of an intravenous urogram, and wishing to be certain that the lower urinary tract is included on the radiograph, may—as a margin against error—open the collimator to extend the 'north–south' dimension of the beam just that much more for good measure. It is not always realized that this action—which may appear to the radiographer merely a small precaution against radiographic mishap—can increase the gonad dose some twenty-five times in the case of a male patient, due to the inclusion of the testes within the primary beam.

The conditions under which chest radiography is undertaken should be even more carefully examined. For example, if a cone or

U

aperture providing coverage for a 35 × 43 cm (14 by 17 in.) film at an anode-film distance of 1 metre (36 to 40 inches) is used for chest radiography at a distance of 2 metres (72 inches), the diameter of the beam reaching the patient has become 1 metre or more. This inevitably will irradiate the gonads in an adult female, is quite likely to do so in the case of a male, and may easily irradiate the whole body if the subject is a child.

At the present time most major X-ray sets are fitted with a beam collimator or diaphragm providing visual evidence of the field size covered by the beam at any anode-film distance. It is important that the radiographer should make intelligent use of this and should by inspection limit the beam to a minimum in every case. If the last use of the unit was made for the same type of radiograph, it is potentially dangerous to assume that the previous setting of the diaphragm will serve again; the new patient may well be smaller than his predecessor.

For chest radiography many departments, in addition to the light beam unit, employ a gonad screen or apron which is suspended at waist level of the patient and will provide protection of the gonads from the primary beam (see page 291). However, the presence of such a device does not release the radiographer from the ethical obligation to limit the area of the primary beam in order to avoid undue irradiation of the gonads from scatter.

With reference to the use of any device for beam limitation, either a variable collimator or a cone, a point of significance is the skill with which it is used. Concomitant with narrow restriction of the beam is its accurate direction. The necessity to repeat several exposures because of careless positioning and poor radiographic 'aim' results in the possibility of increased rather than diminished dose to the patient. It is clear that the proper employment of these devices—which is indeed extremely desirable—requires from the radiographer the utmost precision and care.

Mobile and portable X-ray units present an often unremarked danger, since the cones accompanying them provide a wide film coverage at conventional anode-film distances of perhaps 1 metre. The extent to which these limit the beam is actually slight in most cases, and when using them, particularly for chest radiography, it should be borne in mind that the spread of radiation can indeed be considerable, and is probably much wider than is usually appreciated.

Equipment employed for fluoroscopy whenever possible should incorporate accessory devices designed to give protection to the patient. These are not to be confused with provisions for the safety of the operator, and they include the following.

(i) A fluoroscopic timing switch which indicates the period during which the patient is actually subjected to fluoroscopy. At the end of a preset limit it will open the fluoroscopic circuit, usually to the accompaniment of a warning buzzer or visual signal from a lamp; sometimes both.

(ii) A limiting device which, at any anode-screen distance, prevents opening of the fluoroscopic diaphragms to a field size beyond the margins of the screen. While primarily of value in protecting the operator and his assistants, this device—which provides for a constant visual indication of beam size—clearly operates also in favour of the patient.

In some cases an X-ray set may properly be subjected to one or even a number of trial exposures. This may occur, for example, in using a portable unit in an unfamiliar environment when it is desirable before taking a radiograph to make sure that the line fuses will carry the projected load. Or, again, a number of milliampere-meter readings may have to be obtained to check the output of a unit thought to be faulty in operation.

When tests of this nature are made it is important beforehand to pay attention to the direction in which the X-ray tube may happen to be aimed at the time. It should never be allowed to remain in line with either a patient or indeed any other person in the room. Where an adjustable diaphragm is fitted, this should be fully closed. Alternatively the tube head may be lowered to the surface of the X-ray table, on which is placed a sheet of lead, or the beam may be directed towards an *outer* wall of the room.

These are simple but important points, the observation of which should become automatic by all who handle X-ray sets. Only by continuous attention to the radiation hazard can we diminish its risks. Only by constant care in our work can we discharge fully our responsibility to ourselves, our patients, and the generations which will follow. Though remote in its repercussion, we cannot say that the genetic risk does not matter. We have a responsibility for it, which belongs collectively to our age and rests in particular upon each of us as individuals.

INDEX

Page numbers in bold are important references. Italicized numbers indicate pages which have relevant illustrations.

V

Vacuum uterine cannula 140
Vaginal speculum 139, *141*
Valentine jar 92
Venous haemorrhage 261
Ventilation, pulmonary *see* Pulmonary ventilation
Ventriculography 171
  care of patient 171
  contrast media 36, 43, 171
'Victoria' enema ring 93
Vulsellum forceps 139, *142*

W

Wall plugs 174

Wash-out, colonic 86
  gastric (aspiration) 76
  rectal 240

X

X-ray equipment, mobile and portable 174; *see also* Mobile X-ray equipment
  power 175
  preparation 83, 168, 171, 195
  theatre installation 197
X-ray room, preparation 168, 171, 202
Xylocaine hydrochloride 134, 152